Why Solipsism Matters

WHY PHILOSOPHY MATTERS

Series editor: Professor Constantine Sandis, University of Hertfordshire, UK

Why Philosophy Matters focuses on why a particular philosopher, school of thought, or area of philosophical study really matters. Each book will offer a brief overview of the subject before exploring its reception both within and outside the academy and our authors will also defend different provocative outlooks on where the value of philosophy lies (or doesn't, as the case may be). Why Philosophy Matters is accompanied by an ongoing series of free events (talks, debates, workshops) in Bloomsbury. Podcasts of these events will be freely available on the series page.

Books in this series

Why Iris Murdoch Matters, Gary Browning
Why Medieval Philosophy Matters, Stephen Boulter

Also available from Bloomsbury

Nihilism and Philosophy: Nothingness, Truth and World, Gideon Baker
The Meaning of Life and Death: Ten Classic Thinkers on the Ultimate Question, Michael Hauskeller
The Philosophy of Death Reader: Cross-Cultural Readings on Immortality and the Afterlife, ed. Markar Melkonian

Why Solipsism Matters

SAMI PIHLSTRÖM

BLOOMSBURY ACADEMIC
LONDON • NEW YORK • OXFORD • NEW DELHI • SYDNEY

BLOOMSBURY ACADEMIC
Bloomsbury Publishing Plc
50 Bedford Square, London, WC1B 3DP, UK
1385 Broadway, New York, NY 10018, USA

BLOOMSBURY, BLOCMSBURY ACADEMIC and the Diana logo are
trademarks of Bloomsbury Publishing Plc

First published in Great Britain 2020

Copyright © Sami Pihlström, 2020

Sami Pihlström has asserted his right under the Copyright, Designs and
Patents Act, 1988, to be identified as Author of this work.

For legal purposes the Acknowledgments on p. vii constitute an extension
of this copyright page.

Cover image: Diagram showing blind spots in a field of vision
(© The Book Worm / Alamy Stock Photo)

All rights reserved. No part of this publication may be reproduced or
transmitted in any form or by any means, electronic or mechanical, including
photocopying, recording, or any information storage or retrieval system,
without prior permission in writing from the publishers.

Bloomsbury Publishing Plc does not have any control over, or responsibility
for, any third-party websites referred to or in this book. All internet addresses
given in this book were correct at the time of going to press. The author and
publisher regret any inconvenience caused if addresses have changed or sites
have ceased to exist, but can accept no responsibility for any such changes.

A catalogue record for this book is available from the British Library.

A catalog record for this book is available from the Library of Congress.

ISBN: HB: 978-1-3501-2640-4
PB: 978-1-3501-2639-8
ePDF: 978-1-3501-2642-8
eBook: 978-1-3501-2641-1

Series: Why Philosophy Matters

Typeset by Deanta Global Publishing Services, Chennai, India
Printed and bound in Great Britain

To find out more about our authors and books visit www.bloomsbury.com and
sign up for our newsletters.

CONTENTS

Acknowledgments vii

1 Introduction 1
   Why Solipsism? 2
   Some Varieties of Solipsism 6
   The Structure of the Book 15

2 Metaphysical and Skeptical Solipsism 19
   Historical Preliminaries and Contemporary Issues 20
   Classical Metaphysical and Epistemological
      Solipsism—the Cartesian Legacy 23
   Methodological Solipsism 39

3 Transcendental Solipsism 47
   Kantian Idealism 48
   Phenomenology and the Problem of Intersubjectivity 55
   Transcendental Solipsism in Wittgenstein 64

4 Leaving Solipsism Behind: Pragmatist Considerations 83
   Arguing against Solipsism 83
   Giving up Solipsism 92
   A Realistic *Credo*? 103

5 The Relevance of Solipsism 111
Facing Otherness 112
Solipsism and Death 129
The Suffering Other 145

6 Concluding Remarks 151
A Summary of the Argument 152
Solipsism and the Limits of Philosophical Argumentation 156

Notes 163
References 208
Index 229

ACKNOWLEDGMENTS

I would like to begin by thanking a crucially important philosophical teacher I had in the early stages of my academic life, Heikki Kannisto, without whom this project would never have been begun. It was Kannisto's series of lectures on Wittgenstein at the University of Helsinki in 1993 that triggered my interest in solipsism—to the extent that I wrote a series of essays on the topic in the 1990s and early 2000s (Pihlström 1996b, 2000, 2001, 2004). Some of the results of that early work were later included in my books addressing death and guilt (Pihlström 2011, 2016).

The present investigation obviously takes its departure from my early research on solipsism and related themes, but its approach is different. In the context of this book series, I now primarily seek to show why, and how, the problem of solipsism *matters* to us as human beings, examining this specific issue in relation to the meta-level question about why, and how, philosophy itself matters.

A number of colleagues and friends have over the years considerably contributed to the development of my views on solipsism. In addition to Dr. Kannisto, they include, among others, Hanne Appelqvist, Leila Haaparanta, Sara Heinämaa, Lars Hertzberg, Heikki J. Koskinen, Simo Knuuttila, Olli Koistinen, Ilkka Niiniluoto, Anssi Peräkylä, Panu-Matti Pöykkö, Henrik Rydenfelt, Naoko Saito, Seppo Sajama, Tero Vaaja, Thomas Wallgren, and Kenneth R. Westphal. Some of my reflections in this book may be regarded as responses to discussions with these and many other scholars. I also try to implicitly respond to Richard Schantz's (2008) valuable criticisms of my earlier work on solipsism. Moreover, I am grateful to Constantine Sandis for the initial suggestion that I might propose this book to the *Why Philosophy Matters* book series, and to Liza Thompson, Lucy Russell, and Lisa Goodrum at Bloomsbury for smooth collaboration. I would also like to thank the anonymous reviewers who have evaluated this project both at the book proposal stage and at the full manuscript stage, presenting useful and constructive criticism. Over the past couple of years, some of this material has been presented as talks at the University of Helsinki, University of Turku, and Sapienza University in Rome.

My greatest debt is to Sari Kivistö, with whom I have authored two thoroughly non-solipsistic books and several articles. Her influence may not be as explicit in this work as in some others of mine, but it is implicit in almost everything I write. I also gratefully acknowledge my entire (immediate and extended) family, especially my daughters Meeri and Katri, and their fundamental role in enabling me to avoid solipsism.

Helsinki, Finland
October 2019
Sami Pihlström

CHAPTER ONE

Introduction

While philosophy, especially academic philosophy, might be regarded as an abstract activity far removed from anything that really matters to us as human beings, it is easy to think of philosophical topics that clearly matter. Consider the problem of determinism versus free will, for instance. I suppose most of us would admit that it does matter, perhaps greatly, whether we are (and if so, in what sense exactly) free in our actions and responsible for what we do or somehow "programmed" and determined to behave in the ways we do. Or consider typical problems of ethics: there can hardly be any doubt about issues concerning the good and the right, or their opposites, "mattering" to us. Many of us would also readily admit that even rather technical work in the philosophy of logic or the philosophy of science matters at least to the extent that it clarifies the structure of scientific reasoning, thus contributing to the advancement of science, while philosophers of religion may also be doing work that matters when debating on the criteria for reasonable or justified (or unreasonable and unjustified) religious belief.

Other philosophical topics may seem to matter less. Skepticism, for instance, maintains that we cannot know anything about the external world. Because almost all of our activities would continue as they are even if skepticism were true, many would claim that it matters little whether it is true or not (though it might matter whether we *believe* it to be true or not). Now, if there is any philosophical idea that has generally been considered extremely implausible, or even downright crazy, it is surely *solipsism*, the view that the world is "my world," that is, nothing exists independently of my mind, my thought, or my experience—either in the straightforward sense that everything there is is internal to my mind (e.g., "my dream") or in the slightly more elaborated sense that everything there is depends for its existence on my mental activity and thus would not exist without me.

Indeed, solipsism may seem to be a paradigmatic example of a philosophical position that does *not* "matter" to us at all. It does not appear to play any role in our serious attempts to understand the world, society, and ourselves. Rather, it might be taken to be ridiculous to discuss solipsism with any seriousness. While we might be initially tempted by the radical skeptical scenario that there is no world external to our thought, or the solipsistic view that the world exists only due to our thinking, we usually drop such options as wildly implausible—even insane—from among the philosophical positions we seriously consider soon after having passed the introductory class in philosophy.

In this book I argue that solipsism matters much more than we might think. How exactly it matters can only be explained on the basis of a relatively detailed discussion of the different versions of solipsism philosophers have been preoccupied with.

Why Solipsism?

By arguing that solipsism does matter, after all, this book more generally demonstrates that philosophy, even when dealing with highly counterintuitive and "crazy" ideas, may matter rather considerably—and in unexpected ways. The challenge of solipsism should make us rethink fundamental assumptions concerning subjectivity, objectivity, realism and idealism, and relativism, as well as ethics—that is, our ethical relations to other human beings—and death and mortality.[1] A key to the entire issue of solipsism, elaborated at some length in this book, is the distinction between solipsism as a mere skeptical idea ("for all I know, it is possible, or conceivable, that nothing exists independently of my mind and experience") and solipsism as a "transcendental" idea ("the world is my world" in the somewhat mystical sense of Ludwig Wittgenstein's early work, *Tractatus*

Logico-Philosophicus). The latter idea is argued to be both ethically and metaphysically, or even existentially, fundamental to our self-understanding.

Nevertheless, many readers will find it odd to even consider the issue of solipsism. No sane person is a solipsist anyway, so is there anything interesting to say? Why should one examine solipsism, especially if one is (as I am) a non-solipsist and believes there are other people who will (hopefully) read, understand, criticize, and possibly review a book like this?

As already remarked, there are other philosophical views not actually held by anyone as well, such as radical, all-encompassing skepticism or relativism. A careful consideration of solipsism might teach us something about *other* philosophical positions that we are more likely to adopt and defend, and about the ways in which we may be justified in defending them. The legitimation of an examination of solipsism need not, then, lie solely in the intrinsic importance—if there is any—of solipsism itself. Rather, solipsism may be relevant also, or even primarily, due to its *metaphilosophical* significance. It may teach us something essential about the philosophical quest and philosophical argumentation by, say, forcing us to see the relation between ontology and ethics in a new light. And there *may*, of course, be some philosophical relevance in the very issue of solipsism itself, too; it may "matter" in more than one way.

Not only professional philosophers have been interested in the issue of solipsism. For example, literary theorists may regard solipsism as an expression of extreme human loneliness, the inevitable isolation of an individual consciousness; thus, writers as diverse as Laurence Sterne, William Wordsworth, T. S. Eliot, Theodor Storm, Joseph Conrad, Jean-Paul Sartre, Albert Camus, and Samuel Beckett—not only their "philosophical" views but their literary techniques as well—have been studied from the viewpoint of solipsism.[2] Biologists, psychologists, cognitive scientists, or philosophers of biology and psychology may, in turn, address the empirical question of why living organisms usually are not solipsistically "programmed."[3] Moreover, within sociology or social and political philosophy, solipsism may be understood, more or less metaphorically, as an expression of the insufficiency of human dialogue, or the problems we often have in understanding (or even making sense of our ability to understand) other people and cultures.[4] I will, however, be concerned with more strictly philosophical applications of the notion of solipsism.

Joseph Margolis (1995) suggests that philosophers who regard the social as "constituted" on the basis of the mental should be classified as solipsists. John Searle, among others, qualifies as a solipsist in this sense, according to Margolis—a surprising claim, as Searle (1995) is a self-proclaimed "external realist." Solipsism may, indeed, be more widespread and hence more interesting than it first seems. Even so, it is advisable to avoid loading the term with too much meaning, so that virtually anyone could turn out to be a solipsist. Although solipsism does, as we will see, emerge in quite surprising contexts, it is not met *everywhere* in philosophy. In any case, solipsism may provide an illuminating perspective on the thought of philosophers who would not themselves dream of being or becoming any kind of "ordinary" solipsists. Karl-Otto Apel (1998) may be right in claiming that a form of "methodological" solipsism dominates much of modern philosophy. It seems to have been one of the key assumptions in Western thought at least since René Descartes, although few philosophers have ever subscribed to solipsism. A long and winding development of methodological (or, in the most interesting cases, transcendental) solipsism, finding the proper philosophical starting point in the individual ego and its representations of the world, extends from Descartes's *cogito* through Immanuel Kant's transcendental philosophy to Edmund Husserl's phenomenology and the early Wittgenstein's conception of language and the world (see Chapters 2 and 3).

Moreover, as we will note in Chapters 4 and 5, solipsism is not unproblematically avoided even by those (e.g., the later Wittgenstein) who are often taken to have transcended the (transcendentally or methodologically) solipsistic "egological" approach of mainstream Western philosophy. It begins to seem, then, that given the undeniable importance of the issue from the point of view of our self-understanding as post-Cartesian, post-Kantian, and post-Wittgensteinian philosophers, it is surprising that there are so few comprehensive historical and systematic expositions of the problem of solipsism available.

Furthermore, we ought to recognize that solipsism, despite its emphasis on the "first person perspective," is not simply "my" problem, a challenge to my own philosophical orientation. As C. D. Rollins (1967: 488) remarks, no formulation of the doctrine has denied "the requirement that 'the' self is not just the solipsist's own; that the word 'self' or 'I' is not to be confined to a single, fixed reference," but rather "'the' self is that of any person who is supposedly following the argument and thinking the singular word 'I.'" Solipsism may, then, be a deep philosophical issue for us all (cf. Lafleur 1952). Everyone uses the word "I"; hence, it seems that no one can avoid taking this problem seriously.[5]

Similarly, Alec Hyslop (1995: chapter 2) argues that *the problem of other minds* (which he defines as the epistemological problem of showing that there are others who have experiences and mental states in the way I do) arises no matter which philosophical theory of the mind one holds. Even behaviorists and eliminative materialists, who (in different ways) claim that there are no "inner" mental states at all, must, according to Hyslop, use first-person evidence to ground their theses: they have to argue that there is nothing *in their own case* to justify belief in irreducible mentality, and that this insight can be extended to the case of others. But, Hyslop reminds us, there is an *asymmetry* between the first-person and the third-person points of view, since only in my own case can I have "direct knowledge" about my possessing mental states or being such a creature that no mentalistic assumption is necessary.[6] It is because of this asymmetry that the problem of solipsism—and, more specifically, that of other minds—arises, irrespectively of *who* in particular *I* am or which theories of the mind I hold. This slightly paradoxical feature of our problem will preoccupy us in our discussion in this book.

In sum, while most philosophers would admit that solipsism is (i) *impossible to be conclusively refuted* and claim further that it is (ii) *absurd*,[7] concluding that it is (iii) an *uninteresting* philosophical option hardly requiring critical examination, I would subscribe (tentatively) to (i) and (ii) but insist that (iii) does not follow. On the contrary, both (i) and (ii) teach us lessons worth attending to. While we may end up with the conclusion that solipsism, though wildly implausible, cannot be refuted and that the solipsist's worldview is absurd, we may learn something on the way. If so, then solipsism definitely matters.

In the rest of this introduction, some tentative distinctions between various versions of solipsism will be made, the general significance of the problem (i.e., a preliminary answer to the question why it matters) will be discussed, and the overall plan of the book will be outlined.

Some Varieties of Solipsism

The brief catalog of the varieties of solipsism in this section parallels the discussion of the varieties of realism in Ilkka Niiniluoto's (1999) classification of different realisms; in addition, I will, in order to offer a general overview, cite some helpful encyclopedia definitions of solipsism. I will distinguish between ontological, epistemological, semantic, methodological, and ethical (axiological) versions of solipsism. These and other distinctions will be further explicated in Chapters 2 and 3.[8] Generally, solipsism attaches "prime importance to the self" (Rollins 1967: 487); the solipsist "not only accepts the egocentric axiom but also denies the equivalence of himself and other people" (Dingle 1955: 436). The word, after all, derives from the Latin "*solus ipse*," which can be translated (literally) as "(one) self alone" or (less literally) as "I alone exist" (Borst 1992: 487; Craig 1998: 25). We will now turn to the classifications that define the framework for what follows but which can also be considered steps on a ladder that can later be thrown away.

First, let us begin with the most basic variant. As an *ontological* or *metaphysical* thesis, solipsism states that the world is *my world*, or that everything there is equals to, or depends on, the contents of my thoughts.[9] Clive Borst (1992: 487) defines the metaphysical solipsist's view as the thesis that "he alone *is* (exists, or is real)," while Stephen Thornton (2004) characterizes solipsism as the doctrine that, "in principle, 'existence' means for me *my* existence and that of *my* mental states. Existence is everything that I experience . . . ." The ontological solipsist may maintain, with Arthur Schopenhauer, that the world is "my representation" ("*meine Vorstellung*").[10] Nothing exists independently of me, and perhaps nothing *could* exist independently of me; in Thornton's (2004) terms, "The solipsist can attach no meaning to the supposition that there could be thoughts, experiences, and emotions other than his own." Locating solipsism in the ontological sphere, we may consider it an extreme version of *subjective idealism*, opposed to *realism* (i.e., roughly, the thesis that there is a mind-independent reality). This is too simple, though, as we will see by distinguishing other versions of solipsism.[11]

The thesis of ontological solipsism is ambiguous. The world may be ontologically coordinated to me (my thoughts, experiences, mental goings-on, etc.) regarding its *existence* (i.e., the fact that there is a world at all, that there is something rather than nothing, is ontologically, though not necessarily causally, dependent on me), *structure*, or *determinacy of categorization* (i.e., there are no "natural kinds" or ontological structures out there independently of the way(s) in which I divide the world up into kinds and categories).[12] The latter view allows the existence of a world independently of my mind, while interpreting the determinacy of the ontological structure(s) of reality in a solipsistic fashion, claiming that it is, necessarily, only from *my* point of view that the world *is* ontologically structured, that is, that any "way the world is" ontologically depends on me.

On the other hand, the first variety, ontological solipsism focusing on the existence of the world, can be further radicalized into *solipsism of the present moment*, according to which only what is internal to my mind at this particular moment of time really exists (Borst 1992: 487), or, in a weaker version, everything that exists is ontologically dependent on, or reducible to, my present experiences. My world is something that is *right now right here* and nowhere else; "the world" extends no further.

Another ambiguity concerns the *modal force* of the ontological solipsist's claim. It might be suggested that ontological solipsism (in any of its versions) is a *contingent* truth about the ways things are (i.e., that "the ways things are" are coordinated with what I think or experience). The problem with this view is that it would, broadly interpreted, make the last survivor of a global catastrophe destroying most of humankind a solipsist, as there would be nothing left except a world "for" her/him—but it would obviously be implausible to call such a person a solipsist, even though s/he would be "alone" in the world.[13] Therefore, it could be more strongly suggested that ontological solipsism, if true, is a *necessary* truth. If such a modally stronger version is adopted, one will also have to consider the specific sense of necessity at issue. It would be implausible to claim solipsism to be logically or even conceptually necessary. The *concept* of existence is hardly such that its applicability presupposes a link to my mind or thought (though even this could be contested). On the other hand, solipsism could hardly be conceived as a mere law of nature, either: the necessity characterizing the world's being "mine" is not the same kind of nomological necessity as, say, gravitation. However, with some minimal plausibility, ontological solipsism could be claimed to be a *metaphysical necessity*; any metaphysically possible world would then be claimed to be "mine." While I will avoid heavy modal metaphysics, such modal formulations are relevant when we move on to consider transcendental versions of solipsism.[14]

Secondly, the *epistemological* doctrine of solipsism can also be divided into two broad categories: the *strong* epistemological solipsist claims that there can be knowledge *only* about my private world (in the sense of some of the versions of ontological solipsism), whereas the *weak* epistemological solipsist claims that all knowledge is *based on* and/or *derived from* knowledge about my private world. The latter basically amounts to a form of first-person epistemological *foundationalism*.[15] Borst's (1992: 487) definition of epistemological solipsism is also relatively weak: the epistemological solipsist thinks that "only he *certainly* is (exists, or is real)." If the epistemological solipsist is involved in the traditional "quest for certainty" in epistemology, it follows that s/he cannot be a *fallibilist*, that is, cannot maintain that all human knowledge is uncertain and corrigible and that even our most strongly justified beliefs might be false. Fallibilism and epistemological solipsism, thus defined, seem to be mutually incompatible. However, even what I have called strong epistemological solipsism is compatible with a kind of fallibilism. The strong epistemological solipsist could claim that I can never be certain about anything that takes place in my private world, although that world is all I could know anything about. Solipsism should, then, be distinguished from the quest for certainty and foundationalism.[16]

Moreover, if one investigates solipsism in a fallibilist spirit, one should admit that whichever view one holds—solipsism or its opposite—one could always be mistaken. On the other hand, the epistemological issue of certainty, related to the task of providing a conclusive refutation of "the skeptic," has been influential in the historical development of the problem of solipsism (cf. Chapters 2 and 3). Epistemological solipsism is thus, unsurprisingly, often characterized with reference to skepticism. Craig (1998: 25), for example, defines the "epistemic forms" of solipsism as the skeptical hypotheses that, "for all we know," it might be true that "one is the only self," or that "nothing at all exists apart from one's own mind and mental states."[17]

Thirdly, in *semantics*, the solipsist claims that *my language* is the only meaningful language, or the only language referring to reality and thus the only language in which any truths (or falsehoods) can be expressed. The picture theory of language developed by Wittgenstein in the *Tractatus* is, arguably, a sophisticated example of this view; Wittgenstein's solipsism is labeled "semantical" by, for example, Jaakko Hintikka and Merrill B. Hintikka (1986: 66). The Wittgensteinian *transcendental* solipsism is primarily a subspecies of semantic solipsism, though it accommodates ontological elements as well (see Chapter 3).

Note that Rollins's (1967: 490) definition of "epistemological solipsism" as holding either one or both of the theses that (i) "knowledge about existence and nonexistence of everything outside the self originates in immediate experience, or 'the given,' which is not strictly shared," and (ii) "to any given person, the intelligibility of existential claims originates in his own immediate experience" is, in my terms, a combination of epistemological and semantic aspects of the doctrine. Similarly, Abdur Razzaque's (1995: 208) "linguistic solipsism," which urges that "my sense-data belong to me and the sense-data of others belong to them,"[18] concluding that the language used by me to express my sense experience is privately meaningful only to myself whereas others' languages are meaningful only to them, entangles epistemological and semantic considerations. Furthermore, semantic solipsism can be connected with any of the versions of ontological and/or epistemological solipsism; consequently, various ontologically and epistemologically solipsistic doctrines are compatible with it, though it is not necessary for a semantic solipsist to adopt solipsism either in the ontological or in the epistemological sense.[19]

Fourthly, *methodologically*, the solipsist may claim that the contents of my consciousness, experiences, or mental states are the proper, or the only, place to begin any scientific or philosophical investigation. Again, we have a *strong* version, according to which this thesis holds *globally*, with respect to all cognitive activities (as in Rudolf Carnap's methodologically solipsistic program in *Der logische Aufbau der Welt*, 1928), and a *weak* version restricting the primacy of the solipsistic starting point to the philosophy of psychology and cognitive science, as in Jerry Fodor's (1975, 1980) views on the language of thought and methodological solipsism as a "research strategy," as well as mentalistic philosophy of mind and psychology generally.[20] One may also speak of methodological solipsism more broadly, referring to the subject-centered starting point in much of post-Cartesian philosophy. As we saw, leading philosophers like Margolis (1995) and Apel (1998) find this quasi-solipsistic assumption of the primacy of subjective consciousness a major unfortunate trend in Western thought (cf. Böhler 1984).

Fifthly, and finally, solipsism can be formulated as an *ethical* (or more generally value-theoretical, *axiological*) position coming close to extreme *subjectivism* in ethics (e.g., a metaethical standpoint privileging the states of mind or other subjective characteristics of individual moral agents). Subjectivist and noncognitivist metaethical views like *emotivism* and *prescriptivism* are, however, far from what I mean by ethical solipsism. Generally speaking, the ethical solipsist claims that *my will* is the only ethically—and, in general, normatively—relevant will; the moral world is my world, and other people are mere objects I can only describe, never normatively assess. I can only evaluate my own moral thought and conduct, never that of others.[21] A view not very much unlike this was expressed, according to the New Testament, by Jesus in the Sermon on the Mount, although his point was restricted to our judging other people: "Judge not, that ye be not judged. . . . And why beholdest thou the mote that is in thy brother's eye, but considerest not the beam that is in thine own eye?" (Mt. 7:1, 3) The relevance of ethical solipsism from the perspective of the Christian tradition may be considerable, for the Christian believer should be deeply concerned with the ethical quality of their own soul (in relation to God and other humans). The Wittgensteinian transcendentalist position, to be discussed in detail, is also closely related to this type of solipsism, though Wittgenstein himself may not have held the view.

What I am calling ethical solipsism differs significantly from what Rollins (1967: 488) labels "egoism," or a (theoretical or practical) doctrine of "self-seeking,"[22] which (as he points out) would hardly be consistent as a solipsistic theory; insofar as self-seeking has any significance in one's life, other selves must be assumed to exist as rivals. The ethical problem of egoism will in this sense be neglected in my discussion, although related issues in moral philosophy will be considered in later chapters; indeed, it may be suggested that solipsism is relevant today partly because an excessive prioritization of one's own self—a kind of narcissistic if not egoistic "selfie culture"—is a typical feature of our times. Furthermore, it might be argued that *any* ethical standpoint, solipsistic or non-solipsistic, requires that one is not an ontological solipsist, that is, that one recognizes the reality of other subjects whose needs can and should (or may fail to) be taken into account in an ethical way. In most cases, this is true; in the transcendental framework to be considered later, the transcendental subject may, however, be "without peers" and still view the world (or life) ethically.[23]

The *problem of solipsism* can now be formulated as the conjunction of all the specific questions whether some or any of the five versions or any of their sub-versions is true, plausible, and/ or coherent. Some of the philosophers to be considered in this book, for example, Russell, have understood solipsism as a genuine philosophical issue, whereas others, for example, Wittgenstein, have sought ways of dissolving the problem (along with other philosophical problems). These differences in philosophers' approaches to our topic are not unimportant. We will not merely be concerned with the question of whether solipsism (in its various versions) is true or false but with the question of what sort of an overall philosophical (and metaphilosophical) approach we should choose for examining this issue. The latter considerations will also to a large extent determine our views on whether the problem of solipsism (in some, or any, of its versions) makes sense.

I have freely spoken about *the* problem of solipsism, but it may be argued that there is no such single problem at all. It may not be very useful to define a generic problem of solipsism; the use of the term "solipsism" in philosophical literature may mislead us to think that there is such a fundamental problem underlying seemingly innocent word use. Very different problems (e.g., epistemological and ethical) may be related to our use of this term. Perhaps our habit of classifying various philosophical troubles as instances of "the" problem of solipsism tells us something about ourselves (and, arguably, about the modern individualism in terms of which we are accustomed to think), rather than about the problems that earlier philosophers—especially those who did not use the term "solipsism" but also those who did—dealt with.[24]

The discussions of the problem(s) of solipsism that follow are by no means intended to demonstrate that these problems have a unified core. There may be irreducible plurality in the problem framework we are studying, to the extent that it might indeed be misleading to use the same word in all these cases. But whether this is so can be judged only after we have seen what kinds of problems become relevant under the rubric of "solipsism"—and how they matter to us. Thus, I am not assuming, except as a working hypothesis, that the various problems of solipsism briefly introduced above constitute a kind (although I am inclined to think that they do, in a loose family-resemblance sense). Nevertheless, in order to highlight, for example, the ethical character of the solipsism issue, it is important to say something about the metaphysical, epistemological, and semantic instances of the issue in order to see how the ethical challenge differs from these while being intimately related to them. To some extent it is, then, necessary to treat all this material under the general label "solipsism," although no commitment to any informative general definition of "the" problem of solipsism is made.

There are some further general clarificatory remarks to be made. As is well known, the deconstructionist "death of the subject" was, again in many different versions, announced in twentieth-century Continental, especially French, philosophy.[25] The very issue of solipsism presupposes that there *could* at least be a solipsistic *subject* to *whose* world everything there is would belong if solipsism were true. Solipsism as a philosophical problem could not survive a total disappearance or fragmentation of the subject, although a deep reconceptualization of the very idea of subjectivity does take place in some of the most interesting accounts of solipsism.

It is impossible to deal with the postmodern fragmentation of the subject in this work. I suspect, however, that the solipsism issue will not easily go away. For example, Jean-Paul Sartre, often pictured as the old-fashioned "humanist" target of later (both structuralist and poststructuralist) attacks on the subject, has been argued to have anticipated, already in his existentialist works, the "decentering" of the subject his critics often emphasize; on the other hand, his struggle with solipsism seems to have lasted his entire life (cf. Howells 1992; Fretz 1992). Indeed, the persistence of the problem of solipsism may provide us with a modus tollens argument against radically decentered views concerning the death of the subject. That, at least, is one of my implicit lines of argument: solipsism matters because we still have to take seriously human subjectivity and individuality, the uniqueness of our distinctive points of view. However, the subject presupposed in discussions of solipsism need not be the Cartesian, metaphysically substantial, soul-like one often ridiculed by critics of the modern philosophical tradition. Both Sartre and, in particular, Wittgenstein were concerned with "non-egological" versions of solipsism (cf. Chapter 3). This, indeed, is a key move in their somewhat analogous ways of rethinking subjectivity.

I will suggest that we, like Sartre, may just have to live with the problem of solipsism. Neither the later Wittgenstein nor his followers seem to be able to get rid of this problem for good. One important issue to be discussed throughout this volume is *how* to live with the problem, that is, how it should be conceptualized as a philosophical question relevant to our lives—a question that matters. Furthermore, the fact that solipsism has been a problem (or at least its status as a philosophical issue was and remains problematic) for both Sartre and Russell, for both Husserl and Wittgenstein, as well as for many of these philosophers' interpreters and followers, indicates that solipsism provides an opportunity for a case study of the ways in which rival philosophical traditions in the twentieth century have been preoccupied with similar fundamental questions. The historical part of this work suggests that the Cartesian-Kantian roots of the solipsism issue are common to the main currents of twentieth-century philosophy.

While my examination of solipsism focuses on academic philosophical questions, I want to emphasize the *cultural significance* of the issue we are considering. There are several reasons why a detailed exploration of solipsism may be argued to be relevant today. First, solipsism is analogous to *cultural relativism*, which has even been described as "solipsism with a 'we.'" Secondly, solipsism poses a radical challenge to our understanding of *otherness* in general. There are many kinds of othernesses we need to deal with: other human beings around us, people coming from different cultural and ethnic backgrounds, nonhuman animals, machines and artificial intelligence, fictional creatures such as ghosts and monsters—you name it. A deeper understanding of an extreme position such as solipsism, which in a sense *denies* otherness, may help us deal with our problems of encountering these and other othernesses. Thirdly, it seems to be an increasingly strong feeling among many people in various cultural contexts today, including politics, work places, and business life, that we should strengthen our capacities of *empathy* and *compassion* toward others' experiences. This sounds like a morally good thing to do and a way of taking otherness (or othernesses) seriously; however, excessively empathetic and compassionate attitudes toward others may in fact run the risk of too fully embracing the other, of reducing the other to oneself. At an extreme, this risk may even be called solipsistic. Instead of genuinely responding to the other, empathy may be a way of immersing the other into oneself, and this tendency may, despite good intentions, be dangerously solipsistic.

Finally, the fourth point regarding the significance of solipsism in our societies today is related to what we may call *the culture of narcissism*. By this I mean the tendency—arguably strengthened by the increasing use of social media—of placing oneself at the center of the world and seeing everything else as mere background for one's own experience. This is not merely the widely experienced need to aggressively promote one's own achievements and potentialities in, say, academic or business contexts, and not merely the addiction people have to their cell phones, but also the pressure to share one's own feelings and experiences with, potentially, anyone using social media—as if everyone were really interested in them. Admittedly, there is the element of sharing there, but I suppose it can be argued that at least part of what goes on in the social media today is a kind of solipsistic pseudo-sharing—and the same may hold for the claim to "share" others' emotions in empathy. The whole world is turned into a context *for me*, for my merits and achievements, for my vacation trip posings and pictures. The cultural artifact symbolizing this most vividly is the selfie stick. People walk with a selfie stick everywhere, taking pictures of themselves no matter where they are—not just pictures of, say, the Empire State Building, the Niagara Falls, the Brandenburger Tor, the Tiananmen Square, or some other monumental sight, but *of themselves in such surroundings*. Those places and monuments, as well as other human beings, become mere background for us, *for me*. This is a way of *placing oneself into the center of everything*, and it seems to me that this development—which, undoubtedly, has always been there but has arguably intensified with the development of the internet and smartphones—can be critically analyzed by turning serious attention to solipsism.

The broader cultural relevance of the solipsism issue will remain merely implicit in my discussions, which will focus on the philosophical issues themselves. These at least potentially widely relevant aspects of our problem should, however, be kept in mind throughout the philosophical argumentation.

The Structure of the Book

After this introduction, Chapter 2 will offer selected historical and more recent perspectives on the development of what I call the issue of "classical" solipsism.[26] We must start with reflections on the history of skepticism, especially on Descartes's method of doubt. In brief, Chapter 2 is concerned with (conceptually, not chronologically) pre-Kantian forms of solipsism, namely, classical metaphysical and epistemological—particularly skeptical—varieties of solipsism, through brief accounts of such classical figures as Descartes and Russell. The chapter will conclude with a discussion of the program of methodological solipsism, arguing that the distinction between classical and methodological solipsism is unclear. As Hilary Putnam (1983, 1994) suggests, one should not be a methodological solipsist unless one is prepared to be a "real" solipsist.

As Putnam (1981) also argues, Kant was the first philosopher who rejected "metaphysical realism," the picture of the world as consisting of a fixed totality of mind- and description-independent things. The purpose of Chapter 3 is to reorientate the solipsism discussion in a Kantian, transcendental manner, with special emphasis (after a historical introduction dealing with Kant and German idealism) on Husserlian phenomenology and Wittgenstein's early philosophy. In a deep sense, the history of any philosophically profound problem of solipsism begins with Kant. Solipsism is, arguably, an interesting option only after metaphysical realism has been rejected, although genuine versions of solipsism may be formulated in a pre-Kantian, "classical" (Cartesian or perhaps Berkeleyan) framework. The history of solipsism is thus entangled with the history of the philosophical issue of realism.

Although there is little detailed scholarly discussion of Kant's own views in the present volume, I duly recognize the fundamentally Kantian nature of my inquiry. By this I do not mean merely the fact that the notion of the transcendental subject will be used, but also, more broadly, my aims and goals. By exploring the problem of solipsism, I propose to examine, in a Kantian-like fashion, problems regarding the necessary transcendental conditions for the possibility of not only knowledge or experience but also, and most importantly, ethics. Together Chapters 2 and 3 provide a comprehensive account of different varieties of solipsistic thought. Both historically and systematically, the most interesting version of solipsism is the transcendental one formulated in Wittgenstein's early philosophy, which is deeply indebted to Kant and Schopenhauer.[27]

In Chapter 4, solipsism will be subjected to realistic critique. No simple version of realism will be presupposed, however. Rather, the chapter will examine what kind of non-solipsism should be maintained in a critical dialogue with the solipsist. My main argument for (a rather generic form of) non-solipsism[28] is *transcendental*, modeling Kantian arguments, but I will suggest that transcendental argumentation, like realism, may be *pragmatically* reconceptualized (cf. Pihlström 2003, 2009). This is also to acknowledge its limitations, regarding solipsism and more broadly. Moreover, it will be suggested that solipsistic tendencies are more widespread in philosophy than one would think. For example, various forms of relativism can be seen as varieties of "solipsism with a 'we'" (to use Putnam's apt phrase), and even a pragmatic or late-Wittgensteinian commitment to acknowledging otherness cannot easily leave solipsism behind.

Chapter 5, continuing from the inadequacy of purely theoretical argumentation against solipsism (a result arrived at in Chapter 4), provides an answer to the question of why this book ought to have been written in the first place. Solipsism is an extreme and, for most philosophers, extremely implausible position. Therefore, it is metaphilosophically most interesting. Its relevance is closely related to the nature (and limits) of philosophical argumentation in general. As a highly controversial case, the (transcendental) solipsist's metaethical position is critically discussed. Even a solipsist can entertain ethical concepts and ideas; arguably, the ethical perspective, rather than the metaphysical and epistemological ones, provides *the* motivation for considering the issue of solipsism. Moreover, it is precisely the ethical background that leads to the metaphysical picture developed in Wittgenstein's *Tractatus*. The main proposal of the chapter is that solipsism can eventually only be abandoned through an ethical decision, as a fundamental existential commitment. This, however, reintroduces the issue, for it will always, inevitably, be *me* who is going to give up solipsism and ethically acknowledge others. These themes will in the fifth chapter also be connected with the philosophy of death, dying, and mortality.

Chapter 6 concludes the inquiry by summarizing the argument and raising the metaphilosophical issue of the limits of philosophical argumentation, one of the most significant themes emerging from the theoretical irrefutability of solipsism. I will, thus, critically assess the relevance of both solipsism itself and the various critiques of solipsism to our understanding of the nature of the philosophical enterprise—and thus to our self-understanding as philosophers and human beings today. By the end of Chapter 6, I hope to have been able to show that, and perhaps how, solipsism matters to us.

CHAPTER TWO

Metaphysical and Skeptical Solipsism

This chapter explores in some detail what I label "classical solipsism," a view, or a bunch of views, that is usually a mixture of metaphysical and epistemological claims. The epistemological issue of skepticism about the external world is closely related to this brand of solipsism. Offering historical and contemporary examples (without any claim to scholarly accuracy in historical interpretation), I will outline some typical lines of argument offered in favor of the forms of solipsism I discuss. I will also show why the most interesting philosophical problems remain intact even after the most careful critical considerations of classical solipsism.

While I do, in a way, agree with those who regard most of the solipsisms to be considered in this chapter and the following ones implausible and even absurd, I wish to join David Bell's (1996: 157ff.) campaign against "anti-solipsistic prejudice."[1] Bell introduces certain "initial demands" that any minimally acceptable solipsism must satisfy. First, solipsism must be "*fact-preserving*," that is, it must not assert or imply empirical falsehoods. Solipsism must be compatible with our "normal forms of behaviour": "There must be nothing wrong with a solipsist's talking to other people, playing backgammon, writing books, or even organizing conferences which other solipsists are invited to attend." Secondly, solipsism must be *internally consistent*. Thirdly, solipsism must be "*philosophically* interesting" in order to escape outright rejection (1996: 158–60). In judging how (or whether) these demands are met by specific theories, we must keep in mind that the demands are, indeed, initial. They do not render any theory true, acceptable, or (in closer examination) even meaningful. However, the availability of certain forms of solipsism that do meet these initial demands justifies a closer study of the issue and shows that there are at least some forms of solipsism that do "matter."

Historical Preliminaries and Contemporary Issues

If we insist on the connection between solipsism and skepticism, we may regard the early Greek skeptics as marking the historical beginning of the problem of solipsism. An examination of ancient skepticism would take us far from my main concerns, however. The Greeks did not formulate the question of solipsism in anything like its post-Cartesian form. Their skepticism was primarily a philosophy of life, a method of achieving a peace of mind, rather than an epistemological position. We will, therefore, mainly be concerned with solipsism as a problem in *modern* philosophy, although we must start with a brief look at its "prehistory." We will proceed through some remarks on the Cartesian struggle with skepticism to twentieth-century developments, focusing on philosophers like Russell, who certainly took skepticism seriously. This chapter will conclude with a brief discussion of methodological solipsism, which, I will argue, is conceptually connected with classical solipsism, while seeking to avoid its metaphysical commitments. Methodological solipsism, it will be seen, can only be understood with reference to "real" (classical, metaphysical) solipsism.

A quite different, transcendental, dimension of the solipsism issue will be the topic of the next chapter, in which brief expositions of Kant's and other German idealists' views as well as of Husserlian phenomenology will lead to a more nuanced discussion of Wittgenstein's version of solipsism, which in my (and many others') view is the most important among the historical stages of the development of the solipsism issue. In the present chapter and the next one, I will not even try to present the history of the problem of solipsism in any chronological manner; otherwise I would have to rewrite the history of Western philosophy as a whole, as almost all major figures in the tradition have had something to say about solipsism, or the problems surrounding it. Any historical claims I will make are subordinated to my systematic aims. I will just refer to a few important turning points in the development of the problem, utilizing selected commentaries of the major classics.

In a word, this chapter will examine "*non-transcendental*" (both classical and methodological) forms of solipsism, while the next one will focus on the (in my view more sophisticated and philosophically interesting) post-Kantian, *transcendental* forms one finds in the phenomenological tradition and especially in Wittgenstein. Both chapters make primarily systematic points by examining historical material.

The issue of solipsism is older than the word, and the term "solipsism" has not always been used in relation to what we now see as the philosophical problem of solipsism. Rollins (1967: 488) reminds us that "apparently the earliest use of a cognate of the English term 'solipsist' is ascribable to an apostate Jesuit, Giulio Clemente Scotti, in a work of 1652 titled *La Monarchie des solipses* [*Monarchia Solipsorum*], which depicts a kingdom of self-seekers," being a satire on Jesuits, who were afterward called *solipses* in France. The author uses a pseudonym, Lucius Cornelius Europaeus; in a French translation, the author is identified as Melchior Inchofer.[2] The subsequent history of the term "solipsism" extends, it has been noted, through F. E. Müller's *De solipsismo* (1841), Eduard von Hartmann's *Das Ding an sich und seine Beschaffenheit* (1875) and *Neukantismus, Schopenhauerianismus und Hegelianismus* (1877), as well as Alfred Barrett's *Physical Metempiric* (1883).[3] It was only in the latter half of the nineteenth century that the term acquired its present meaning (Gabriel 1995: 1018). Earlier Kantians and other idealists had spoken about "egoism" rather than "solipsism." In the 1870s, especially thanks to von Hartmann, the new usage was established (Gabriel 1995: 1020). Only in the twentieth century did "solipsism" become widely used in philosophical literature. Indeed, many of the major philosophers whose ideas and arguments are important in the history of solipsism never used this word.

Rollins (1967: 488), among many others, maintains that the metaphysical problem of solipsism is not ancient; Descartes can be considered its father. The issue, Rollins explains, develops through

Locke's and other classical empiricists' as well as Kant's reactions to Cartesianism to Fichte's and other post-Kantian idealists' systems and, finally, to G. E. Moore's, Russell's, and Wittgenstein's criticisms of those views in the twentieth century (1967: 488–89). Thus, while some Greek skeptics and sophists did consider something perhaps slightly resembling the doctrine of solipsism, they had nothing like the problem of solipsism in the modern sense. The history of solipsism essentially belongs to the history of modern philosophy. That is why it is also *our* problem in a way many ancient and medieval problems are not. While some early Greek writers' views might be seen as experimenting with the possibility of something like solipsism,[4] the Greeks generally seem to have almost entirely avoided solipsism.[5] It would be anachronistic to read the problem of solipsism into Greek conceptions of skepticism, too, or into the views held in other Hellenistic philosophical schools. Even the skeptics were not preoccupied with this problem in the form in which it was construed after Descartes and Kant (see, however, also Johnstone 1991).

Presumably the only ancient thinker to whom a view not very much unlike solipsism might be ascribed was Protagoras, the sophist famous for his *homo mensura* (*anthropos metron*) doctrine: what is true is always true-for-me, true for an individual human being; hence, there is no independent world common to us all, but only (for each of us) a world-as-I-conceive-it, a world whose ontological "measure" I, like any other individual, am. However, distinct subjects can entertain this doctrine. There can be multiple subjects in the Protagorean world, even though that world, again, "is" in a way or another only as a world *for* some such subject. Protagoreanism is usually regarded as an extreme form of *subjectivism* or *relativism* rather than solipsism, but the idea of all truths being radically perspectival truths-for-me suggests a close relationship among these positions.[6]

More generally, the fact that the ethical focus of the Greek philosophical schools lay in the cultivation of one's character and in the idea that the subject's personal virtue and peace of mind are the key foci of ethical thought might be seen as an early indication of the intimate connection between solipsism and ethics (cf. Chapter 5). In a not entirely irrelevant sense, the Greek philosophers emphasizing the virtue and happiness of a single human being were ethical quasi-solipsists, though there is another sense in which they, living in a *polis*, certainly were not solipsists. The good life of the individual was not to be separated from the well-being of the community.

We now can, after these preliminary historical remarks, move directly to the (early) modern period of Western thought, that is, to the way in which the work of Descartes, in particular, set the stage for later discussions of solipsism.[7] We will be concerned with the ontological and epistemological aspects of the issue.

Classical Metaphysical and Epistemological Solipsism—the Cartesian Legacy

Solipsism, Skepticism, and Subjectivity

As defined in Chapter 1, ontological solipsism maintains that reality ontologically depends on something "subjective": my mind, my thoughts, my experience, or the contents of my consciousness. This can be taken to amount to a metaphysical world picture in which I am the only genuine subject there is and the world is "mine"— or perhaps "my dream"—in a strict ontological sense. Thus construed, solipsism is a version of *idealism*. In her classification of realisms and antirealisms, Susan Haack (1987: 281) speaks about "solipsistic constitutional idealism" as a version of the antirealist thesis of the "dependence" of truth on us (or me).[8] Karl Popper, one of the twentieth-century champions of realism, formulates the doctrine of solipsism (as a species of "subjective idealism") as follows:

> Solipsism is the theory that I, and only I, exist. According to this theory, the rest of the world—including all of you, and also my body—is my dream. Thus, you do not exist. You are only my dream. This theory cannot be refuted by you. (Popper 1994: 106)

Popper famously regards the irrefutability of a theory not as a virtue but as a vice. His definition of solipsism is, however, superficial—certainly it fails to be "fact-preserving" in Bell's sense. More generally, the solipsist's and the realist's interpretations of what "facts" are and what it means to "preserve" them differ.[9] Yet, solipsists may have rational arguments in their favor. This is how

Rollins summarizes what he takes to be the central argument for metaphysical solipsism:

> Every claim concerning the existence or nonexistence of anything is grounded in experience and could not possibly extend beyond it. An existential claim which seemed to reach beyond experience could have no basis or reference; it would apparently be unintelligible and not strictly a claim at all. But experience is essentially immediate; in itself it is never mistaken (only inferences from it can be mistaken), and it is had by one person only and is private to him. Hence, existential claims can never truly, and perhaps never with full intelligibility, claim more than the existence of the experiencing self and its states, and indeed perhaps never claim more than this as of the moment of the experience. (Rollins 1967: 488)

Thus, metaphysical solipsism, whenever backed up by a serious argument, is usually intertwined with epistemological considerations, typically of a strictly *empiricist* sort, which seem to lead to global skepticism concerning anything external to the experiencing subject.[10] It may be impossible to keep metaphysical and epistemological solipsism separate, if we insist on this empiricist starting point. Rollins notes this: the very formulation of the latter seems implicitly metaphysical (Rollins 1967: 490). I will call this combination of metaphysical and epistemological viewpoints *classical solipsism*.[11] If the metaphysical dimension of this doctrine is emphasized, classical solipsism claims that my experiences exhaust reality; if the epistemological dimension is taken to be central, the claim is rather that I cannot know (certainly, at least), or even justifiably believe, that they don't.

Historically, empiricistically motivated classical solipsism can be regarded as a radicalization of the Berkeleyan phenomenalist doctrine, "*esse est percipi*" ("to be is to be perceived"). The perceiver upon whom the existence of everything ontologically depends is, of course, me—the only perceiving subject whose perceptions are directly given to me. It is relatively easy to slide into this form of solipsism, if one begins from the strongly empiricist premises assumed by someone like Berkeley. Moreover, it might be speculated that the threat of solipsism has been one of the reasons why major thinkers from Descartes and Kant to those in our days have rejected the idea that all human knowledge is reducible to sense experience—despite the enormously appealing case for empiricist epistemology constituted by the advancement of empirical science. Yet, the slide into solipsism is possible also in a non-empiricist (Cartesian, rationalist) framework. Although twentieth-century discussions of classical solipsism (such as Russell's) have been empiricistically oriented, this is not inevitable.

Epistemologically, the classical view has, as Rollins's summary suggests, been defended by referring to the trivial fact that we must start from our own minds in order to obtain knowledge about the environing world. This primacy of the first person can be either empiricistically or rationalistically grounded. Ernest Gellner, speaking about "solitary confinement" instead of solipsism, formulates the crucial argument in a way worth quoting at length:

> If you accept the cognitive authenticity of nothing other than your own directly accessible data, in the end you are confined to a prison whose limits are indeed those data. If they are constituted by *your* immediate consciousness, by *yourself* in effect, then your self eventually becomes your prison. The self is your world, the world is your self. Nothing else is allowed you. . . .
>
> Assume that one realm only is accessible to you (it is in effect defined [by Descartes] as that which is indisputably accessible to you, and, *as* itself, not open to doubt). Furthermore assume that another realm, of external reality, in principle is *not* directly accessible. Can you infer, from the entities drawn from within the first category . . ., either to the mere existence, or the character and distribution, of entities of the second kind? . . . You only have access to the first lot, but never to the second. How could you check connections between what you can see and what you can never see?
>
> Call the first lot "experiences of the individual" and the second lot "external reality." Inescapable conclusion: neither the pattern, nor even the mere existence, of external reality, can ever be substantiated. All you have is your own data, *yourself*. . . . This is the Loneliness of the Long-Distance Empiricist. (Gellner 1998: 43–44)[12]

As Thomas Nagel puts the same Cartesian-cum-empiricist idea in the beginning of his introductory text-book, "If you think about it, the inside of your own mind is the only thing you can be sure of" (Nagel 1987: 8). He goes on to elaborate on the solipsist's situation as follows:

> The most radical conclusion to draw from this would be that your mind *is* the only thing that exists. This view is called solipsism. It is a very lonely view, and not too many people have held it. . . . If I were a solipsist I probably wouldn't be writing this book, since I wouldn't believe there was anybody else to read it. On the other hand, perhaps I would write it to make my inner life more interesting, by including the impression of the appearance of the book in print, of other people reading it and telling me their reactions, and so forth. I might even get the impression of royalties, if I'm lucky. (Nagel 1987: 11)

Nagel goes on to note a connection between solipsism and skepticism about the external world, but he distinguishes between the two (Nagel 1987: 12). Solipsism is not in itself a skeptical position, but (extreme) skepticism about the external world may be defined as the view that ontological solipsism (or even solipsism of the present moment) *may* be true and we cannot know that it isn't; that is, we do not have any rational, epistemologically sound reasons for being non-solipsists.

Nevertheless, if Nagel's definition says that solipsism is the view that "your mind" is the only thing that exists, a rather peculiar dialectical situation follows. Shouldn't (classical) solipsism be rather construed as the view that *my* mind only exists? Nagel, a non-solipsist, is trying to tell me that *I might* be a solipsist (and that he might also have been).[13] Popper, as we saw, is more straightforward: according to solipsism, "you do not exist." Indeed, if we take seriously the notion of *subjectivity* in metaphysics and the philosophy of mind, we cannot easily avoid the issue of solipsism. If my experience is fundamentally subjective, inescapably mine, can I ever justifiably believe that there are other genuinely subjective points of view, or loci of experience? From my own perspective, I cannot occupy anyone else's—hence, why should (or even could) I think that there *are* any others? How can *I* so much as arrive at a conception of my occupying only one specific point of view among others, located in a common, objective world? As a subject, I occupy my own perspective on the experiential reality given to me—

and others are, after all, *objects* from that subjective perspective. Accordingly, whenever philosophers of mind and experience speak about subjectivity and its irreducibility, we should observe their attachment to the problem framework of metaphysical and epistemological solipsism.

The idea that everything, particularly the existence of an external reality and other minds, can be doubted is of course the key to Descartes's "methodological doubt," a method developed in *Discourse on the Method* (1637) and *Meditations on the First Philosophy* (1641). Descartes supposes that solipsism (or skepticism regarding the existence of an external world) *might* be true. Of course, such skeptical solipsism plays for him only the role of the argumentative opponent. He seeks to show that we *do* have knowledge about an external reality, about mathematics, God, and other souls. The method of doubt is sketched in a well-known passage at the end of the meditation on "the things of which we may doubt":

> I will suppose, then, not that Deity, who is sovereignly good and the fountain of truth, but that some malignant demon, who is at once exceedingly potent and deceitful, has employed all his artifice to deceive me; I will suppose that the sky, the air, the earth, colours, figures, sounds, and all external things, are nothing better than the illusions of dreams, by means of which this being has laid snares for my credulity; I will consider myself as without hands, eyes, flesh, blood, or any of the senses, and as falsely believing that I am possessed of these; I will continue resolutely fixed in this belief, and if indeed by this means it be not in my power to arrive at the knowledge of truth, I shall at least do what is in my power, viz. [suspend my judgment], and guard with settled purpose against giving my assent to what is false, and being imposed upon by this deceiver, whatever be his power and artifice. (Descartes 1641: Meditation I)

Descartes's solution to the problem of skeptical solipsism, that is, the possibility that I might be deceived by an evil demon (the modernized form of which is the hypothesis that I might be a "brain in a vat"),[14] while seeking to demonstrate the reality of my own body, of God, and of a reality external to me, begins from the first-person perspective already expressed in the method of doubt itself. It is from the subjective insight—*cogito, ergo sum* ("I think, therefore I am")—that all knowledge about myself and the rest of the world flows (as argued in Meditation II). It is, thus, only on a *methodologically* solipsistic basis that metaphysical and epistemological solipsism (or skepticism) can be avoided, in Descartes's view.

As we have seen, it is common to think that the problem of solipsism is fundamentally based on the Cartesian possibility of skepticism and the *cogito* argument aiming at refuting it, and that our issue is thus closely connected with the mind-body problem also originated by Descartes.[15] We may call this view the *Cartesian conception* of the problem of solipsism. While we must acknowledge Descartes's crucial importance in the development of our problem,[16] we will later see that there can be fundamentally non-Cartesian ways (e.g., Wittgenstein's) of reacting to it. In a word, the Cartesian conception is not "transcendental" in the way post-Kantian approaches to the solipsism issue are. We might say, following Jean-Pierre Schachter (1997: 447, 454), that an ontologically substantial conception of the mind, a view according to which "at least some reality is mental," grounds Descartes's epistemic challenge, implying, together with Descartes's introspective method, the inconceivability and unimaginability of a plurality of minds. Still, this inconceivability is not transcendental, and the transcendental formulations of solipsism we will explore later are *not* skeptical in the Cartesian sense.

This is not the right place to examine in detail the historical traces of solipsism in modern philosophy after Descartes. We may briefly note that, among Descartes's followers, Spinoza's (1677) rationalistic metaphysics might be regarded as analogous to solipsism in some respects. This is because Spinoza's substance, unlike Leibniz's monads, is *one* and unique: it is both God and Nature (*Deus sive Natura*), the totality of everything that is (including me).[17] It would be a gross exaggeration to claim that Spinoza or Leibniz (any more than Descartes) was a solipsist. Their metaphysical constructions are, nevertheless, parts of a tradition that turned solipsism into a genuine option. It is possible for a Cartesian soul or a Leibnizian monad to view the world as if it were "its own" (and God's), that is, to view it from its private, absolutely unshareable point of view. This possibility remains while none of these great rationalists endorsed solipsism. In Spinoza's case, this idea is more problematic, though, for his all-encompassing substance is not even distinguished from the world and can, thus, hardly conceive of the world as "its own."

Turning briefly from early modern rationalism to British empiricism, it should be pointed out that, while George Berkeley and David Hume are, among Descartes's empiricist critics, the most important empiricist classics regarding solipsism, their common background lies in Locke's epistemology, particularly the *tabula rasa* doctrine, that is, the view that the human mind does not possess any innate ideas or principles but receives everything through sense experience (see Locke 1690: Book I). It is this doctrine that made possible later empiricist formulations of the main argument for metaphysical and epistemological solipsism. This argument is a "slippery slope": once you acknowledge that knowledge can only be based on the stimulation of your senses, you may be easily led to maintain that all you can ever know is (reducible to) the contents of your own sense experiences.

Berkeley radicalized the empiricist position by claiming that there are no external, material, mind- or sensation-independent things at all: the being of any objects consists in their being perceived—*esse est percipi* (cf. Berkeley 1710: Part I, especially §3). Berkeley's rejection of the material substance naturally opened doors for solipsism, though Berkeley himself, as a Christian theist, did not embrace it.[18] If there were only one mind (i.e., mine) whose perceptual faculty guaranteed the existence of objects, solipsism would follow. In a Berkeleyan context, it naturally becomes hard to explain why I, construing the world solely on the basis of my sense experiences, should believe in other, independently existing minds—even God's. It has, indeed, been suggested that Berkeley's immaterial world is reminiscent of the "nightmare" world that Descartes imagines in his methodological doubt (Tipton 1992). Hume (1739–40, 1748), in turn, as is well known, went even further than Berkeley and argued that the traditional notion of a substantive self as the one entertaining ideas and perceiving objects cannot be maintained. The self is just a bunch of ideas or representations; there is nothing more substantial or permanent behind them.[19]

The historical twists and turns of the rationalist and empiricist epistemological traditions need not concern us here further. What we have observed is that the Cartesian conception of the problem of solipsism is crucial in discussions of classical solipsism, while the threat of solipsism is usually formulated in empiricist rather than rationalist terms. For Descartes and for later philosophers alike, skeptical solipsism amounts to a kind of *horror metaphysicus*, revealing our insecurity regarding the fundamental nature of reality.[20]

Debates Over Solipsism, Skepticism, and Other Minds: Bradley and Russell

In early twentieth century, solipsism discussions became more explicit. Unlike in classical works such as Descartes's, the term "solipsism" has since then been in wide use especially in interpretive literature on such twentieth-century figures as Wittgenstein and Husserl (see Chapter 3). Meanwhile, there are additional points to be made about the epistemological disputes over solipsism and skepticism. In particular, Russell's worries concerning skeptical solipsism must be examined in order to arrive at a satisfactory account of classical solipsism. Solipsism as a philosophical problem appears to have been somewhat different for early twentieth-century British analytic philosophers, Continental philosophers, and thinkers influenced by American pragmatism.[21] I do not want to emphasize any problematic "analytic versus Continental" divisions, but it will be helpful to devote this subsection mainly to British analytic philosophy, continuing the epistemological discussions of the empiricist tradition, in which skepticism is seen as a major problem.

First, we may, following Borst (1992), note conceptual distinctions cutting across the ones made in Chapter 1. In particular, there is Russell's (1948: 191–92) distinction between *dogmatic solipsism* and *skeptical solipsism*, which parallels the one between atheism and agnosticism (i.e., denial and doubt regarding God's existence) in the philosophy of religion.[22] According to Borst (1992: 487), this roughly coincides with the distinction between metaphysical and epistemological solipsism (cf. Bouveresse 1987: 111; Craig 1998). More generally, what we have here is a distinction between two meta-epistemological attitudes to the acceptability of solipsism.[23]

Secondly, among the possible radicalizations of solipsism, the one known as solipsism of the present moment (again to be held either dogmatically or skeptically) is a key issue in Russell's contributions to the topic, as we will see. Another one, *conceptual solipsism* (which can be contrasted with "factual" versions of solipsism), is not. With reference to Wittgenstein, Borst explains that the conceptual solipsist holds not only that there in fact are no other minds, or no reality external to my mind, but that the existence of other minds is *inconceivable*.[24] He argues that "a dogmatic solipsist had better be a conceptual solipsist and that a conceptual solipsist had better not be a sceptical solipsist," since the view that there in fact are no other minds but there might have been some "has nothing whatsoever going for it" (Borst 1992: 487–88). It is hardly the case that dogmatic solipsism, strictly speaking, implies conceptual solipsism or that conceptual solipsism implies the denial of skeptical solipsism. Why, after all, couldn't the conceptual solipsist adopt a view close to "meaning skepticism" and *doubt* (instead of denying) the conceivability of there being other minds or the significance of the concept of another mind—or, correspondingly, of the concept of an external world in the realist's sense? These, however, are not the issues Russell or his followers seem to have been interested in. The avenue of conceptual solipsism opens in Wittgenstein.[25]

Around the turn of the twentieth century, solipsism, skeptically and "factually" (rather than conceptually) considered, was a major issue for both British Hegelians and later analytic philosophers. The latter, in particular, found solipsism as a species of skepticism—a sort of ultimate skepticism questioning the existence of a reality external to the experiencing mind and of other minds. It was against this kind of Cartesian skepticism that G. E. Moore's famous defense of common sense and his "proof" of an external world were aimed at.[26] Russell, early and late, also tried to *refute* solipsism (in particular, solipsism of the present moment), that is, to show that it is false or at least that we are justified in believing that it is false. Among Russell's writings, *Human Knowledge* (1948) is the most important from the viewpoint of the solipsism issue, although earlier works, especially *The Problems of Philosophy* (1912) and the 1913 manuscript *Theory of Knowledge* (Russell 1983), unpublished during Russell's lifetime, also contain discussions of solipsism.[27]

Already before Russell made his lasting contributions to epistemology, the Hegelian absolute idealist F. H. Bradley had construed the solipsist's argument, in its simplest form, as follows: "I cannot transcend experience, and experience must be *my* experience. From this it follows that nothing beyond my self exists;

for what is experience is its states" (Bradley 1893: 218). Now, if the solipsist insists on the continuation of experience beyond the present moment, s/he falls into an incoherence. If I am justified in believing in the existence of my self beyond the present moment, I have a similar right to believe in the existence of other selves; it is by means of a similar fallible process of inference that I arrive at the belief in my past self (Bradley 1893: 224–25).

Nevertheless, there are three grains of truth in solipsism, on Bradley's account. First, the world appears in my experience and "*is* my state of mind," so is "the real Absolute, or God himself" (the central concept in Bradley's metaphysics). Secondly, in order to know the universe, I must fall back upon my own sensational experience, contacting reality through "the felt 'this.'" Thirdly, although my own self is by no means identical to the Absolute, the latter would not be itself without my self. If the solipsist merely insists on the "essential necessity of his self to the Universe and every part of it," s/he cannot be refuted (Bradley 1893: 229–30, 557–58). These points are naturally related to Bradley's metaphysics of the Absolute and receive whatever plausibility they may have only within that framework.[28]

Although Russell was, at least most of his life, opposed to Hegelian metaphysics, he shared with Bradley the view that we must push solipsism into its extreme. There is nothing to be said in favor of a partial solipsism, which accepts the past and future of my self, as such a solipsism relies on principles of inference that it must reject in order to shun any inference to other minds. To be coherent, the solipsist must confine her-/himself to the mental states s/he is *presently* aware of. Thus, Russell distinguishes between more and less drastic versions of solipsism. The former (i.e., solipsism of the present moment) is defined as the thesis that "the universe consists, or perhaps consists, of only the following items; and then we enumerate whatever, at the moment of speaking, we perceive or remember" (Russell 1948: 9, 192–94). Here, perceptions and memories must be construed as instantaneous; according to the solipsist of the present moment, they do not have any external, spatiotemporal referent either in the past or in the present.

This way of formulating solipsism is important, for the traditional "I alone exist" has, according to Russell, no definite meaning unless what it says is false. By speaking about myself I exclude and delimit. Thus, the solipsist must say rather "data are the whole universe," defining "data" by enumerating them, and adding, finally, "this list is complete; there is nothing more," or (skeptically) "there is not known to be anything more" (Russell 1948: 191).[29] Russell summarizes the argument for skeptical solipsism as follows:

> From a group of propositions of the form "A occurs," it is impossible to infer by deductive logic any other proposition asserting the occurrence of something. If any such inference is to be valid, it must depend upon some non-deductive principle such as causality or induction. No such principle can be shown to be even probable by means of deductive arguments from a group of propositions of the form "A occurs." ... Therefore if, as empiricists maintain, all our knowledge is based on experience, it must be not only based on experience, but confined to experience: for it is only by assuming some principle or principles which experience cannot render even probable that anything whatever can be proved by experience except the experience itself. (Russell 1948: 194–95)

Russell thus arrives at a dilemma: either we must accept a very strong form of skeptical solipsism or, alternatively, we must accept a nonempirical principle, or a group of such principles, by which we may infer events from other events, at least probabilistically—and thus we must, in a sense, *reject empiricism* by allowing knowledge not logically inferred from experience (Russell 1948: 195). Russell, of course, opts for the latter, although it is a high price for an empiricist to pay.[30] The solipsistic position is just too much to believe; the other option, a partial rejection of empiricism (conjoined with the fact that empiricism itself could not be empirically known to be true, if it were true),[31] is, though perhaps not wholly pleasant to accept, at least believable (Russell 1948: 195–97). Indeed, the best argument against solipsism seems to be the "proof" (which Russell thought to have provided) that it can only be held in its most drastic form (Russell 1948: 196). This, in effect, is what makes it so *unbelievable*—for Russell and a number of more recent philosophers following his general orientation.[32]

Before leaving the Russellian treatment of solipsism, I want to draw attention to the most interesting American philosopher from the point of view of the issue of solipsism, George Santayana.[33] In Santayana, we find an argument echoing the thesis common to both Bradley and Russell, that is, that only extreme solipsism of the present moment can be a coherent version of solipsism. This argument is developed as a critique of what Santayana calls "romantic solipsism":

> Romantic solipsism, in which the self making up the universe is a moral person endowed with memory and vanity, is ... untenable. Not that it is unthinkable or self-contradictory; because all the complementary objects which might be requisite to give point and body to the idea of oneself might be only ideas and not facts; and a solitary deity imagining a world or remembering his own past constitutes a perfectly conceivable universe. But this imagination would have no truth and this remembrance no control; so that the fond belief of such a deity that he knew his own past would be the most groundless of dogmas; and while by chance the dogma might be true, that deity would have no reason to think it so. . . . Romantic solipsism, although perhaps an interesting state of mind, is not a position capable of defence; and any solipsism which is not a solipsism of the present moment is logically contemptible. (Santayana 1923: 13–14)

Don't we have here an early version of the Wittgensteinian private language argument? Santayana seems to tell us that there could be no normative standards by means of which the memories of the solipsistic deity could be assessed—"no control." Therefore, only solipsism of the present moment, in which the solipsist becomes "an incredulous spectator of his own romance, thinks his own adventures fictions," is "an honest position" and cannot be refuted by standard arguments (Santayana 1923: 15).

In accordance with his anti-skeptical philosophy of "animal faith," Santayana argues that this kind of solipsism can hardly be accepted by human beings:

> So far is solipsism of the present moment from being self-contradictory that it might, under other circumstances, be the normal and invincible attitude of the spirit; and I suspect it may be that of many animals. The difficulties I find in maintaining it consistently come from the social and laborious character of human life. A creature whose whole existence was passed under a hard shell, or was spent in a free flight, might find nothing

paradoxical or acrobatic in solipsism; nor would he feel the anguish which men feel in doubt, because doubt leaves them defenceless and undecided in the presence of oncoming events. A creature whose actions were pre-determined might have a clearer mind. He might keenly enjoy the momentary scene, never conceiving himself as a separate body or as anything but the unity of that scene, nor his enjoyment as anything but its beauty: nor would he harbour the least suspicion that it would change or perish, nor any objection to its doing so if it chose. Solipsism would then be selflessness and scepticism simplicity. . . . For men, however, who are long-lived and teachable animals, solipsism of the present moment is a violent pose, permitted only to the young philosopher, in his first intellectual despair. (Santayana 1923: 17)

Santayana's argument is *pragmatic*: because we have no choice but to engage in our various practical activities, being concerned about the past and the future, we cannot endorse solipsism (of the present moment) and still continue to be the kind of creatures we are. Solipsism might be an option for beings very different from us; for us it is a nonstarter. It would be highly *unnatural* for us, a violation of human nature.[34] As we will see later, the kind of naturalistic (albeit non-reductive) pragmatism developed by William James and other nineteenth- and twentieth-century pragmatists may provide a fruitful—though not unproblematic—framework for criticizing solipsism. My own view is not very far from Santayana's in this respect, although it must be informed by (Wittgensteinian) transcendental and ethical considerations that dig deeper into the problem of solipsism than Santayana's plainly naturalist reliance on our "animal" nature.

Russellian Formulations of Classical Solipsism

Given his enormous influence in twentieth-century analytic philosophy, it is hardly surprising that Russell's engagement with the solipsism issue has been adopted as a model among several more recent treatments of classical solipsism. I will provide two examples, both construing the problem in a skeptical and factual (as distinguished from conceptual) manner. These examples will enrich our understanding of the varieties of (classical) solipsism.

In a Russellian tone of voice, Helier J. Robinson maintains that solipsism follows from the hypothesis that there are no "imperceptibles," that is, nothing of which I am not conscious now (but only "strict perceptibles") (Robinson 1978: 162). One of the consequences of this view is that time does not exist; instead, only the "specious present" exists (Robinson 1978: 163). Thus, Robinson's solipsism, just like the version of solipsism Russell considers, is inevitably a solipsism of the present moment.

Robinson argues that the denial of this metaphysical and epistemological solipsism must lead to its opposite, "rationalism," that is, the view that "it is humanly possible to obtain a truth or wisdom that is an opposite of solipsism" (Robinson 1978: 166). Such truths, we are told, include "ontological optimism" (Leibniz's doctrine of the world being the best possible world) and the principle of sufficient reason (Robinson 1978: 165). These are opposites of solipsism, because the compossibility of possible worlds (which, according to Robinson, is taken to be something good) is, if solipsism is correct, minimal, and because the principle of sufficient reason takes everything to be explicable, whereas for solipsism nothing is explicable (since no reference to imperceptibles is allowed). Now, Robinson argues that solipsism cannot be shown to be false but is psychologically impossible to believe; accordingly, it must be escaped by means of belief. The critical question is where one should stop. From a slight skepticism there is a slippery slope leading all the way down to solipsism. Only arbitrary fiat or dogma can stop the slide. If we let common sense or some other dogma prevent us from being solipsists, we are, in Robinson's view, *unphilosophical*. Hence, we must not take our first step on the slippery slope at all. In order to rationally and undogmatically, that is, philosophically, avoid solipsism, we must believe what Robinson finds its opposite (Robinson 1978: 167–68).

This seems to me problematic. Why is the rationalistic belief itself not a groundless dogma? I fail to see how Robinson, any more than Russell, Popper, or Nagel, offers any easy escape from solipsism. For many contemporary philosophers, the rationalist, ontologically optimistic "opposite" of solipsism Robinson recommends is as unbelievable as solipsism.[35]

An at least equally rationalistic and metaphysically biased perspective on the issue of solipsism has been provided by Albert A. Johnstone who, in the subtitle of his book *Rationalized*

Epistemology (1991), encourages us to "take solipsism seriously." What Johnstone offers us is perhaps the most elaborate and comprehensive formulation of the classical skeptical problem of solipsism we have inherited from Descartes. He carefully distinguishes between various forms of solipsism, all of which are essentially skeptical, questioning our warrant in believing their opposite (which, in this case, is not claimed to be rationalism but something like ordinary commonsense realism about the mind-independent, external world).[36] Johnstone's solipsisms are thus skeptical (Cartesian-Russellian) variants of classical solipsism. In each case, the solipsist questions our entitlement to the belief that the everyday world we take ourselves to be experiencing exists independently of our experiencing it. S/he claims that there are no good grounds to support such a realistic position (1991: 15). Thus, a more proper title for Johnstone's investigations is perhaps "warrant skepticism" (see 1991: 17) rather than solipsism. Johnstone proposes that we return to the foundationalist project in epistemology, meeting the skeptic and the solipsist on their own ground.[37] This is obviously something that Descartes and Russell, in their different ways, attempted to do.

However, Johnstone's consideration of solipsism in terms of probabilities (1991: chapters 12 and 13) strikes me as flatly irrelevant. Let us, for example, take a look at his critique of "monopsyche solipsism":

> What is being claimed is that the intimate mirroring relationship experienced in one's own case is unique and is not to be found in the case of any other person. It is a very implausible claim that such a state of affairs should exist within the structured world .... In an orderly world, given the regularities in behavior and similarities between one's own behavior and that of others, it is highly anomalous that there should be such a huge difference in nature between oneself and others. (1991: 305–06)

This reasoning, clearly resembling Russell's rejection of solipsism, is hopeless. No interesting solipsist is convinced by the argument that solipsism is a highly improbable state of affairs. What the solipsist rejects is the realistic conception of a regular, "orderly" world as something that covers her/his specific point of view or structuring activity.

Something similar happens when Johnstone sets out to defend the reality of the world against what he calls "unreal world solipsism." Pointing out (again like Russell) that the solipsist is committed to an ontology more complex than the ontology of common sense, he notes that the commonsense position has no epistemological superiority over the solipsistic one (1991: 315–17). But then he goes on to argue that there are "several modest but distinct advantages enjoyed by the commonsense position over its solipsistic rivals" (1991: 319), the most important of them being the improbability and arbitrariness of the solipsistic hypothesis:

> The egocentricity of the world involves a particular individual, the solipsist. The latter is the one who has the illusion, or who awakes to find it was all a dream, or who is being deceived by a demon. The reference to the individual solipsist introduces an arbitrary element into the solipsistic thesis. ... There is no good reason to appoint one particular subject rather than another to the position of hub of the universe. ... What good reason (if any) does one have to embrace a solipsism with oneself, rather than someone else, as the dreamer or the person perceiving the vast illusion or the butt of a demon's hoax? (1991: 322; see also 326, 328)

It is hard to believe that anything like this is offered as a serious argument. The solipsist obviously begins from her/his own first-person point of view, from which there is nothing arbitrary in the solipsistic thesis. The claim that it is arbitrary for me to choose myself as the center of the universe, or that it would be highly improbable if I instead of someone else were the subject upon whom the world depends in a solipsistic fashion, is convincing only if I am *not* a solipsist, already believing in a realistic world in which I am just one individual among many. For a genuine (prospective) solipsist, there is no other choice than solipsism "with oneself." Very simply, there are no other selves, if solipsism is correct. Johnstone's appeal to the arbitrariness of the solipsistic subject and the resulting improbability of solipsism is itself arbitrary and has no force against anyone who seriously considers being a solipsist. Embracing or rejecting solipsism is not a matter of probability and improbability; solipsism, if worthy of acceptance, is inescapable.

Johnstone admits, however, that the specific identity of the solipsist might be renounced in favor of "a vaguely worded . . . proclamation on the unreality of the world, one that specifies nothing regarding the mode of unreality," in which case "unreal world solipsism" would be transformed into "the skeptical doctrine that the world is unreal in some way or other." Then, however, no one—no epistemological self—could rationally and warrantedly hold a solipsistic belief (1991: 329). I believe Johnstone is right in admitting "the permanent possibility of unreality," the fact that no argument logically demonstrates the falsity of the skeptical scenarios he investigates (1991: 329), but he does not acknowledge the more sophisticated philosophical resources the solipsist might have in keeping her/his identity out of the question. The solipsist, instead of being an identifiable and hence arbitrary individual *in* the world, might be a transcendental ego *to whom* the world is given as a world, that is, a condition for the possibility of a structured, representable world.

In short, the transcendental, essentially non-skeptical—and conceptual rather than factual—problem of solipsism I wish to encourage (in the next chapter) us to "take seriously" is very different from Russell's, Johnstone's, and others' classical skeptical problem of solipsism. Before moving on to this transcendental problem, we must, however, conclude our discussion of classical solipsism by taking a short look at its spin-off, a "merely methodological" form of solipsism that is sometimes regarded as less radical than the traditional metaphysical and epistemological forms we have considered.

Methodological Solipsism

The epistemological solipsist's thesis that all human knowledge originates in some private or "given" experience is close to what has come to be known as *methodological solipsism* in the philosophy of mind and language. Indeed, Descartes's methodological doubt can be interpreted as a species of methodological solipsism (Borst 1992: 487). Methodological solipsists typically *endorse* such an epistemological approach, emphasizing the primacy of the first-person point of view; this, of course, distinguishes their views from the traditional treatments of classical solipsism, in which the solipsistic scenario is usually seen as a threat to be avoided by philosophical arguments.

The modern classic of the program of methodological solipsism is Rudolf Carnap's *Aufbau* (1928), one of the landmarks of the early stages of logical positivism. For Carnap, it is vital to distinguish between metaphysical solipsism and mere methodological solipsism, which is just the adoption of an "autopsychological" (*eigenpsychische*) basis for the construction of scientific concepts.[38] The physical, "heteropsychological," and cultural realms are constructed out of the autopsychological (Carnap 1967: §§58–67). In a true Vienna Circle style, no metaphysical views are allowed: methodological solipsism is neither realistic nor idealistic (let alone solipsistic) in the bad metaphysical sense (Carnap 1967: §§64, 175–78). This is a problem that other logical positivists were preoccupied with as well: A. J. Ayer (1946: 168–75) argued that his epistemology does not commit him to a solipsistic denial of other selves,[39] while Hans Reichenbach (1951: 267–68) claimed that the solipsist thinks s/he can "prove the existence of his own personality," the "ego," although empirical knowledge about the ego and about the physical world are on the same footing.[40]

Carnap (1963: 864) tells us that he used the term "methodological solipsism" in the *Aufbau* in the sense of "methodological individual phenomenalism," but gave it up later, fearing the misreading that would construe him as a metaphysical solipsist. This is how Carnap characterized his system in 1928:

> The expressions "autopsychological basis" and "methodological solipsism" are not to be interpreted as if we wanted to separate ... the "*ipse*," or the "self," from the other subjects, or as if we wanted to single out one of the empirical subjects and declare it to be the epistemological subject. At the outset, we can speak neither of other subjects nor of the self. Both of them are constructed simultaneously on a higher level. ... The basic elements are to be called experiences of the self *after* the construction has been carried out; hence, we say: in our constructional system, "my experiences" are the basic elements. ... Likewise, the characterizations of the basic elements of our constructional system as "autopsychological," that is, as "psychological" and as "mine," becomes meaningful only after the domains of the

nonpsychological (to begin with, the physical) and of the "you" have been constructed. . . . Before the formation of the system, the *basis is neutral* in any system form; that is, in itself, it is neither psychological nor physical. (Carnap 1967: §65)

Hence, no preexistent ego is postulated before the construction of the system of concepts. The elementary experiences out of which the world is logically constructed are not experiences of a Cartesian soul. Rather, they are experiences by a Humean non-self-identical "self" whose identity remains indeterminate. Carnap does not postulate any "transcendental subject," either; rather, he wishes to maintain metaphysical neutrality regarding realism and (transcendental) idealism (Friedman 1999: 139 and *passim*). The extent to which the Viennese positivists' solipsism was merely methodological can also be appreciated by recalling Moritz Schlick's (1936: 471ff.) treatment of solipsism as a "pseudo-thesis" and his claim that "true positivism" is characterized by an "antisolipsistic attitude" (1936: 472).

However, the dichotomy between harmless methodological solipsism and bad old metaphysical solipsism cannot be swallowed easily. Putnam, one of the founders of modern externalist philosophy of mind and language, was one of the key critics of methodological solipsism.[41] He develops his criticism of methodological solipsism as an analogy to his argument against cultural relativism,[42] offering us this:

> The "methodological solipsist"—one thinks of Carnap's *Logische Aufbau* or of Mach's *Analyse der Empfindungen*—holds that all our talk can be reduced to talk about experiences and logical constructions out of experiences.[43] More precisely, he holds that everything he can conceive of is identical (in the ultimate logical analysis of his language) with one or another complex of his own experiences. What makes him a *methodological* solipsist as opposed to a real solipsist is that he kindly adds that *you*, dear reader, are the "I" of this construction when *you* perform it: he says *everybody* is a (methodological) solipsist.
>
> The trouble . . . is that his two stances are ludicrously incompatible. His solipsist stance implies an enormous asymmetry between persons: my body is a construction out of my experiences, in the system, but *your* body isn't a construction

out of *your* experiences. It's a construction out of *my* experiences. And your experiences—viewed from within the system—are a construction out of your bodily behavior, which, as just said, is a construction out of *my* experiences. My experiences are different from everyone else's (within the system) in that they are what *everything* is constructed from. But his transcendental stance is that it's all symmetrical: the "you" he addresses his higher-order remark to cannot be the empirical "you" of the system. But if it's really true that the "you" of the system is the only "you" he can understand, then the transcendental remark is unintelligible. Moral: don't be a methodological solipsist unless you are a *real* solipsist! (Putnam 1983: 236–37)

Something analogous is, according to Putnam, true about the cultural relativist who attempts to acknowledge other cultures' right to consider their viewpoints as the background to which everything must be relativized. There is, he argues, no transcendental standpoint available for such a claim. Putnam's criticism of Carnap, introducing the distinction between the transcendental and the empirical levels of investigation, paves the way for our later discussion of Wittgenstein's attitude to solipsism.

In a later reflection on Carnap, Putnam repeats the charge that the distinction between metaphysical and methodological solipsism collapses. The argument is slightly different, however. Putnam now questions Carnap's claim that different "reconstructions" of scientific language, for example, autopsychological and physical, are "equally possible." In what sense, he asks, can two incompatible theories be "equally possible"? (Putnam 1994: 88–89). What Carnap's answer boils down to is his statement that the methodological solipsist's autopsychological basis enjoys an epistemic priority (Carnap 1967: §§54ff.). According to Putnam, all this can mean is that "the methodological solipsist [reconstruction] is the one we can *understand*; that it is *by* seeing that they are in some sense 'equivalent' to the methodological solipsist one that we understand the others" (Putnam 1994: 90). Again, the illusion that the methodological solipsist avoids "real" solipsism, the view that "language is just a device for anticipating *my* experiences" and does not refer to anything external, disappears (Putnam 1994: 90; cf. Putnam and Putnam 2017: 22). What Carnap offers us is a "pseudosocial" dimension of language within a solipsistic world

(Putnam 2012: 81). Moreover, it is only Carnap's (incoherent) belief that "elementary experiences are 'private' in a sense which implies that I *cannot* refer to the elementary experiences of other people" that motivates his methodological solipsism (Putnam 1994: 97).[44]

The extent to which Carnapian methodological solipsism is quite as radical as "real" solipsism can be appreciated by taking a look at how William Todd defines what he labels "analytical solipsism" (a "modern" form of solipsism close to Carnap's view, although Todd makes few explicit references to Carnap). Todd characterizes analytical solipsism as a reinterpretation or radicalization of traditional empiricist skepticism about the external world:

> [The solipsist] does not deny that there are reasons for believing in the existence of the external world and the existence of other persons. In fact, he admits the truth of statements asserting the existence of these things. Rather, he is saying that one can admit all this and still not commit oneself ontologically to anything beyond the occurrence of one's own sensations and certain principles governing them. Thus, while the modern solipsist would never deny the existence of the world, his hypothesis is that we can assert its existence just by talking ultimately about our own sensations and making very complex assertions about them. His view is that we never have beliefs which commit us to anything more than this . . . . Instead of denying the existence of an irreducible physical world he tells us that we never believed in it anyway. (Todd 1968: vii)

Accordingly, the solipsist holds that "everything which can ordinarily be said could, in theory, be said in a language which referred only to one's own sensations" (Todd 1968: 24)—that is, in a "private language." If, as analytical solipsism maintains, statements of common sense purportedly referring to causal and temporal facts, or facts about other minds, can be reinterpreted as complex statements about one's own mental states, then there is no reason to deny that what we have here is a doctrine as radical and as difficult to maintain (though also as hard to overcome) as any thesis the classical solipsist might put forward.[45]

Putnam offers no direct argument against "real" solipsism. I am not saying that he (any more than Todd) should. Obviously he takes solipsism to be highly implausible and considers a reduction of any view to it a sufficient *reduction ad absurdum*. What he does show us is that the gap between metaphysical and methodological solipsism is considerably narrower than philosophers hostile to metaphysics, including Carnapian empiricists, may have thought.[46] Carnapian methodological solipsism, while seeking to avoid skepticism and other traditional metaphysico-epistemological difficulties, seems to be entangled with the very same classical issues it was supposed to set aside. This is a point we may grant to Putnam.

Occasionally, for example, in recent treatments of methodological solipsism in the philosophy of psychology and biology, the connection between external world skepticism and methodological solipsism is affirmed more clearly than in Carnap's allegedly non-skeptical and non-metaphysical methodological solipsism. Thus, Elliot Sober (1995) considers the evolutionary question of *why* living organisms usually are not solipsistic: "*Why* are our minds so constituted that we spontaneously think in nonsolipsistic terms?" This amounts to a question of function: "Why is it *useful* to an organism for it to have beliefs that describe a world outside its own mind?" (Sober 1995: 548). Here the definition of solipsism parallels those discussed in relation to semantic or methodological solipsism: "Solipsistic organisms have beliefs that are solely about their own experiences; these beliefs make no reference to a world that exists outside the mind. A solipsist may think something like *I am experiencing a bitter taste* or *bitterness is now occurring*. However, the solipsist cannot think *this tastes just like the lettuce I ate yesterday*" (Sober 1995: 551).

Here, as in the classical Cartesian-Russellian case, solipsism is identified with a broadly skeptical position denying the existence of (or reasons to believe in) an external, independent reality.[47] However, we will see in the next chapter that solipsism, in its transcendental version, can be a *non-skeptical* interpretation of the world—and can even be based on an ethical motivation. Therefore, both Sober's explanatory project and the debates over methodological solipsism we have considered are, in the end, to some extent irrelevant for our purposes. Indeed, Sober's phrase "solipsistic organisms" would be strange or even oxymoronic from the transcendental standpoint. What we are interested in here is not the question of why we do have beliefs about external reality rather than just about the states of our own minds, but the question of whether or not even those beliefs that we take to refer to objects outside our thought ought to be reconstructed solipsistically.

Borst (1992: 488) observes that methodological solipsism as a "research strategy" in cognitive psychology is far removed from "orthodox solipsism," since it is supposed to be used in the study of other minds. This fact further illuminates the irrelevance of most of the arguments *pro* and *contra* methodological solipsism from the point of view of our problem. On the other hand, methodological solipsism, at least in its Carnapian form, depends on metaphysics—on a kind of picture that makes classical solipsism possible, too—despite, or even because of, its insistence on avoiding such metaphysics. Its metaphysical commitments remain implicit, however. I do take Putnam's arguments to show that it is not obvious that one can adopt the first-person starting point in one's epistemological pursuits without making heavy metaphysical commitments. Methodological solipsism is conceptually tied to classical solipsism, although it is precisely the metaphysical and epistemological (skeptical) framework of the latter that it seeks to overcome. Both presuppose a kind of *metaphysical realism*—to use Putnam's (1981, 1983) expression that he later (e.g., 2012) largely gave up—or transcendental realism in Kant's sense (cf. Chapter 3), attempting to view the world from a "God's-Eye View," through metaphysical spectacles, or claiming (as Carnap did) that wearing such spectacles is not desirable or even possible.

Pace methodological solipsists for whom solipsism amounts to a mere "research strategy," the issues we will, at least mainly, consider in the rest of this inquiry are not empirical, let alone natural-scientific. Ours is, crucially, a transcendental problem. Thus, in the next chapter, we will move on to a Kantian stance critical toward the kind of pre-Kantian approaches we have considered in this chapter. I hope it has become clear that neither classical solipsism nor its methodological alternative is satisfactory or even a particularly relevant way of approaching the topic.

Some philosophical relevance may be gained, however, by relating methodological solipsism to broader topics. In its general form, methodological solipsism can be understood as the view that other minds or other human beings (*if* there are any) must be investigated and understood by means of an analogy to myself (i.e., my mind and my mental activity), from my standpoint or perspective. Thus, the methodological solipsist adopts a first-person point of view to the understanding of others.[48] But then it is, again, unclear whether this view can remain merely methodological, or metaphysically neutral.[49] Putnam's abovementioned argument against Carnapian methodological solipsism can be reconstructed as an application of Charles S. Peirce's and William James's "pragmatic maxim": there is, it turns out, no *practical* difference between methodological and "real" (classical) solipsism. At least *ethically*, one might argue, they collapse into one another: my perspective on others is, whether I am a classical or merely a methodological solipsist, a first-person perspective (see Chapters 4 and 5). I do not, then, let others be genuinely other to me.[50] This is a metaphysico-ethical difficulty for me, a problem about the structure of the world I live in, instead of being simply a deficiency in my methodological procedures. The value of methodological solipsism might lie in the dialectical result that the very attempt to adopt a consistently first-person perspective will lead to unbearable metaphysical and ethical difficulties.

If Putnam (or my construal of him) is correct in his diagnosis of Carnap's failure to satisfactorily defend methodological solipsism without succumbing to something like "real" solipsism, then solipsism is, indeed, a much more widely relevant philosophical issue than one might initially think. Many of us, perhaps all of us to some extent, are in the grip of the seeming inevitability of the first-person point of view. Solipsism is, consequently, a problem— perhaps primarily an ethical problem, a moral threat—not only to epistemologists working in the Cartesian-Russellian tradition but to us all. The next step in the argument is to explain what the transcendental perspective to the issue of solipsism amounts to and what its relevance is. My problem, then, is transcendental and conceptual, not merely epistemological or methodological, and certainly not simply factual, skeptical, empirical, scientific, or evolutionary. At the transcendental level, our investigation of solipsism will focus on the fundamental structure of our world-engagement as such.

CHAPTER THREE

Transcendental Solipsism

Having discussed classical solipsism (and its "merely methodological" alternative), I will next explain why a quite different variety of solipsism is more interesting and relevant. Special attention will be drawn to the Wittgensteinian brand of solipsism, which I will call *transcendental solipsism*, and to its close relatives.

In terms of my introductory classification, transcendental solipsism roughly amounts to a combination of (weak) ontological solipsism, semantic solipsism, and methodological solipsism.[1] There is, thus, a methodological element involved, although the position is not "purely" methodological or non-metaphysical. The reason why the transcendental solipsist's ontological commitment to solipsism may be rather weak is that such a solipsist might hold that it is only the way the world is that depends on the solipsistic subject, not the mere existence of the world (which may be conceived as analogous to the existence of Kant's things in themselves).[2] Furthermore, transcendental solipsism is often, though not necessarily, semantically motivated; this is, at least, the case with Wittgenstein's version. Finally, transcendental solipsism is, in terms of the distinctions introduced in the previous chapter, a "conceptual" rather than a "factual" thesis: the world, or its ontological structure, depends on the subject (me) conceptually or necessarily, not just accidentally as a contingent matter of fact. There is, according to transcendental solipsism, no *sense* in claiming that the world *could* possess its own ontological structure independently of me (my experiences, my thoughts, etc.) while it actually *doesn't*.

Kantian Idealism

Such a conceptual dependence can be explicated by means of the transcendental vocabulary we have inherited from the father of modern transcendental philosophy, Kant. Any discussion of transcendental solipsism must begin with a recapitulation of some central characteristics of Kant's transcendental approach, even though Kant himself cannot be interpreted as a solipsist (nor can this book be any kind of study on Kant).

Kant: The Rise of the Transcendental Ego

While the Cartesian skeptical framework is a central background of the classical problem of solipsism, it is only with Kant that we face a transcendental way of overcoming skepticism. Kant famously sought to explain how we are able to cognize an objective, structured reality—though not the "things in themselves." According to Putnam (1981: 60), Kant was the first philosopher to seriously question the dogma of metaphysical realism, according to which the world consists of a fixed set of mind-, description-, theory-, scheme-, or discourse-independent objects that can be, at least in principle, completely captured in one single true theory or description (in a non-epistemic correspondence sense), from a God's-Eye View. This makes Kant a crucial historical figure from the point of view of the realism issue in general and the problem of solipsism in particular.

As is well known, according to Kant, we ourselves construct, at a transcendental level, the empirical world (i.e., phenomena, appearances) that can be the object of our cognition. It is we ourselves that impose spatiality and temporality (as forms of pure intuition) as well as causality and other categories of understanding into that world, or structure the world in such a way that it is, for us, spatiotemporal and consists of causally connected events and processes. Independently of our cognitive capacities and the transcendental constitution of reality based thereupon, there would be no empirical world, no experienceable objects, no nature. Famously, Kant maintained that we can have no experience whatsoever of the things in themselves that transcend the subjectively (transcendentally) constituted empirical world. We must only postulate their existence.

From the idea of a transcendental subject actively constructing the object(s) of its experience—that is, the world or nature—it is only a small step to the basic idea of solipsism, namely, that the world is my world, ontologically dependent on my subjective activity (though not causally or empirically, but transcendentally, dependent). Since the prefix "I think" (*Ich denke*) must, according to Kant, be able to accompany all my representations (*Vorstellungen*),[3] there is a sense in which everything I can represent in the experienceable world is represented as belonging to a world-for-me. Indeed, in his celebrated commentary on Kant's first *Critique*, P. F. Strawson (1966: 196) explicitly claims Kant's transcendental idealism to slide into "transcendental solipsism." Such a reading can be questioned, with good reasons (see Beiser 2002; Allison 2004; and especially Collins 1999), but we cannot deny Kant's fundamental importance in the development of the solipsism issue.[4]

The central position of Kant's *Kritik der reinen Vernunft* can also be expressed by saying that organized experience, as distinguished from a mere Humean "rhapsody" of individual sense impressions, is possible and that we can show, transcendentally, *how* (i.e., on the basis of which conditions) it is possible. These conditions include the forms of pure intuition and the categories of understanding. That a kind of first-person perspective is Kant's starting point is manifested in his way of relying on the "formal" principle that any representation is potentially accompanied by the "I think"; indeed, this can be seen as his main premise in the Transcendental Deduction, whose purpose is to demonstrate the objective validity and necessary applicability of the categories to experienceable objects and events, or appearances (*Erscheinungen*). In this sense, Kant's approach might be regarded as methodologically solipsistic (like Descartes's), albeit operating at a transcendental level (unlike Descartes's).

Kant does not view the world, and the human capacity to cognize the world, from a God's-Eye View or an Archimedean point, as Descartes still tried to do. Kant's argumentation begins *from within* the cognitive activity whose conditions of possibility he is examining. His transcendental idealism is distinguished from the "transcendental realism" of both his rationalist and his empiricist predecessors by being strictly confined to an anthropocentric perspective, with no hope of providing any non-anthropocentric account of the possibility of knowledge—and with no skeptical disappointment naturally following the realization that such accounts are impossible (see Allison 2004: chapter 2).[5] If the center of the perspective from which the possibility of knowledge is established is a single human ego (me), the Kantian position becomes almost indistinguishable from a kind of solipsism. The transcendental subject constitutes the empirical world, whose objects and events (including other subjects) are, however, empirically real, that is, not imagined or fictional.

However, little explicit treatment of the problem of solipsism in its modern sense can be found in the first *Critique*. For example, in his Refutation of Idealism (Kant 1781/1787: B274ff.), Kant does not consider the issue of other minds at all. Instead of solipsism in the sense of the other minds problem, he is here interested in the more general Cartesian (methodological) skepticism about the material world (see Allison 2004 [1983]: 295).[6] Nevertheless, the "Refutation" is an important document of Kant's struggle with his Cartesian heritage. It contains the essence of Kant's critique of Descartes, the originator of the modern problem of solipsism. Kant, famously, regarded it as a "scandal" in philosophy that the reality of the external (empirical) world, which is the object of our external, spatiotemporal perceptions, could not have been proved and that its existence remained controversial in relation to the existence of the objects of our inner mental states.

It should be noted, in contrast to Descartes in particular, that Kant's notion of the inner sense (*innere Sinn*) is not equivalent to the Cartesian assumption of an epistemically privileged cognitive capacity. The contextuality of this notion in Kant's epistemology is one of the elements of his critique of the Cartesian skepticism and the resulting possibility of solipsism. The inner sense, according to the "Refutation," depends on there being real objects of the outer sense in the empirical world.[7] These outer objects must not, however, be confused with things in themselves. They are empirical external objects whose transcendental structure is constituted by the subject; their independence is empirical, not transcendental.

Hence, while the problem of solipsism in a sense becomes possible as a transcendental problem only due to Kant's transcendental idealism and its central insight that the empirical world is at a transcendental level constituted by the activity of the subject, Kant himself was a sharp critic of the kind of solipsism that seemed to be possible for Descartes and for his empiricist followers preoccupied with skepticism. Thus, Kant's general philosophical approach is very different from the approaches to the skeptical problem of solipsism. In the "Refutation," Kant persuasively argues in a resolutely anti-Cartesian manner that inner experience in general is only possible if outer experience of external objects in space and time is. According to Kant, the Cartesian possibility of solipsism—that is, the possibility that, in an empirical or factual sense, I might be the one and only existing mind and my experiences of a structured world with other minds might be caused by a deceiving demon—is not a real possibility at all. There is, indeed, no distinction between the transcendental and the empirical to be found in Descartes, nor in any other pre-Kantian philosopher. The transcendental solipsism that becomes an option after Kant is much more subtle than the solipsism Descartes and his earlier followers were preoccupied with.

On the other hand, one might legitimately wonder whether Kant actually touches the problem of solipsism at all. As the Kantian transcendental ego, operative in the original synthetic unity of transcendental apperception, is not a Cartesian substantial soul but the merely formal "I think" which must be able to accompany all my representations, "it" is not "mine" (or "me") in any ordinary sense of these pronouns. It is something superindividual or intersubjective—in a word, transcendental rather than empirical. It is *our* common human cognitive capacity, structuring the empirical, experienceable world *for us*.[8] Yet, despite Kant's own anti-solipsism, he *was* a precursor to the kind of transcendental solipsism that later philosophers have been preoccupied with. Thus, while there may be no specifically Kantian problem of solipsism, Kant sets the transcendental framework for later philosophers considering this issue.[9]

We may conclude that while the first *Critique* leaves the solipsism issue (almost) unexamined (at least insofar as it invokes the question of the uniqueness of my ego as compared to others), one may move from the concept of transcendental subjectivity to the uniqueness of such an ego—perhaps even more so in moral philosophy, where the motivation for ethical action can only arise, according to Kant's rigid rationalist deontology, within *me*, from my pure practical reason and my unqualified respect for the moral law whose absolute commandment is, in effect, comparable to ("as if") God's. There is a sense in which the Kantian moral subject is solipsistic by being the only ethically relevant and evaluable subject.[10] Yet, again, this subject represents the rational core of *anyone's* moral self. It is "me" only in the transcendental sense, not as a distinct object in the world.

Solipsism in Post-Kantian Idealism

J. G. Fichte and Arthur Schopenhauer are presumably the most significant post-Kantian idealists whose complex views are relevant to our problem—though one could easily mention several others as well, for example, G. W. F. Hegel, Karl Reinhold, and Solomon Maimon.[11] Fichte, in particular, is famous for his quasi-solipsistic view, developed in the *Wissenschaftslehre* and elsewhere,[12] that the absolute, primordial, all-sufficient, transcendental self (I, ego) "posits" (*setzt*) both itself and the "not-self," that is, the world external to the self (cf. Fichte 1794–95: §§1–2). Clearly, then, Fichte is an important post-Kantian figure in the development of the transcendental problem of solipsism. This is one of his descriptions of the ego's transcendental activity:

> The self's own positing of itself is thus its own pure activity. The *self posits itself*, and by virtue of this mere self-assertion it *exists*; and conversely, the self *exists* and *posits* its own existence by virtue of merely existing. It is at once the agent and the product of action; the active, and what the activity brings about; action and deed are one and the same, and hence the "I am" expresses an Act, and the only one possible. (Fichte 1794–95: §1:6; I, 96)[13]

Fichte's transcendental idealism is based on Kant's, but it can be regarded as a radicalization of the Kantian account, in which the "I think" remains, as we saw, a formal principle, and substantializations of the self are attacked as metaphysical illusions.[14] The activity of the Fichtean self is primordial: the positing of the not-self depends on the self-positing of the self. For Fichte, as one commentator explains, "the undifferentiated primordial being that is the source of all is actually a self" (Lachs 1987: 189); hence, his view can legitimately be considered transcendentally solipsistic.[15] Fichte's idealism is clearly transcendental, as the self's "positing" cannot be reduced to any causal, empirical, or factual production.

Fichte seems to have maintained that while solipsism (or "egoism," as it was then called) is theoretically acceptable, it should be avoided in the practice of human life, especially moral life with other persons. The transcendental nature of his solipsism explains why the primordial self is not an individual human being, that is, not me, as distinguished from other persons.[16] If it were, no moral life together with others would be possible. It is in the realm of morality, in particular, that Kant also needed to abandon the quasi-solipsistic dimensions of his transcendental idealism in order to construe the moral law as demanding justice for all human beings, all inhabitants of the "kingdom of ends," all rational beings who were to be treated as "ends in themselves"—although it is not clear that even Kant succeeded in this effort (Kuhlmann 1990). While Kantian moral philosophy, with its affirmation of the existence of God as a postulate of practical reason, appears to be clearly non-solipsistic, even religion (as subordinated to the requirements of morality) is, Kant seems to be claiming in his latest work, essentially constituted by an individual's (i.e., my) inner truthfulness, without any assumptions about an external metaphysical deity.[17] Such a conception of religion is solipsistically interpretable, although Kant himself was, in his moral theology, a theist, believing in a personal God whose role (we may hope) is to secure a moral world order (cf. Beiser 2006). Moreover, as already observed, the fact that Kant's ethical system imposes obligations on me, rather than anyone else, may make his approach (quasi-)solipsistic in practical philosophy.

Be that as it may, Fichte's starting point is (methodologically) solipsistic even more clearly than Kant's, as demonstrated by the 1797 introduction to the *Wissenschaftslehre*: "Attend to yourself: turn your attention away from everything that surrounds you and towards your inner life; this is the first demand that philosophy makes of its disciple. Our concern is not with anything that lies outside you, but only with yourself" (Fichte 1794–95: I, 422). He goes on to say that the philosopher's "self-constructing self is none other than his own" and that the philosopher can intuit the act of the self "in himself only" by carrying it out her-/himself (Fichte 1794–95: I, 460). Consequently, a kind of solipsism seems to be built into the very enterprise of philosophy. The philosopher her-/himself must, Fichte appears to claim, bring about the act of the self that is the transcendental ground of everything, both of the self and of the not-self. It is not easy to see how the transcendental activity of the self can be brought about by a philosopher who after all must be a flesh-and-blood human being. Yet, it is clear that Fichte is a major figure in the history of transcendental solipsism.

Schopenhauer's importance in the development of transcendental solipsism is as considerable as Fichte's, and he was also crucially indebted to Kant's philosophy, especially transcendental idealism. In his great work, *Die Welt als Wille und Vorstellung*, one finds a discussion of "theoretical egoism" (his word for what we now call solipsism) leading to the unethical position of "practical egoism."[18] Theoretical egoism, according to Schopenhauer, "regards as phantoms all phenomena outside its own will, just as practical egoism does in a practical respect; thus in it a man regards and treats only his own person as a real person, and all others as mere phantoms." It is impossible to refute theoretical egoism "by proofs," because it can be found, as "a serious conviction," "only in a madhouse," where it needs cure rather than refutation (Schopenhauer 1969 [1844]: 104).[19] Hence, Schopenhauer might appear to be a severe critic of solipsism, and he even seems to provide strong moral reasons for avoiding solipsism (cf. Atwell 1995: 96; see Chapter 5).[20]

However, there is a strong solipsistic element in Schopenhauer's central thesis that "the world is my will"—even stronger than in his Kantian-like idealist view that "the world is my representation" (with which his major book begins). His ethical opposition to solipsism is also compromised by the search for a union with All (other willing beings), which is akin to the Hinduist doctrine *tat tvam asi* ("this art thou"). John E. Atwell's (1995) study on Schopenhauer makes these points clear: he argues that Schopenhauer's doctrine can be condensed in a fundamental "single thought," his idea of the world as a *macranthropos*, as an analogy of a willing human being.

Hence, just as in Kant and Fichte, albeit in a different way, there appears to be a tension between solipsism and anti-solipsism in Schopenhauer's transcendental philosophy. None of these great German idealists can be called a "solipsist"; yet, none of them has shown us any easy escape from the problem we are considering, but all have, on the contrary, offered insightful formulations of transcendental solipsism.[21] Together they set the stage for the kind of solipsism that major twentieth-century thinkers like Husserl and Wittgenstein were concerned with.

Phenomenology and the Problem of Intersubjectivity

The sources of the "Continental" tradition in twentieth-century philosophy can largely be found in Husserl's *phenomenology*. The important role played by the issue of solipsism in this tradition can be explicated in the context of the Husserlian methodology of "bracketing" the external, transcendent world (i.e., the phenomenological *epoche*) in order to be able to focus on the experience itself, on the way in which what is experienced is given to me (the subject of experience), or to my consciousness. Indeed, the issue of solipsism is largely parallel in Husserl and Wittgenstein.[22] One of their shared questions was whether, and how, a common world and genuine intersubjectivity among human beings are so much as possible—or whether we should even seek to explain how they are possible.[23]

Husserlian phenomenology has been considered problematic precisely because of the solipsism issue (cf. Jacques 1982). Because of his transcendental idealism, starting not from external ("transcendent") objects but from their being given to the subject, me (Mensch 1988), Husserl has been regarded as a (transcendental) solipsist, or necessarily committed to solipsism, despite his own claims to the contrary. It is, in other words, his phenomenological reinterpretation of the Kantian notion of a transcendental ego that is usually taken to force him into a solipsistic position in which other egos remain problematic (Carr 1977). At least he is generally seen as a "methodological solipsist" roughly in Descartes's sense: his point of departure in phenomenological reflection is the first-person perspective; hence, his phenomenology, early and late, is a kind of "egology."[24] Husserl himself saw the danger of solipsism and asked,

> Wenn ich, das meditierende Ich, mich durch die phänomenologische Εποχη auf mein absolutes transzendentales Ego reduziere, bin ich dann nicht zum *solus ipse* geworden, und bleibe ich es nicht, solange ich unter dem Titel Phänomenologie konsequente Selbstauslegung betreibe? Wäre also eine Phänomenologie, die Probleme objektiven Seins lösen und schon als Philosophie auftreten sollte, nicht als transzendentaler Solipsismus zu brandmarken? (Husserl 1931: §42 [91])[25]

This result seems natural, as in Husserlian phenomenology the world (in which I live and which I experience) receives whatever meaning or objective validity it has *from me* (Husserl 1931: §§8, 11 [22, 27]). But, of course, the transcendental solipsism that results is, we are told, only methodological, "eine philosophische Unterstufe," and "als solche in methodischer Absicht abgegrenzt werden muß, um die Problematik der transzendentalen Intersubjektivität als eine fundierte, also höherstufige in rechter Weise ins Spiel setzen zu können" (Husserl 1931: §13 [32]).[26] Still, in such a methodological approach, others remain "modifications" of myself (Husserl 1931: §52 [118–19]). The *alter ego* must be found "innerhalb der erfahrenden Intentionalität meines Ego" (Husserl 1931: §62 [152]).[27] Husserl thus acknowledges (at least in the *Cartesian Meditations*), as Wittgenstein had done in the *Tractatus* a few years earlier, that there *is* a kernel of truth in (transcendental) solipsism and that a critical philosophical attitude ought to recognize this: "Der Schein eines Solipsismus ist aufgelöst, obschon der Satz die fundamentale Geltung behält, daß alles, was für mich ist, seinen Seinssinn ausschließlich aus mir selbst, aus meiner Bewußtseinssphäre schöpfen kann" (Husserl 1931: §62 [154]).[28]

While some major Husserl scholars are happy to read Husser's phenomenology in terms of transcendental solipsism (e.g., Bell 1988, 1990: 153ff.), the solipsistic account of Husserl's philosophy has been emphatically contested by Dan Zahavi, who notes that what Husserl aimed at was a transcendental theory of intersubjectivity.[29] In particular, the concept of *lifeworld*, central in Husserl's later philosophy, is "intersubjective through and through": objects, events, and actions experienced by the self (me) are public, not private, and "the source of all real truth and being" lies in an "intersubjective-transcendental sociality." I am only one among the many subjects of experience there are; there are perspectives on the world other than my own (Zahavi 1996: 228–32). According to Zahavi, Husserl maintains that the categories of transcendence, objectivity, and reality are "constituted intersubjectively," "by a subject that has experienced other subjects"; the same is true about the categories of immanence, subjectivity, and appearance (Zahavi 1996: 233; see Zahavi 2003: 109–25).

While Zahavi may be correct about this "intersubjective transformation" in Husserl's transcendental philosophy,[30] I am not convinced that the problem of solipsism will have gone away as soon as we adopt his reading of Husserl. It seems that the problem comes back when we admit that "intersubjectivity cannot be examined adequately from a third-person's view, but must be analysed in its manifestation in the life of the individual subject," "through a radical *'mich-selbst-befragen'*" (Zahavi 1996: 230). My experience of an intersubjectively experienceable transcendent object is "mediated by my experience of its givenness for another transcendent subject, that is, by my experience of a foreign world-directed subject" (Zahavi 1996: 231). Isn't this kind of intersubjectivity still possible for the solipsist, insofar as the solipsism at issue is transcendentally construed? Couldn't the "I" who observes that "only insofar as I experience that Others experience the same objects as myself, do I really experience these objects as objective and real" (Zahavi 1996: 231), be a solipsistic "I"? Couldn't the other be her/his own transcendental construction?

This "return of the solipsist" is further strengthened by Zahavi's remarks on the "egological attachment of intersubjectivity": "Intersubjectivity, my relation to an Other, always passes through my own subjectivity. Only from this point of view is intersubjectivity and the plurality of constitutive centers phenomenologically accessible" (Zahavi 1996: 237). Intersubjectivity thus unfolds from my transcendental ego, the condition of all intersubjectivity. This is stated by Husserl *expressis verbis*: transcendental intersubjectivity must be "rein in mir, im meditierenden Ego, rein aus Quellen meiner Intentionalität für mich als seiend konstituiert" (Husserl 1931: §56 [133]),[31] albeit in a way that brings with it subjective experiences other than mine and an objective constancy of the world experienced. It is *me*, in any case, to whom others as experiencing beings are given; remove me, the ego, the first person, and no intersubjectivity will remain. Intersubjectivity is, thus, phenomenologically and transcendentally grounded in subjectivity, the mineness of all experiences. As Zahavi (2005: chapter 6) shows in his more comprehensive explorations of historical and contemporary phenomenology, this need to develop a philosophy of intersubjectivity by examining the relation between the self and the other is a fundamental trend in the phenomenological tradition.[32]

Obviously I do not think that Zahavi—a leading Husserl scholar—has misrepresented Husserl by emphasizing intersubjectivity rather than the solipsistic predicament. But I do not think that he, or any other commentator, has shown that Husserlian phenomenology *silences* the solipsist. Solipsism is still an issue in phenomenology, even in Husserl's late work on the transcendental role of the lifeworld (Husserl 1935).[33] Husserl, from his early phenomenology all the way to the late transcendental phenomenology, starts from "egology"; the notion of intersubjectivity available in his philosophy depends on the constitutional role of transcendental consciousness, and can be accounted for only from within the framework of a "transcendental subjectivism" (Husserl 1935: 109).[34] As Søren Overgaard (opposing solipsistic readings of Husserl as well as Wittgenstein) puts it, "For me, intersubjective space opens only here, in me, and nowhere else" (Overgaard 2007: 88).

Another commentator, James Mensch, discusses at length the way in which the threatening solipsistic situation is overcome by Husserl's phenomenological reduction itself, when carried out far enough. True, the phenomenological reduction, reducing statements about external objects to my experiences, seems to be transcendentally solipsistic (Mensch 1988: 17), at least in *Cartesian Meditations*. The transcendental ego is "given to itself" as a "*solus ipse*," as Mensch (1988: 18) explains (cf. Steeves 1998: 9ff.). The reality of other egos thus becomes problematic. However, in his later writings on the phenomenology of intersubjectivity, Husserl postulated an "original level" of (transcendental) constitution, a level not individualistic but prior to the ego, a level at which there can be an "immediate access" to others (whose existence is left problematic in the phenomenological reduction). This level grounds both subjectivity and intersubjectivity, and it is referred to as the "depth of life" prior to any plurality of subjects (Mensch 1988: 18–22 and *passim*).[35]

At the level of this pre-individual ground of experience, I am in a sense identical to the other. Mensch claims that this identity, precisely because it is prior to the individuality of a subject producing a private world, is not solipsistic (Mensch 1988: 21). The claim that there is an original, primordial "ground" prior to any world-constituting transcendental subjectivity seems, however, to postulate just a more basic, underlying, deeper kind of transcendental ego to whom the world—in its subjective and intersubjective aspects—is given. The primary identity between me and the other is, at least, quasi-solipsistic. Why couldn't the primal ground, life, be given to itself as a "me," too? Isn't life always *someone's* life?[36] It could be argued that we are still operating within a transcendentally solipsistic system.

Hence, we may note here the persisting tendency of the problem of solipsism to *return*, to come back to the one who believes it has been left aside—a tendency to be investigated at some length later. Even if the phenomenologist claims that the ego and the other arise together, or are constituted equally primordially, the very notion of the other as external to me (and equally primordial) requires the prior notion of *my* self, the standpoint from which the other *is* an "other" in the first place (Steeves 1998: 28). Indeed, as Byong-Chul Park (1998: 48) notes, "solipsism is built into the idea of phenomenology," since phenomenology is concerned with objects being given to *me* in my experience.[37]

Largely due to Husserl's influence, solipsism as a potential—and threatening—outcome of the kind of transcendental idealism associated with phenomenological world-constitution has been a key problem for later phenomenologists, including Sartre.[38] Sartre's analysis of the ontology of being human is, again, presented from the first-person point of view. I, as a "being-for-itself," experience my existence as unrestricted freedom requiring choice and responsibility, resulting in anxiety. Popular expositions of Sartrean existentialism usually emphasize the individual's ultimate responsibility for choosing their moral values and other basic commitments in an absurd and meaningless world to which they have been "thrown," as well as their need to make the choice continuously, all over again, since even refusing to choose is to make a choice. A tension between solipsism and non-solipsism results as soon as one observes that one's absolutely free individual choices are always made in historically contingent situations, among other human beings and the factual, material world. One is, by always "choosing oneself," a kind of (ethical) solipsist; yet, insofar as one chooses "for the whole world," standing up as a model for everyone, one already postulates the existence of others. Sartre's novels and plays could also be read from the point of view of this philosophical tension.

Part III of his major philosophical work, *Being and Nothingness* (1943), entitled "Being-for-Others," contains a section on solipsism (303–15). Sartre points out that,

> if [solipsism] is formulated in conformity with its denomination as the affirmation of my ontological *solitude*, it is a pure metaphysical hypothesis, perfectly unjustified and gratuitous; for it amounts to saying that outside of me *nothing* exists and so it

goes beyond the limits of the field of my experience. But if it is presented more modestly as a refusal to leave the solid ground of experience and as a positive attempt not to make use of the concept of the Other, then it is perfectly logical; it remains on the level of critical positivism. (1943: 311)

He refers to behaviorism, observing that realistic and idealistic attempts to overcome solipsism, beginning with the premise that the other is "the one who is not me and the one who I am not," seem to lead to one another (1943: 312) and cannot avoid our being separated from the other "by a real or ideal space" (1943: 313). In this dead end, he suggests that the problem should be approached differently:

It seems therefore that a positive theory of the Other's existence must be able simultaneously to avoid solipsism and to dispense with a recourse to God if it envisages my original relation to the Other as an internal [rather than external] negation; that is, as a negation which posits the original distinction between the Other and myself as being such that it determines me by means of the Other and determines the Other by means of me. (1943: 315)

Sartre arrives at a phenomenological theory of how intersubjectivity, being-for-others, is constituted by the being-for-itself. My certainty of the existence of others—other consciousnesses—results from my being an object of the other's *look*, an experience resulting in *shame* (1943: 340ff.). These central existentialist notions are taken to establish a non-solipsistic human ontology; yet, the experience of being looked at is, phenomenologically, again irreducibly mine. Hence, it seems that while Sartre, like Husserl, tried to overcome the threat of solipsism through a phenomenological analysis of an experience (i.e., that of being looked at) inherently involving the reality of another consciousness, his phenomenological starting point problematizes this attempt from the beginning.[39]

Things were perhaps somewhat different in the work of Martin Heidegger. In contrast to Husserl and Sartre, Heidegger offers in *Sein und Zeit* (1927) a penetrating critique of the persistence of the "problem of reality" in Cartesian and Kantian philosophy. In a way, he seems to assume non-solipsism right away, for *Mitsein* ("being-together") is, for him, an aspect of *Dasein*'s (viz., an individual human being's) *in-der-Welt-Sein* ("being-in-the-world").⁴⁰ However, since Heidegger, too, begins his reflections from the individual human being, with their being thrown into the world, and approaches this being-in-the-world by means of a phenomenological method, the solipsistic option only appears to be alien to his overall position.

Admittedly, as *Dasein* I am already in the world, together with other people and objects ready-to-hand, and my existence as such a being is thoroughly temporal. Therefore, solipsism of the present moment, in particular, is a nonstarter. Nevertheless, *Mitsein* is an "existential" feature revealed by phenomenological investigation; it is one of *Dasein*'s modes of being-in-the-world. Its status as such a mode is discovered through a phenomenological method fundamentally similar to Husserl's and Sartre's accounts of intersubjectivity and otherness. Insofar as one takes seriously the idea that *Dasein* is *my* being (in the world, with others), or *jemeinig*, as Heidegger puts it, one begins to wonder whether the solipsistic situation is really avoided at all. Sartre's ways of formulating his views are perhaps more Cartesian than Heidegger's and thus more easily vulnerable to the solipsistic charge; yet, Heidegger's view as a whole may not be much farther away from ("existential") solipsism than Sartre's.

Yet, one might try to argue that the phenomenologist does have resources to combat solipsism. In particular, Maurice Merleau-Ponty's conception of phenomenology may seem to lead to a vigorous critique of the Husserlian-Sartrean problem of solipsism and hence to a truly intersubjective transcendental philosophy. In Merleau-Ponty, the living and moving human body, rather than an abstract, immaterial ego, is the "transcendental subject" constituting the experienced world. From Merleau-Ponty's perspective, Sartre's problem with solipsism resulted from his Cartesian refusal to see human beings primarily as embodied and situated in the world (cf. Matthews 1996: 102). As Merleau-Ponty states in the preface to his major 1945 work, *Phenomenology of Perception*, Husserl's problem is that of other people, and "the *alter ego* is a paradox" for Husserl (Merleau-Ponty 1962: xiii). In contrast to Husserl's and Sartre's consciousness-centered phenomenology, Merleau-Ponty offers us the following (somewhat Heideggerian-sounding) formulation: "The world is not what I think, but what I live through. I am open to the world, I have no doubt that I am in communication with it, but I do not possess it; it is inexhaustible" (Merleau-Ponty 1962: xviii–xix).

Solipsism hardly seems possible in this framework. The primary locus of phenomenologically analyzed significance is our acting, living, bodily existence. From this insight one only needs to take the obvious-seeming step to the ineliminable sociality of all human action and world-engagement. Even so, Merleau-Ponty's phenomenology of the body has also been regarded as an egocentric, foundational method that is not, in the end, fundamentally different from Husserl's phenomenological reduction (see, e.g., Baldwin 1988: 36–43). While phenomenology, for both Husserl and Merleau-Ponty, is "a philosophy for which the world is always 'already there'" (Merleau-Ponty 1962: vii), this philosophy is distinguished by its method that views me as "the absolute source" (Merleau-Ponty 1962: ix), in the sense that the world (which is already there) is something that "I rediscover 'in me'" (Merleau-Ponty 1962: xiv). Although Merleau-Ponty claims that this "does away with any kind of idealism in revealing me as 'being-in-the-world'" (Merleau-Ponty 1962: xiv), the world I share with others "is still a project of mine" (Merleau-Ponty 1962: 415). The existence of the other is "a fact *for me*" (Merleau-Ponty 1962: 417). His further reflections, seeking a phenomenological way out of the solipsistic situation, manifest a genuine struggle with solipsism:

> We are thus brought back to solipsism, and the problem now appears in all its difficulty.... I escape from every involvement and transcend others in so far as every situation and every other person must be experienced by me in order to exist in my eyes.... Consciousnesses present themselves with the absurdity of a multiple solipsism.... Solitude and communication cannot be the two horns of a dilemma, but two "moments" of one phenomenon, since in fact other people do exist for me.... Reflection must in some way present the unreflected, otherwise we should have nothing to set over against it, and it would not become a problem for us. Similarly my experience must in some way present me with other people, since otherwise I should have no occasion to speak of solitude, and could not begin to pronounce other people inaccessible.... How, then, can I who perceive and who, *ipso facto*, assert myself as universal subject, perceive another who immediately deprives me of this

universality? The central phenomenon, at the root of both my subjectivity and my transcendence towards others, consists in my being given to myself. *I am given*, that is, I find myself already situated and involved in a physical and social world—*I am given to myself*. . . . Contrary to the natural world I can always have recourse to my thinking nature and entertain doubts about each perception taken on its own. The truth of solipsism is there. (Merleau-Ponty 1962: 418–19)

This transcendental reasoning finally leads to the conclusion that transcendental subjectivity is intersubjectivity, as existing is "being in and of the world" (Merleau-Ponty 1962: 421), and thus a solipsistic philosophy could only be developed in a community (Merleau-Ponty 1962: 420). There surely is a level at which the argument, just like Husserl's, Heidegger's, and Sartre's parallel ones, seems to succeed. A shared natural and social world appears to be a precondition for the possibility of conceiving oneself as a subject (even a solipsistic subject). However, at another level, the argument that Merleau-Ponty, with other phenomenologists, launches against the solipsism he sees as a problem with the phenomenological method is based on the first-personal use of that method itself. Solipsistic consequences can only be avoided by inquiring into how "I am given to myself"—and it is right here that there is a "truth of solipsism" to be reached. Far from avoiding solipsism, phenomenological investigations, even Merleau-Ponty's, thus appear to rely on a fundamentally transcendental interpretation of it.

We have in this section briefly dealt with the ways in which major phenomenologists (Husserl, Heidegger, Sartre, Merleau-Ponty) saw solipsism as a transcendental problem arising from their philosophical method. I have not tried to present novel historical interpretations of these thinkers' views; what I hope to have achieved is a sense of what I take to be a key feature of the solipsism issue, namely, its tendency to return when one thinks one has arrived at a position within which it has ceased to be threatening. Whether or not these phenomenologists succeeded in saving their method from transcendental solipsism (which I doubt), all of them regarded solipsism as an unwelcome potential consequence of phenomenological investigations of subjectivity. It is time to turn to a thinker for whom transcendental solipsism was not (I believe) unwelcome at all.

Transcendental Solipsism in Wittgenstein

David Pears, one of the leading scholars of Wittgenstein and his solipsism, writes as follows:

> Sympathy is the most striking characteristic of Wittgenstein's treatment of solipsism. Other philosophers find the doctrine embarrassing, like a family ghost haunting the subject and sending down its value. But Wittgenstein treats it with respect and understanding. You might almost think that he was a solipsist himself or, at least, that he had been one. But that . . . would be wrong. His sympathy was the sympathy of a therapist. (Pears 1996: 124)

This comment touches a number of intriguing themes we will be preoccupied with in this section and the next chapter. Wittgenstein's attitude to solipsism was different from most other philosophers' attitudes, although he belongs to the tradition of transcendental solipsism. I disagree with Pears's interpretation, according to which Wittgenstein never was a solipsist of any kind, but I believe he makes an important point by noting that Wittgenstein's main novelty in comparison to earlier critics of solipsism (e.g., Russell and others concerned with classical solipsism) was that he focused on the *sense*, rather than the *truth*, of solipsism (Pears 1996: 124).[41] Thus, the first thing to notice is that Wittgenstein struggled with solipsism as a conceptual instead of a merely factual problem. Moreover, I agree with Pears's embedding Wittgenstein in a Kantian-Schopenhauerian context: according to Wittgenstein, "the solipsist suffered from the transcendental illusion that he still had a criterion of identity of his ego, when really he did not have one" (Pears 1996: 124). Nevertheless, the *Tractatus* view, rejecting the ego as an inhabitant of the world, may be seen as fundamentally solipsistic. The basic insight of this solipsism, transcendentally viewed, is that a (semantically but also ontologically) solipsistic framework is required for linguistic meaning to be possible. Solipsism emerges as a transcendental principle, a necessary condition for the possibility of something that we take to be actual, namely, meaning. The issue concerns not only the sense of solipsism but also the solipsistic grounding of any sense whatsoever.

Wittgenstein's Reconceptualization of the Issue of Solipsism

I will approach Wittgensteinian transcendental solipsism as a systematic philosophical topic rather than a question of interpreting Wittgenstein's writings. I hence avoid taking any stand on the controversy regarding the "new Wittgenstein" (see, e.g., Crary and Read 2000; Hacker 2001; Wallgren 2006); I will examine how the solipsism issue itself emerges in both Wittgenstein and some of his relevant commentators. My starting point is the controversial remark in the *Tractatus* (1921: §5.64) about the solipsistic self "shrinking" to an extensionless point. In the German original, this central passage reads as follows: "Hier sieht man, daß der Solipsismus, streng durchgeführt, mit dem reinen Realismus zusammenfällt. Das Ich des Solipsismus schrumpft zum ausdehnungslosen Punkt zusammen, und es bleibt die ihm koordinierte Realität." Thus, taking solipsism seriously—subscribing to the views that the world and life are one, that the limits of my language are, for me, the limits of my world, and that "I am my world" (1921: §§5.6–5.63)—leads, according to Wittgenstein, to a situation in which "pure" realism and solipsism "coincide." The idea is more fully developed in Wittgenstein's early (1914–16) notebooks:[42]

> *The limits of my language* stand for the limits of my world.
> There really is only one world soul, which I for preference call *my* soul and as which alone I conceive what I call the souls of others.
> The above remark gives the key for deciding the way in which solipsism is a truth. (Wittgenstein 1961: 49)

> The I makes its appearance in philosophy through the world's being *my* world. (Wittgenstein 1961: 80)

> Here we can see that solipsism coincides with pure realism, if it is strictly thought out.
> The I of solipsism shrinks to an extensionless point and what remains is the reality co-ordinate with it.
> . . .
> *I* have to judge the world, to measure things.

> The philosophical I is not the human being, not the human body or the human soul with the psychological properties, but the metaphysical subject, the boundary (not a part) of the world. (Wittgenstein 1961: 82)

> This is the way I have travelled: Idealism singles men out from the world as unique, solipsism singles me alone out, and at last I see that I too belong with the rest of the world, and so on the one side *nothing* is left over, and on the other side, as unique, *the world*. In this way idealism leads to realism if it is strictly thought out. (Wittgenstein 1961: 85)

There is a related passage in *Zettel*, where Wittgenstein (1967a: §413ff.) considers the question of whether there might be any difference in the realist's and the idealist's ways of teaching their children. When they disagree about the independent existence of a chair, for example, the difference between the realist and the idealist seems, we are told, to lie only in their different "battle cries" (1967a: §414).

If Wittgenstein is right, one can be a solipsist (or, less radically, an idealist) and still view the empirical world precisely as the realist does. The combination is reminiscent of Kant's attempt to reconcile transcendental idealism with empirical realism, and it has been plausibly argued that Wittgenstein was, in a peculiar way, a Kantian transcendental philosopher.[43] Erik Stenius, one of the first scholars to note this link between Kant and Wittgenstein, points out that what Wittgenstein calls "solipsism" is his "linguistic turn of Kantian idealism," which can also be labeled "transcendental lingualism" (Stenius 1960: 220–22). In an early paper, Jaakko Hintikka (1958: 160) argued, more strongly, that Wittgenstein's "solipsism" does not have much to do with what is ordinarily called solipsism: the point is not the "*impossibility* of getting 'beyond the boundaries of myself,'" but the contingency of all boundaries of myself.[44] According to Hintikka, Wittgenstein's "solipsism" is best compared to methodological solipsism, which is unavoidable in Wittgenstein's phenomenological approach, since in phenomenological languages the person her-/himself serves as a reference point (Hintikka 1996: 75; cf. 192, 217, 223). Hintikka and Hintikka (1986: 65–67) claim that the Tractarian solipsism is based on the doctrine of objects as objects of (Russellian) acquaintance;[45] accordingly, objects must be given to *me* in *my* experience (and, hence, life), but there is no metaphysical assumption of their being phenomenal or mind-dependent. What Wittgenstein, as a phenomenologist (on the Hintikkian reading), investigates is the way in which objects (whatever they are) are given to me in immediate experience. Methodological solipsism is compatible with realism about the objects of experience; by no means does it lead to phenomenalism (Hintikka 1996: 138, 211).[46]

Hence, Wittgenstein was clearly no classical metaphysical or epistemological solipsist. Even emphatically *non-solipsistic* readings of the *Tractatus* have been proposed by distinguished scholars, and they ought to be taken seriously. Pears's seminal *The False Prison* (1987–88) is presumably the most significant among these; thus, I will draw some attention to his interpretation (cf. Pears 1996, 2001, 2006).

Pears reads Wittgenstein in a Kantian context as a critical philosopher. In the *Tractatus*, a distinction between factual language presenting a picture of the world, on the one hand, and "the mystery of the world," on the other, is drawn. What makes the factual picture possible cannot be expressed in factual language (Pears 1987–88, vol. 1: 4–7). Solipsism, of course, is a metaphysical theory, inexpressible in factual language; therefore, the Russellian epistemological emphasis on truth and evidence in relation to the solipsism issue is wrong (Pears 1987–88: 34–36).[47] The fundamental question, according to Pears, is this: "But who does he [the solipsist] think he is?" The solipsist's problem is the one of identifying her-/himself independently of the objects (the world) s/he is aware of (Pears 1987–88: 35ff.; see also chapter 7).

This problem forms the basis of the critique of solipsism in the *Tractatus*, on Pears's reading—a critique out of which Wittgenstein's later considerations of sensation language and the problem of private language grow. The critique is an attack on "ego-based" solipsism, but it applies to "Humean" views as well, since they provide no criterion of identity for the subject, either (Pears 1987–88: 36). The problem, more explicitly, is that the solipsist "wants to use his ego as a reference-point in order to draw his personally restricted boundary, but he cannot use it, because in his theory it is not independently identifiable. . . . If this ego is never identified as his, it could be anybody's" (Pears 1987–88: 39). Solipsism emerges naturally from the use of "I" as a subject, but the solipsist does not "refer to himself as a complete person, mind and body," and hence fails to make a significant statement (Pears 1998: 386).

Hence, whereas the ego is usually taken for granted in treatments of solipsism, its status (especially its identity) is the main problem for Wittgenstein (Pears 1987–88, vol. 1: 153–54).[48] Pears offers a dilemma: either the ego is a part of the world, in which case solipsism is self-refuting, or it is not a part of the world, in which case the doctrine collapses to emptiness (Pears 1987–88: 157–58).[49] If, in particular, one refuses to attach the ego to one's body (which is a part of the world), solipsism turns out to be empty (Pears 1987–88: 169). The "empty or self-refuting" dilemma is summarized in propositions 5.64 and 5.641 of the *Tractatus* (Pears 1987–88: 184; cf. vol. 2: 228–30). The problem is semantical or meaning-theoretical (and partly epistemological) rather than metaphysical.

Pears's transcendental concerns with the identifiability of the solipsistic ego in the *Tractatus* are different from the issue of personal identity which, at least since Locke, has been on the agenda of metaphysicians and philosophers of mind and has been debated, non-transcendentally, by many philosophers. Non-transcendental metaphysicians have—in vain—attempted to say something metaphysical about the subject, understood as belonging to the world, whereas for Wittgenstein there *is* no such subject; the subject he considers philosophically interesting is a limit of the world instead of belonging to the world (Wittgenstein 1921: §§5.631–5.632; cf. Pihlström 2016: chapter 3).

Nevertheless, even Pears cannot overlook the fact that Wittgenstein thought there had to be a genuine insight in solipsism, "something right," a deep "truth" underlying all trivial factual truths about the world. This insight is captured by acknowledging the *linguistic* character of Wittgenstein's treatment of solipsism: the crucial idea is that "any language has to be understood from a point of view which cannot be captured in that language" (Pears 1987–88, vol. 1: 165). The subject is a "limit"; it cannot be described in factual language. Thus, it is not an object among empirical objects but "the inner limit of the world, a point without magnitude" (Pears 1987–88: 178–79). This can only be shown, not stated; moreover, this view was, according to Pears, *not* given up by the later Wittgenstein but only traced back to "its origin in ordinary human life and language" (Pears 1987–88: 188). Hence, we should not read the later Wittgenstein as criticizing the kind of solipsism "accepted" by the early Wittgenstein.⁵⁰ Rather, the critique of solipsism that was begun, in Pears's view, in the *Tractatus* is *continued* in the later critique of phenomenalism and sensation language (cf. Pears 2006: 114 and chapter 5). Just as the solipsist cannot identify her/his ego without self-refutingly assuming realism, the phenomenalist cannot "start by identifying his sense-data empirically within the common world, and then go on to claim that language was limited to sentences about his sense-data" (Pears 1987–88, vol. 2: 234; cf. 295).

Pears (1996: 126) rightly emphasizes that Wittgenstein "drew on the legacy of Kant" in his critique of solipsism: the solipsist's assumption that her/his ego somehow corresponds to an individual person even in the absence of the body is a "transcendental illusion," confusing an abstract principle of unity with an empirical principle of individuation.⁵¹ Wittgenstein's later reflections on solipsism after his return to philosophy in 1929 were, on Pears's reading, merely developments of his earlier critique, with the additional motivation drawn from his new interest in the philosophy of mind and its relation to the philosophy of language (1996: 128–29).⁵² The celebrated private language argument is, again, argued to be an outgrowth of the Tractarian treatment of solipsism (1996: 131; cf. Pears 1987–88, vol. 2: chapters 13–15), although there is a difference between the scope of Wittgenstein's early and late critiques of solipsism.⁵³

H. O. Mounce (1997: 11) also reads the remark in the *Tractatus* on solipsism coinciding with "pure realism" as an *elimination* of solipsism: "I cannot say that I alone exist, as against the world, for without the world I cannot distinguish my own existence. Consequently what is true in solipsism cannot be expressed without recognizing the truth in realism."⁵⁴ What is correct in solipsism is the idea that we can only know the world from a human perspective, reflected in our language and experience. This is compatible with realism. The mistake is to "deny the reality of the world" (1997: 12). Hence, Wittgenstein in the *Tractatus* "was not advancing any form of solipsism" (1997: 14).

Now, Mounce's remarks on the correlation between subject and object, and on the world's being known only from a human perspective, as well as his claim that "I cannot step outside language and consider the world and language independently of one another" (1997: 7), are, in my view, on the right track. What Mounce misses is the peculiar *transcendental* feature of the Tractarian solipsism. The transcendental solipsist does not "eliminate" or deny the reality of the world, for s/he is an empirical realist. Correspondingly, Pears is surely right in insisting that Wittgenstein's critique of solipsism, focusing on the sense of the solipsistic claim, takes a revolutionary step forward from Russell's standpoint, which was merely concerned with showing that solipsism is false (or that it need not be believed to be true)—"Where Russell saw falsehood, Wittgenstein saw meaninglessness" (Pears 1996: 130; cf. Pears 2006: 100–01). Russell's mistake was precisely the one of employing inductive argumentation against solipsism, as if it were a factual thesis (Pears 1987–88, vol. 1: 164).[55] Indeed, Russell's argumentation is remarkably superficial in comparison to Wittgenstein's. We may agree that the *Tractatus* is not concerned with a solipsist claiming, in an empiricist fashion, that one "cannot penetrate the veil of his own sense-data and so cannot establish the existence of the physical world or of other people inhabiting it" (Pears 1987–88: 187–88); nor does Wittgenstein subscribe to solipsism in the sense that he would accept it as true, and thereby as a theory that *can* be true or false in the sense in which factual statements are true or false (Pears 1987–88: 188).

The claims that Wittgenstein was, "of course, a realist" (Pears 1987–88) and that he "did not have any earlier solipsism to recant" in his later philosophy (Pears 1996: 128) are unconvincing, however. Indeed, his solipsism *was* (in a manner compatible with empirical realism) of a transcendental variety,[56] and I am not sure whether Pears and other non-solipsist interpreters have drawn due attention to this. If Wittgenstein is interpreted as a truly transcendental solipsist, his "realism" cannot be regarded as "uncritical" in the way Pears (1987–88, especially vol. 1: chapter 5) does. Rather, whatever realism there is in the Tractarian position, it is subordinated to the "second-order," meta-level, transcendental thesis of solipsism— which, however, cannot be stated (as Pears and others correctly note)—and it is this subordination that makes the (empirical) realism "critical." The problems of Pears's account become explicit when he says that the unidentifiability of the ego becomes a problem for the solipsist insofar as solipsism is "offered as a philosophical theory to be assessed for truth and falsehood" (Pears 2001: 17). Isn't it clear that the kind of transcendental solipsism we may read into the *Tractatus* is *not* offered as *such* a "theory" at all, precisely because it is something that cannot be put to words? For the same reason, it seems to me that Pears's (2006: 97–98) discussion of solipsism in terms of the problem of "drawing a line" between "you" (the solipsist) and "what is not you" is misleading.

Moreover, isn't Pears's "argument from identifiability," as we may call it, just an argument against *any* factual-language treatment of the solipsistic insight? Isn't the claim that the solipsistic ego is not identifiable just the claim that solipsism cannot be stated in factual language (which everybody following Wittgenstein here accepts)? What still remains, for Wittgenstein, is the inexpressible, transcendental task of "drawing limits" to the world and language. Far from depending on the possibility of identifying the ego for whom language and the world are possible, the "truth" of solipsism lies in the linguistic describability of the world in general.[57] In this sense, solipsism is not only true, but there is no alternative to it. For me there can be no other world than mine, the one I am able to describe (Vossenkuhl 1995: 51, 176, 181).[58]

In particular, what remains correct, or "true," in solipsism, according to Wittgenstein, seems to be the transcendental, limiting role of the ethical. Like some other commentators (e.g., Hintikka), Pears recognizes Wittgenstein's temptation to think that there is a deep insight in solipsism (although, as we saw, it cannot be stated) while, in my view, failing to appreciate the way in which Wittgenstein's treatment of this insight is connected with his conception of ethics. In brief, Pears pays no attention to Wittgenstein's peculiar *ethical solipsism* (cf. Chapter 5). The subject—the point of view which cannot be mentioned in a factual description of the world—is the locus of all value and meaning; only my will is ethically engaged. *This* view can hardly collapse to realism, for otherwise Wittgenstein's sublime ethics would collapse to a banal, trivial factuality. Insofar as there *is* such a thing as ethics, it will have to be *mine* (just like the world and life are). This, I take it, is what Wittgenstein would have regarded as *the* inexpressible but fundamentally important insight in solipsism.[59] What is more, the fact that Wittgenstein took seriously the possibility not only of solipsism but of solipsism of the present moment, even in its strongest form as a conceptual thesis, suggests that his underlying concern was ethical: it must have seemed to him that what *I* am doing *right now*, at this crucial moment of my life, is the only thing that matters, ethically.[60]

This ethical reason for being critical about Pears's non-solipsistic reading only serves as an initial motivation, though. We should take a look at some genuinely solipsistic discussions of Wittgenstein and build our exploration of the problem on them. Richard W. Miller (1980), among others, defends a much more explicitly solipsistic reading of the *Tractatus* than Pears, Mounce, et al., emphasizing that Wittgenstein's view *is* a linguistic version of solipsism. More recent commentators who see Wittgenstein as subscribing—in a problematic and qualified sense, to be sure—to a form of (linguistic, transcendental) solipsism include Bell (1996), Wilhelm Vossenkuhl (1995, 1999, 2009), and Brian McGuinness (2001).[61] Similarly, Heikki Kannisto (1986) takes seriously the Kantian analogy and construes the Tractarian position as a combination of transcendental solipsism and empirical realism (see also Glock 1999: 443–49). I will shortly refer to these and other scholars' interpretations in more detail.

I hope, however, that my sympathy to the solipsistic readings of the *Tractatus* will not be misunderstood. Within a book like this, I am not in the position to judge whether these or any other commentators are, historically, right or wrong about Wittgenstein.[62] The scholarly literature on Wittgenstein, early and late, is so enormous that almost *any* interpretation appears to be supported by *some* evidence; conversely, almost *any* interpretation conflicts with *some* (suitably interpreted) evidence. I am not concerned with correct readings of the *Tractatus*, nor with finding a right answer to the question of whether the author of the *Tractatus* actually was committed to any "views" at all or just to the practice of offering ironic, imaginative therapeutical suggestions (cf. again Crary and Read 2000; Hacker 2001).[63] The philosophical issue of transcendental solipsism that can be formulated on a Tractarian basis goes beyond these historical disputes.

Hence, whatever Wittgenstein's actual position at various stages of his philosophical development was, the "Wittgensteinian" solipsism—not just the endlessly disputable view cryptically put forward in the *Tractatus* but a more widespread position whose elements can be found in many of the scholarly contributions cited in this chapter—which I find genuinely problematic and am concerned with here (and which I think genuinely "matters") is a blend of transcendental idealism and empirical realism. Here

I basically follow the interpretive lines proposed by Kannisto (1986). While admitting that Wittgenstein does argue against the expressibility of solipsism in the *Tractatus*, we should not fail to notice that solipsism is, for him, in some sense the *preferred* view in comparison to realism. It should be obvious by now that there is, in his early work, an acknowledgment of a deep "insight" in solipsism that even non-solipsistic interpreters like Pears cannot deny. *Pace* Pears, Wittgenstein *affirms* solipsism, or its unsayable "truth," in the *Tractatus*, far from refuting it (cf. McGuinness 2001: 1). In the later works, presumably, solipsism is no longer preferred or affirmed in this way—although we must be careful even here, as we will see.

The Subject of Transcendental Solipsism

Turning from scholarly debates to a more general exploration of the Wittgensteinian position, we may first observe that no simple non-solipsistic attacks are effective against this transcendental view. For example, Popper's (1983: 83–84; 1994: 106–07) argument that (classical) solipsism cannot be true because he could never himself have composed Bach's music or written the *Iliad* or Shakespeare's plays (nor the stupid books on the justification of induction he has to read and criticize), and that the solipsist would thus have to be a "megalomaniac," does not impress the Wittgensteinian solipsist at all. There is nothing in the world that the realist can say or think but the solipsist cannot.[64]

The metaphysical subject of solipsism constitutes her/his— that is, *my*—world, and the entire world thus ontologically, or transcendentally, depends on the subject. Against this idea, the realist is helpless: in Kannisto's (1986: 147) words, Wittgenstein wants to say that "if the ball is red, the ball is red, whether I am a solipsist or a realist." In a Kantian fashion, the transcendental solipsist can be an empirical realist (1986: 147). S/he does not disagree with the non-solipsist "about any practical question of fact" (Wittgenstein 1958: 59).[65] The solipsist replies to the realist (who claims that "there is more in the world than you can ever think of") that if s/he (the solipsist) cannot think or experience such facts, then "neither can the realist, and what he says is accordingly without sense. The world of the realist extends no further than the world of the solipsist. And this is what the solipsist has meant all the time, although his attempt to put it into words has only resulted in confusion" (Kannisto 1986: 148–49).

The solipsist maintaining that "nothing exists save myself and my mental states" tries, then, according to Wittgenstein, to capture something which is "correct in its intention," though it cannot, strictly speaking, be said (Kannisto 1986: 146; see Brockhaus 1991: chapter 11; Cook 1994: chapter 5). Realism without solipsism would, for Wittgenstein, be *naive* (Vossenkuhl 1995: 200)—and thus realism not worth defending. Of course, consistently with the idea of *transcendental* solipsism, the world's being "my idea" is not just a fact obtaining in the world; it is for this reason that solipsism cannot be stated in fact-stating language, but must rather be understood, ineffably, as "an interpretation of the world as a whole" (Kannisto 1986: 147–48). The distinctive character of the language whose "center" (*Mittelpunkt*) I am lies in its use and cannot itself be linguistically expressed (Wittgenstein 1967b: 50).

Wittgensteinian transcendental solipsism might even be developed as an interpretation of solipsism of the present moment. It is tempting to say, again, that the transcendental solipsist (of the present moment) can be an empirical realist: just like the redness of the ball, the temporality of worldly events (i.e., their taking place at one moment instead of some other moment in the succession of time) can be regarded as an empirically real feature of the world. Temporality is, hence, not illusory or fictitious, any more than Kantian appearances are; it is a characteristic of the solipsist's transcendentally constituted—and at the transcendental level non-temporal—reality, grounded on the ontologically prior timelessness of the present experiences of the solipsistic subject, and possible only within the transcendental framework established by the subject (me). In other words, the transcendental solipsist of the present moment need not claim time to be unreal; s/he can simply regard the transcendental, atemporal setting provided by her/his experiences *now* as the sine qua non of any empirically real temporality of world-immanent objects and events. The temporal world of the realist "extends no further" than the transcendentally timeless yet empirically temporal world of the solipsist. Neither "ordinary" solipsism nor solipsism of the present moment need, thus, be construed as a naive, empiricist idealism or skepticism, if the transcendental perspective is taken seriously. From the eternal, timeless point of view of the transcendental subject, solipsism and realism coincide.[66]

On the other hand, the transcendental versus empirical distinction may not extend to the solipsism of the present moment in the way suggested—at least not according to the *Tractatus*. Wittgenstein himself may have favored temporal solipsism over some periods of his life, but the solipsism of the *Tractatus* seems to be of a non-temporal variety. Time, after all, is said to be one of the forms of things (Wittgenstein 1921: §2.0251). While there might be something ethically appealing in the "eternity" (or timelessness) of the present moment insisted on by the temporal solipsist, it can be argued that such basic ethical notions as duty and conscience are irreducibly temporal notions not accommodated by a solipsist of the present moment.

I cannot formulate any firm position here. Temporal solipsism may be at home in the empiricist tradition where it can be construed as a radicalization of classical solipsism. If this is correct, Wittgensteinian transcendental solipsism cannot be radicalized into solipsism of the present moment, after all. We may leave the issue open. There is still something to be said in favor of the latter radicalization, too; in particular, there is the ethical point that it is only *now* that I can choose to act, ethically or unethically.

At any rate, the full extent to which the notion of a metaphysical (transcendental) subject in the *Tractatus* is very peculiar gradually emerges. This subject, unlike the one assumed in classical solipsism, is not a Cartesian substantial soul (or any of its more materialist alternatives). The transcendental solipsistic subject is not such a thing, or *any* thing, in the world, but the world in which it is embedded (without being a part of it) is *its* world.[67] Kathleen Wider (1991) suggests that Wittgenstein's notion of the subject resembles Sartre's concept of consciousness. Just like consciousness is, for Sartre, "nothing" in the sense that it "*is* no *thing*," always requiring an object to exist (Wider 1991: 326–27), the solipsistic self, for Wittgenstein, "vanishes into nothing" (Wider 1991: 332). This "nothingness" has a deep significance for both Sartre and Wittgenstein, as both step beyond a mere Humean denial of the substantial Cartesian ego by treating the self, which is nothing, as a Kantian-like transcendental condition of the world (cf. Wider 1991: 337–38).[68]

The self of Wittgenstein's solipsism is a "non-egological" self. The solipsism in question is, in a way, a "solipsism without the self"—thereby coinciding with realism.[69] True, "I am beyond the world as the one for whom there is a world" (Ehman 1966: 23), but, in describing the world, I describe it ("my world") simply as the world, not as "mine" in any distinctive sense. I am always already there in the world (in the empirical sense); at the transcendental level, there is no distinction to be made between me and non-me. On the one hand, everything in the world is mine, since the metaphysical self is the persistent form of all experience; on the other hand, "my world is just *the* world, whoever I am" (Coyne 1982: 314).[70] The world's being present to me—its inevitable "present-to-meness"—does not lead to a loss of the world or to the world's being "swallowed up into the self"; the world is still "out there" (Petrik 1988: 323). The "I" or self cannot be encountered in the world; it is "the centre of life, or the point from which everything is seen" (Anscombe 1959: 168). In other words, there is no philosophically interesting (metaphysical) ego or "soul" to be found in "the realm of the sayable," in which only the empirical ego resides (cf. Brockhaus 1991: 285–86). Wittgenstein's solipsism is an "Ich-Exorzismus" (Vossenkuhl 1995: 192), an "Ich-tilgenden Solipsismus" (Vossenkuhl 2009: 94).[71]

It cannot be overemphasized that Wittgenstein wrote within a tradition, not in intellectual solitude. P. M. S. Hacker (1986: chapter 4) is one of the scholars who have drawn due attention to the Kantian-Schopenhauerian background of his transcendental solipsism (see also Hacker 1996: 30, 280 and chapter 2 *passim*), to the extent that "the clue to Wittgenstein's concern with solipsism lies in the notion of the metaphysical self as derived from Schopenhauer's transcendental idealism" (Hacker 1986: 92). Schopenhauer also claimed that the transcendental self is a presupposition of all experience of the world, yet an "indivisible point" and not a substance (Schopenhauer 1969 [1844], vol. II: 15, 278).[72] It is, presumably, this Schopenhauerian, profoundly non-Cartesian background that led Wittgenstein to entertain the idea that the solipsist is right in maintaining "that the world and life are one, that man is the microcosm, that I am my world" (Hacker 1986: 99). Where Wittgenstein significantly differed from his great predecessor was in thinking that the quasi-solipsistic ideas are literally inexpressible—though no less important for that reason (Hacker 1986: 100).

Having offered a preliminary characterization of Wittgenstein's non-egological solipsism and its sources, let us review Wittgenstein's anti-Cartesian argumentation in some more detail and trace some of its implications for our understanding of the subject. I find the following summary of the argument for solipsism in the *Tractatus* (drawn from O'Brien 1996: 176–77) helpful:

1. Everything in the world can be represented.
2. That there is a representing self is a precondition of (the possibility of) representation.
3. The world is (must be) represented.
4. There is (must be) a representing self. (From 2 and 3.)
5. The self cannot be represented.
6. The self is not in the world. (From 1 and 5.)
7. There can be nothing outside the world.
8. Even if there were something outside the world, the world could be nothing to it.
9. The self is not outside the world. (From 4 and 7.)
10. The self does not belong with the world but is a limit of it, or coincides with it in its entirety. (From 4, 6, and 9.)

The key premise is (5), which Wittgenstein supports by means of several arguments (O'Brien 1996: 179–85). However, O'Brien points out that his arguments against the possibility of self-representation depend on a "perceptual model of representation"; as far as this model is avoidable, solipsism also is (O'Brien 1996: 188–90).[73]

Wittgenstein's anti-Cartesianism—his refusal to postulate any substantial, soul-like self whose inner states are given to us in introspection and can be known and represented—as a key element of his attitude to solipsism has been emphasized by other commentators as well. As Wittgenstein's solipsism drops the Cartesian picture of subjectivity, rejecting the very idea that there is a representable thing called "the self" in the world (cf. (5) and (6) in O'Brien's scheme), what we have here is a revolution in the history of the solipsism debate (with some resemblance to the revolutions that took place in Kant, Schopenhauer, and the phenomenological tradition)—a revolution whose full moral needs further elucidation.

Hans Sluga (1996: 327ff.) finds the roots of Wittgenstein's anti-Cartesianism in a deeper position he labels *anti-objectivism*. What this means is that the "I" is "not subject to scientific theorizing" and "not objectively given as part of the world." It has not been reduced away, that is, it is not "nothing," but it is not "something," either (cf. Wittgenstein 1953: I, §304). Hence, there can be no objective (scientific) account of the subject.[74] The transcendental character of Wittgenstein's solipsism results precisely from the fact that the solipsistic self remains "unindividuated" (Sluga 1996: 328–30). As Hölscher (1998: 57) puts it, Wittgenstein provides a "view from within"; the solipsistic "I" is "internally transcendental" (and, hence, Wittgenstein's form of transcendentalism is "inverted," refusing to describe the subject from any external standpoint)—though this "view from within" characterizes transcendental reflection generally.

Sluga (1996: 330ff.) regards Wittgenstein's later thought as an argument attempting to show how to keep anti-Cartesianism and anti-objectivism while avoiding (transcendental) solipsism. Moreover, he connects Wittgenstein's anti-objectivism with his ethically grounded anti-theoretical attitude to the self: philosophical questions about subjectivity (or what Wittgenstein called the "problem of life") cannot be resolved theoretically, scientifically, or objectively. Therefore, we cannot have any "positive," theoretical account of the self at all: neither a Cartesian, Russellian, Freudian, or a behaviorist one, nor any other such account (Sluga 1996: 342–45).[75] Sluga's interpretation, according to which Wittgenstein thought we must focus, instead of metaphysical theorizing about the self, on practical action and particularly our ethical attitudes in attempts to understand ourselves (and others) as subjects, points toward a larger question about the relation between ontology (or metaphysics) and ethics, to which we will return in Chapter 5. The internal link between Wittgenstein's specific worries about solipsism and his more general anti-objectivism about the self demonstrates, in any case, how the solipsism issue, in its transcendental manifestation, matters.

Bell seems to agree with Sluga on the idea that a kind of anti-objectivism is the key to Wittgenstein's anti-Cartesian conception of the self:

> Genuine subjectivity is not something that, as it were, *has* a place in nature; my own consciousness is not something I ever come

across *in* the world; it is not the sort of thing that I can refer to, identify, describe, have acquaintance with, or knowledge of. And its elements are not any kind of "things"—whether events, processes, objects, properties, or facts. Subjectivity, according to Wittgenstein is more pervasive, and far more important than anything of *that* kind. Genuine subjectivity . . . is that to which the entire conceptual machinery of objectivity is ultimately inapplicable. (Bell 1996: 156–57)

The fundamental point here is almost trivial: *the subject is not an object* (in the world). It is, indeed, "no thing." This very simple idea is, for Wittgenstein, the basis of ethics. It is also, we might say, the "truth" in solipsism. Even though the later Wittgenstein does not endorse the early solipsistic picture of subjectivity (at least not without qualifications), there is no change in the view that the "I" or the self is not an object (Sluga 1996: 344; see Vossenkuhl 1995: 178ff.). When I refer to myself as a subject (and not merely as a piece of flesh with, say, a broken arm), I refer to something that lies beyond the scientific description of natural (objective) reality—to a uniquely perspectival, world-engaging, and morally responsible agent. This irreducibility and unobjectifiability of agency now emerges as a key insight of transcendental solipsism. It is an insight to be taken seriously anywhere where agency is a central theme.

Solipsism and Realism

If, for the sake of simplicity, we define *realism* as the commonsensical thesis that reality (the world) exists ontologically independently of our perceptions, language(s), concepts, beliefs, and theories (i.e., it would still be there, even if all minds—mine included—were destroyed), we can construe Wittgenstein as saying that this kind of realism is, paradoxically, indistinguishable from such an extreme form of antirealism as solipsism, which says (at the transcendental level) that the world is "my world."

Bell (1996: 161) suggests that "metaphysical solipsism," that is, the thesis that "I am the world," can be read from right to left (in which case the world is identified with me) or from left to right (in which case I disappear and leave behind the world).[76] The world is here "independent" in the realistic sense, since it "depends" only on me—that is, on itself (1996: 162). This is still "full-blooded" solipsism, in Bell's view (1996: 162). True, according to the solipsist there is no world independently of *my* thoughts or mental states. But I, or my language, am/is now the measure of what there is: I am the (real) world. Whatever the realist wants to say about the allegedly independent world, the solipsist can say the same about "her"/"his" world.

But *can* we make sense of what the solipsist means to say? After all, *we* (I assume) are not solipsists. At least *I* am not, and solipsism would be true (for me) only if the world were indeed my world; moreover, if it were true, the words "for me" would be redundant (for me), since I would be the only one who would be able to believe in it, or even to find it meaningful. What we find here is a very short argument against solipsism: since solipsism can be true only if *my* world really is all there is, and since *I* am not a solipsist, solipsism must be false—*it is not true in my world*.

This, of course, is far too simple—partly because I might be mistaken about my not being a solipsist. Solipsism might be a correct reinterpretation of my philosophical outlook at a transcendental level even if I were empirically unaware of this. An adequate treatment of the solipsism issue is not achieved by noting that I cannot de facto doubt the existence of a world external to myself. Similarly, it is too simple to argue, as Child (1996: 146–47) does, that solipsism results from a misconstrual of the genuine distinctiveness of the subject's first-person point of view—that is, from the illegitimate step from the correct idea that the first-person point of view is unique (from that point of view) to the mistaken idea that there is something unique about that point of view in contrast to other points of view. How could there be any "contrast" to other points of view, if the solipsistic thesis were taken seriously? The solipsist need not say that her/his point of view is unique or distinctive *in contrast to* others' but that there are, in the relevant sense, no other points of view.

There is no short cut available. To approach our theme from a slightly different standpoint, we can, I think, consider the problem of solipsism as a dimension of the heavily disputed general issue of realism. Over the past few decades, straightforward distinctions between "realism" and "antirealism" (in the philosophy of science and elsewhere) have often been replaced by attempts to formulate sophisticated intermediary positions, often by philosophers who represent, for example, some strand of phenomenology or one or another form of neopragmatism (see Chapter 4). Philosophers like Putnam have argued that metaphysical realism, the view that the world possesses its own ontological basic structure independently of the structuring activity of language-using beings, is deeply problematic, perhaps even incoherent. Now, if there is something wrong with such strong realism, and if transcendental solipsism is a coherent alternative that cannot be refuted, why shouldn't we embrace such solipsism? For example, neopragmatist attempts (e.g., Putnam's) to find a via media between realism and antirealism have often been considered unsatisfying (cf. Pihlström 1996a, 2003, 2009, 2020). Why not simply make things easier by adopting the other extreme?

Moreover, wouldn't solipsism appear to be a natural solution to inconclusive philosophical debates, if we applied Occam's Razor—the weapon of all friends of ontological parsimony—far enough? Solipsism is, arguably, much more parsimonious than any parsimonious version of realism.[77] One might even claim that those realists who insist on ontological parsimony, and thus on the need to use Occam's Razor, are not fully coherent. They ontologically postulate elementary particles, magnetic fields, forces, and so on, while they could confine themselves to the simple postulation of the theorizing subject and then conceive of the physical world as the subject's "own." Does anything but a non-solipsistic prejudice prevent them from doing so? It seems that we still need an explanation of why we really should *not* be solipsists. There is no easy escape from the transcendental predicament I have described with reference to Wittgensteinian ideas.

Most of the philosophers I have cited in this section discuss the issue mainly as an interpretive one, seeking to determine what Wittgenstein himself (at various stages) thought about the matter. This has not been my main concern. Still, I claim, we can make some important systematic (i.e., not merely historical) points by discussing such solipsism and its relation to realism in the Wittgensteinian transcendental context. At least Wittgenstein taught us how to approach solipsism with philosophical respect and understanding—whether it is the respect and understanding of the therapist, as Pears supposes, or the respect and understanding of a puzzled human being who wonders whether there might be some fundamental truth lying at the core of the solipsistic claim, despite its absurdity. Respect and understanding will also be needed when we move on to arguments against (transcendental) solipsism and to the ethical bearings of the issue. In the next two chapters, I will make a (perhaps desperate) effort to *both* respect the "truth in solipsism" (and how this truth matters) *and* argue against solipsism in favor of a form of realism pragmatically committed to a common human world that is needed for us to be able to rationally or argumentatively appreciate any such (or indeed any) "truths."

CHAPTER FOUR

Leaving Solipsism Behind: Pragmatist Considerations

Arguing against solipsism presupposes that the problem itself is taken seriously. I hope to have been able to establish this through a transcendental (as distinguished from the "classical") conceptualization of the issue. Convinced, by now, that solipsism "matters"—at least by threatening our ability to share a common world—we may turn to a possibly promising, though in the end inconclusive, way of arguing against it. By taking seriously this inconclusiveness, we will deepen our understanding of the way in which the solipsism issue is still present even in post-Wittgensteinian philosophy. Hence, I will in this chapter examine some conceivable counterarguments to solipsism, focusing on a certain kind of "pragmatist" argument. Further (primarily ethical) arguments will be investigated in the next chapter.

Arguing against Solipsism

One of the possibilities of arguing against solipsism that might immediately occur to us (as it did to Descartes) is an appeal to *God*. Famously, Descartes tried to overcome epistemological (skeptical) solipsism by offering an *a priori* proof of the existence of a benevolent God, who cannot deceive me. Success in this argument would guarantee success in the rejection of solipsism. If there is a

God who has created the world, including me, then there certainly is something outside my thoughts and experience, that is, God and his creation. As a perfect being, God is necessarily more perfect than I am. Therefore, my world cannot be everything there is. The Cartesian approach is not entirely absent from contemporary discussions, either: Clement Dore (1989), for one, attempts a basically similar maneuver as Descartes.

Invoking God will hardly help, however, against the solipsist. The obvious reason is that the solipsist hardly believes in God, at least if the concept is interpreted in the standard theistic fashion. Moreover, God could be a solipsist. After all, wouldn't God, as the creator of all there is, in a sense *have to* be, if we take his presence to be a necessary condition of the continuous existence of all created things?[1] On the other hand, God may just be our (or my) fictional creation, as atheist critics of religion maintain. Whether or not there is a God, the problem of solipsism remains—at least in its Wittgensteinian setting examined in the previous chapter. From Wittgenstein's point of view, God can be identified with the world as a totality. The ineffable sense (*"Sinn"*) or value of life, which again is equivalent to the sense of the (my) world, is based on my (the transcendental subject's) attitude to that world.

A very different way of countering solipsism could begin from *materialism*. However, it is difficult to see why the (e.g., Wittgensteinian) transcendental solipsist would find materialist dogmatism any more plausible than theistic dogmatism. The empirical reality of matter is in no conflict with transcendental solipsism. But if neither theistic nor materialist metaphysics helps the anti-solipsist, what about the simple postulation of other human beings? Arguments from *analogy* are typical among philosophers dealing with the problem of other minds (Hyslop 1995; Avramides 2001): my ego is analogous to those of the others; so, I should assume that the others have experiences roughly in the way I do. It might be suggested that certain "axioms of symmetry" between my ego and those of the others have to be assumed (Plaut 1962), but such lines of argument seem inconclusive. The solipsist could always just interpret the otherness of the others as a feature of my experiences and my world.

In fact, it seems that anyone offering an "argument from analogy" as a justification of our non-solipsistic belief in other minds must rely on a profound *asymmetry* between one's own case and those of others. This is demonstrated in Alec Hyslop's (1995) careful study of the other minds problem. We have, Hyslop argues, direct (though not infallible or incorrigible) knowledge of our own mental states but no such knowledge of others' mental states, and this is what gives rise to the problem of other minds (1995: chapter 1).[2] The analogical inference must proceed, inductively, from a sample consisting only of one's own case (1995: chapter 4). Hence, the analogical arguer is a methodological solipsist, building the case for other minds on an assumption of the primacy of her/his own perspective, on "the first person."[3] S/he starts from, instead of refuting, the "truth in solipsism."

Solipsism cannot be directly refuted by means of a *transcendental argument*, either (though such arguments are important in philosophy generally).[4] For example, P. F. Strawson's (1959) famous demonstration of the existence of persons (in addition to material bodies) and of a non-solipsistic world aims at explicating our actual conceptual scheme, the one we de facto use, and have to use, in speaking about the world. J. N. Findlay (1984: 113–14, 122), in turn, rejects Wittgenstein's solipsism on the grounds that it destroys the contrast between me and other selves, or between subjectivity and objectivity.[5] If, however, we begin from solipsism, for example, in a Wittgensteinian fashion committed to ineffable transcendental subjectivity, these arguments will not convince us. In transcendental arguments, something is already taken for granted: objective cognition, communicable language, experience, or thought, a genuine subject-versus-object contrast, or something similar. The solipsist could always refuse to take for granted what their transcendentalist critic takes for granted.[6] More importantly, the solipsist can always remind their opponent that one of the key arguments *for* solipsism—the Wittgensteinian one considered in the previous chapter—is itself a transcendental argument, in which solipsism (albeit its transcendental form coinciding with realism) emerges as a result of an investigation of the necessary conditions for the possibility of representing the world. Thus, transcendental considerations might actually seem to offer equally strong support for solipsism and non-solipsism; at least it looks like they cannot settle the matter either way.

We should now see how the non-solipsist could provide some counterarguments without relying on theism, materialism, ad hoc assumptions of analogy, axioms of symmetry, or *a priori* given transcendental standpoints. The project of transcendental argumentation will not be abandoned, however. On the contrary, the main argument pursued in this chapter is itself a kind of transcendental argument, albeit a *pragmatic* one. Needless to say, it does not conclusively secure its thesis. Nevertheless, in a more modest sense it might establish at least the prima facie legitimacy of non-solipsism.

My argument is confined to the transcendental kind of solipsism, which claims, with Wittgenstein, that solipsism is not incompatible with, but rather indistinguishable from, realism. This is the kind of solipsism I find most important to examine critically, as the solipsist who claims to be a realist, too, is by no means an ordinary solipsist. Such a solipsist is like a spy in the realists' camp. In a sense, the transcendental solipsist hardly offers any less radical perspective on the topic of subjectivity (and objectivity) than the classical solipsist. Her/his perspective is only more subtle. The insight of solipsism, its "truth" in the Wittgensteinian ineffable sense, is, if genuine, something that ought to be taken into account in any serious consideration of our ability to encounter a common, objective reality.

To make the point I wish to develop as clear as possible, we should first, once more, try to see how one might argue, on the basis of Wittgenstein's views, *for* what we may call the indistinguishability thesis, that is, the thesis that solipsism and realism "coincide." One might use the following introspective experiment, which might also serve as a summary of the Wittgensteinian ideas already discussed.

Let us first be realists. Then, let us look at the world around us. We see trees, cars, tables, houses, and so on, and if we look more carefully, we can also see cells, bacteria, viruses, and similar small objects unobservable by mere naked eye. Using theoretical instruments, we can even detect atoms and electrons. When we look upon the sky, we find enormous objects very far away from us, such as stars and galaxies. We also see, in our everyday life, other human persons, and we communicate and cooperate with them in our practical affairs. Most of these objects we perceive or think and talk about exist independently of us, that is, they would continue to exist if we ourselves suddenly disappeared from the world. Such is our world, if we are realists.

However, let us now, the experiment continues, be solipsists and look at our world again. The point is that *nothing changes*. We experience the same trees, cars, tables, houses, cells, bacteria, viruses, atoms, electrons, stars, galaxies, and persons as we did when we still were realists. There is absolutely no difference between the realist's and the solipsist's worlds. As noted in Chapter 3, according to Kannisto's (1986) interpretation of the *Tractatus*, the realist's world "extends no further" than the solipsist's. Anyone can recognize this indistinguishability by being, or pretending to be, first a realist and then a solipsist. Consequently, Wittgenstein was right in insisting that solipsism leads to "pure realism," as the solipsistic self shrinks to a point without extension. We may call this the Wittgensteinian indistinguishability argument for solipsism (and for the coincidence of solipsism and realism).

We now have several options. We can adopt realism, which might be considered a rather unparsimonious choice, however: it postulates various (kinds of) independently existing objects out there in the world, though there would be a more parsimonious alternative available, equally well accounting for the world as we experience it. We could employ Occam's Razor in order to embrace "real," metaphysical solipsism.[7] We can also reject the entire controversy, having shown that there is no practical difference between the two rival positions. In any case, we have to *do* something, to *engage* the matter—and this is something we do in a context in which there are always already other voices in the discussion.

The Wittgensteinian temptation to solipsism seems to oscillate between the latter two alternatives. On the one hand, solipsism, in its metaphysical formulation, *attempts* to say something that is right in its intention but collapses because of the transcendentally fixed limits of what can be said in language; on the other hand, there *is* something wrong with the ordinary realistic (non-transcendental) picture of the independently existing world, and hence transcendental solipsism must be preferred (cf., e.g., Miller 1980; Lalla 2002). The situation may be resolved by adopting the Kantian-inspired version of transcendental solipsism Kannisto (1986) examines: we may embrace solipsism at the transcendental (linguistically inexpressible) meta-level, when interpreting the world as a whole (and our being able to represent the world in language), but maintain realism within that world-interpretation. This is, indeed, a kind of "internal" (or, as Kant put it, empirical) realism.[8]

This argument can, I believe, be questioned, though perhaps not conclusively refuted, by means of a transcendental counterargument.

The key idea is that one cannot compare the points of view of realism and solipsism from a third, neutral point of view. When reflecting on the philosophical problem of the external world, we must take a stand, arguing for the indistinguishability of realism and solipsism either *as* realists or *as* solipsists. (One might adopt an intermediary idealistic position, but that does not really change much, since solipsism is basically a radicalization of idealism.) We must start *somewhere*, and some philosophical standpoint must be assumed in any case.

If I enter the argumentative situation as a (transcendental) solipsist, the comparison between realism and solipsism by means of the introspective experiment introduced above could be claimed to yield a performative inconsistency. *To whom* does the solipsist *show* that solipsism and realism coincide? *To whom* does s/he even *tell* that s/he is a solipsist? Showing, arguing, experimenting, and demonstrating necessarily belong to a socially constrained, irreducibly normative, and purpose-oriented language game, a *practice*. A transcendental condition of such a language game is a linguistic community capable of a normative evaluation of its actions.[9] The indistinguishability of solipsism and realism could be demonstrated only within such a community and to such a community; therefore, there is no possibility of demonstrating such an indistinguishability at all (or, for that matter, of coherently arguing for solipsism), since solipsism must be assumed to be false, if one wishes to demonstrate anything. One cannot (*pace* Kekes 1971) directly "refute" solipsism, since the solipsist would, of course, interpret all attempts of refutation as constructions based on her/his own complex mind, as empirical manifestations of a transcendentally primary subjectivity, but—so our counterargument goes—this is nothing that we should be worried about, either. The crux of the matter is that the solipsist cannot even so much as *state* her/his own position; a fortiori, s/he cannot provide any arguments in order to demonstrate anything.[10] Nor is there any such external standpoint from which the solipsist could claim that her/his view and the realist's coincide. And who else would even want to claim anything like that, after all?[11]

Solipsism cannot be refuted or proved incoherent but possibly, rather, shown to be argumentatively pointless and irrelevant by means of an argument like this. There is, according to this meta-level argument, no viewpoint for the solipsist available from which s/he could genuinely engage in anything like a philosophical dialogue. This applies both to the classical metaphysical and epistemological versions of solipsism and to transcendental solipsism. In the latter case, it is particularly problematic to determine from which point of view the distinction between the transcendental and the empirical viewpoints is made in the first place.

The kind of argument formulated here is mainly directed, pragmatically, to the *purposes* allegedly served by the solipsistic position. The solipsist may remind the realist that it is not impossible to meditate, even philosophically, in solitude. This suggestion can be countered by asking what purposes such meditation could possibly serve. There may be a sense of "possible" which makes the solipsist's internal dialogue possible, after all, but it is also legitimate for the non-solipsist to question the relevance of such a possibility. At least the "point" of the internal meditation available for the solipsist cannot be captured by the non-solipsist; so, again, there is little for the solipsist to do to defend her/his position.

Needless to say, I am not here aiming at any conclusive argument against the solipsist. I am only, in a preliminary fashion, investigating the argumentative strategies that the main parties to the debate might adopt. In fact, Oliver (1970: 33) points out that solipsism can only be arrived at through a "leap" or a "fall."[12] If the solipsist complains that the critic, in attacking solipsism, uses such key metaphysical terms as "the world" or "reality" somehow equivocally (i.e., means by "reality" something different from what the solipsist, *qua* solipsist, means by it), there is little more to say. This complaint is perfectly possible, but it makes the solipsist's view of reality arbitrary and irrelevant. Now the solipsist can offer no real alternative, nothing to be taken seriously by the realist. The philosophical dispute is over, and the solipsist can close the windows of the monad.

An analogous argument against the epistemological relevance of cognitive relativism has been given by Olaf Tollefsen. We might say about solipsism what Tollefsen (1987: 210) says about relativism, that is, that it escapes self-refutation only by being self-defeating. Accordingly, either there is no reason to be a solipsist in the first place, or else the solipsist, in trying to demonstrate the indistinguishability of solipsism and realism and in criticizing the realist's use of the notion of "reality," presupposes non-solipsism. We might, indeed, conceive of Wittgenstein's entire work as a passage from (linguistic) solipsism to the rejection of solipsism, based on considerations of the indispensable *normativity* of language-involving human practices.[13] As Pears (1993) suggests, Wittgensteinian solipsism "loses its intended meaning" in trying to achieve its truth.[14]

The upshot seems to be, in any event, that the best thing the solipsist can do is rest silent. There is nothing to say. Or s/he can just talk to her-/himself. But to say that s/he can (in a monologue) even understand the introspective experiment presented above, and employ it in argumentation, is to beg the question against the critic by assuming that the solipsist's own unarticulable conviction that solipsism is "true" is sufficient to convince the critic. Again, *who* would be able to *say*, in what kind of language, and *to whom*, that the solipsist would be able to understand (and be convinced by) the introspective experiment?

We cannot engage here in the well-known and endlessly disputed argumentation against the intelligibility of the idea of a private language in the *Investigations*.[15] The key points, to the extent that they concern us here, are familiar enough from the main works of Wittgenstein's (1953, 1956, 1969) later philosophy. The non-solipsist could argue that the solipsist cannot, for instance, play chess (although s/he may *claim* to possess that skill—but to whom?), at least not in the genuinely intersubjective sense in which we non-solipsists think we play chess; thus, more generally, the solipsist cannot fully engage in any normative, rule-governed practice (cf. also Wittgenstein 1993: 227, 258). There can hardly be any chess boards, chess pieces, and chess positions in the solipsist's monadic hell, since these presuppose an opponent, another subject. Nor can there be any arguments, demonstrations, or experiments— even introspective ones—there. But now, once again, the solipsist may counter the critic's suggestions by saying that s/he *can* easily play chess, argue, and engage in other normative practices within the empirically real intersubjective world constituted by her/his solipsistic transcendental subjectivity. We do not, then, seem to get much further in our argumentative encounter with the solipsist.

Let us briefly return to the idea of arguing transcendentally against solipsism. We may add an important dimension to our picture by modifying our notion of a transcendental argument. We might suggest that while traditional transcendental arguments are ineffective against solipsism, suitably "pragmatized" and "naturalized" transcendental arguments may be more plausible.

These arguments start from our human practices, from what we as human beings naturally do, and from the purposes those practices serve—as we already did by referring to the practices of normative engagement, argumentation, and communication. What is established by a transcendental arguer naturalizing transcendental philosophy is not an *a priori* framework of metaphysical necessity but a pragmatically inescapable structure of our human being-in-the-world. If we do start with real-life human practices, as pragmatists (among others) encourage us to do,[16] there will, arguably, be little argumentative space left for solipsism.

Such practices include normative, rule-governed modes of behavior that cannot be reduced to mere causal regularities in the natural world. As naturalized, transcendental arguments are inevitably self-reflectively circular, if construed as being directed against skeptical doubts concerning what is stated in their conclusions. The very possibility of meaningful human discourse or experience such arguments try to secure will be presupposed in their premises, for without such premises the arguments could not get off the ground. But this circularity—or, rather, reflexivity—is beneficial rather than vicious (cf. Pihlström 2003, 2011), manifesting the self-constituting nature of the (pragmatically structured) transcendental subjectivity whose constitutive powers are examined in transcendental reflection.

The chief non-solipsistic transcendental argument relevant here, to be found (arguably) in the later Wittgenstein and in some forms of pragmatism, for instance, can perhaps be expressed as follows. What is "given" (i.e., plays the role that the actuality and hence possibility of cognitive experience plays in Kant) is, simply, our (or my) use of language. There is no doubt about the fact that we (or at least I) do use language meaningfully. From this given actuality, I may proceed, transcendentally, to the necessary conditions of its possibility. What can be found in the course of such an investigation is the rule-governed nature of our (my) language use. No meaning would be possible unless there were normative rules according to which linguistic expressions are used. What makes such rule-following possible, again, inevitably involves a community, at least a potential one: language can only be used within shared, habitually structured forms of life in which language users agree about many things, including many contingent facts of the matter. Certain natural facts must also actually remain (relatively) unaltered in order for such rule-governed use of language to be possible.[17] This argument arrives, then, at non-solipsism in a pragmatic and naturalistic spirit.

Even here, of course, the solipsist can *claim* that the realist's (or pragmatist's) world "extends no further" than her/his own and that even argumentation and other normative activities are not for realists only. The solipsist may, in a word, refuse to share the pragmatic starting point and the irreducibly intersubjective normativity of human practices. But, again, is there something either to share or to refuse to share here? How can the solipsist *compare* the pragmatic starting point of her/his (imagined) critic and the non-pragmatic idea of an isolated, solipsistic universe? How can s/he offer any reasons for preferring the latter to the former—and, even if it were possible to do so, what would be the *point* of the argument, that is, again, *to whom* would it be directed?

A scholarly point I wish to emphasize here is that commentators may still have not drawn sufficient attention to the way in which the traditions of transcendental philosophy and (what we may call) non-reductively naturalistic pragmatism meet in (the later) Wittgenstein.[18] In my view—although I am unable to document this in any detail here—it is precisely Wittgenstein's "pragmatist" willingness to start with our given human situation, with our forms of life which are in order as they are, that makes his (later) thought truly transcendental, and it is this very pragmatism that enables us to give up solipsism. The argumentation we find in the later Wittgenstein's philosophy provides a paradigmatic example of pragmatized transcendental argumentation or, better, of "transcendental anthropology" (Lear 1998: chapter 11). It does not begin from a vacuum but with ordinary life and language use. Human life and its normative practices cannot be solipsistically understood according to this picture.[19]

Giving up Solipsism

Transcendental solipsism clearly seeks to overcome the traditional distinction between realism and idealism. Wittgenstein, to be sure, *seems* to save realism by affirming that I "belong with the rest of the world." However, this is, according to him, something that shows itself only within "my world"—something I cannot meaningfully say.

If we are persuaded by the pragmatic-transcendental approach very briefly sketched in the previous section, we can hardly find the idea that solipsism and realism "coincide" promising or even coherent. We then basically view human beings, including their (our) practices of cognizing and speaking about the world, as parts of the natural and cultural world that we also help to constitute, or at least shape, through those normative practices. It is in this sense that pragmatism (broadly understood) can be regarded as a possible background of a plausible transcendental philosophy. The pragmatist starts by admitting that there are other irreducible subjects in the world sharing normative practices with me, and there is an obvious sense in which the later Wittgenstein can be considered such a pragmatist.

The pragmatist I am imagining here must nevertheless admit that, from each subject's point of view, the world is experienced as "my world." In a sense, it is certainly correct, though trivial, to claim that the realist's world extends no further than the solipsist's. However, the pragmatist's image of the "constitution" of the world through human practices is irreducibly social. There are other subjects whose "worlds" must be taken into account in our experience and action. There is no abstract transcendental subject of human practice as such; on the contrary, our practices are engaged in by, and composed of, *real* individuals (as well as communities or networks of individuals) purposively interacting with each other and with their *real* natural environment in order to solve practice-laden problems emerging from changes in the environment they need to adjust to.[20]

The need to recognize the reality of other subjects and thus the reality of the world external to ourselves is, then, an overwhelming *pragmatic need* that we cannot just set aside, though we have to admit (by using our normatively governed public language) that it is not *logically* contradictory or inconceivable that I *might* be the only being equipped with consciousness, all others being soulless "zombies." The pragmatic (in)conceivability at issue is *ethical* rather than logical—yet "conceptual" rather than just factual or empirical. Our being always already involved in interaction with other people "under a common sky" (Nuttall 1974) leads us to doubt the conceivability of both the "zombie" idea and any form of solipsism.

In the spirit of this kind of pragmatism, Putnam points out that, "contrary to Wittgenstein's celebrated remark in the *Tractatus* about consistent solipsism and realism coming to the same thing,"

> there is a difference—*a difference in what justifications of conduct make sense viewed from within our language and thought*, and not from some impossible Archimedean point—between regarding other people merely as convenient intellectual devices for coping with one's own experiences and (to borrow a term from Stanley Cavell) *acknowledging* them. This is the difference the later Wittgenstein tries to capture with his remark "My attitude towards him is an attitude towards a soul. I am not of the *opinion* that he has a soul." (Putnam 1994: 299)[21]

From this ethical point of view, what we practically *do* in the world with (and especially to) other people is inescapably significant for us, creating the practical necessity of leaving solipsism behind.[22] As self-reflective human beings, we must view ourselves as responsible for what we do, even when engaging in philosophical inquiry. The point the pragmatic critic of solipsism tries to make is that solipsism is an *irresponsible* philosophical choice—regardless of whether there might be, for example, transcendental or meaning-theoretical considerations in its favor. We may read Putnam as emphasizing (in the quote above) that the transcendental (or methodological) solipsist's position only gives us the *illusion* that the situation is symmetrical (see also Chapter 2): the solipsistic self still claims privilege at the meta-level, and this is not a genuine acknowledgment of another "soul."

Yet—and here comes an observation crucial for the success of the argument I have sketched—it is the subject, the first person, who has to become convinced by the pragmatic-transcendental argumentation examined above. It seems that ultimately we cannot avoid relying on our "private moments" of (ethical) decision, to borrow another phrase from Cavell, even in giving up solipsism.[23] In the end, I have no one else except myself to rely on when following, and continuing to follow, a practice or a normative rule, even if that rule-following entails the rejection of solipsism. My (and others') essentially private decisions to go on following any given socially institutionalized rule cannot be overlooked if we truly aim at an adequate picture of what it is to learn, understand, and use a language, even though such a picture as a whole must anti-solipsistically emphasize the public and social character of language use. Anyone who fails to take this privacy seriously ignores the permanent possibility of what Cavell (1979: 19) calls an "intellectual tragedy," the impossibility to appeal beyond "us" in a disagreement between two or more Wittgensteinian "bedrock" situations where, as it were, "our spades are turned." Such an intellectual tragedy is possible, however strongly we try to be ontologically responsible. Private bedrocks may be hard places to rest on.

The ultimately personal (or even private) non-solipsistic choice available to us may be regarded as a pragmatic "will to believe" commitment *à la* James (1897): the falsity of solipsism cannot be established on purely intellectual or evidential grounds, since the solipsist may always reinterpret the critic's arguments from the solipsistic perspective; thus, avoiding solipsism (which must be at least as live, forced, and momentous an option for us as belief in God's existence may have been for James's audience) requires an existential commitment, a leap of faith. A Jamesian pragmatist cannot merely escape solipsism by means of philosophical arguments but must actively *push* solipsism away. There is a crucial difference between these two attitudes to the rejection of solipsism. At the core of the "will to believe" idea lies the need for active, though necessarily uncertain, decision-making. In choosing to give up solipsism, I partly decide what kind of a human being I am, particularly in my relations to other people.

Quoting Cavell again, I sometimes have to "rest upon myself as my foundation" (Cavell 1979: 125)—and there is, arguably, no firmer ground for giving up solipsism. I *just* refuse to be a solipsist and *simply* acknowledge others. Here, I am "thrown back upon myself," recognizing that there are limits to my understanding, limits that I have to draw on my own grounds (Cavell 1979: 115). Putnam (1992: 73–76) remarks that the Wittgensteinian argument against the possibility of a private language and thus against "first-person relativism" (which, on Putnam's definition, simply relates truth to what oneself agrees with—a view almost equivalent to solipsism) is *not* an argument, at least not an argument the first-person relativist or solipsist would accept. What we need, instead of further theoretical arguments, is, precisely, "acknowledgment."

However, Putnam as well as Cavell draws attention to Wittgenstein's use of such first-person points of view as the one employed in the *Investigations* (1953: I, §217): "If I have exhausted the justifications, I have reached bedrock, and my spade is turned. Then I am inclined to say: 'This is simply what I do.'"[24] When I act with "complete certainty," Wittgenstein tells us, "this certainty is my own" (Wittgenstein 1969: §174). It is not, and cannot be, based on others' actions. It has no "basis" at all. As Heinrich Watzka (2000: 166) explains, our certainty in rule-following is practical and "without grounds" ("ohne Gründe"); it is, indeed, "my certainty." We may even speak about "solipsistic certainty," as Watzka does, following Vossenkuhl (1995: 223, 284–85).

One's bedrock—in this case, the refusal to accept solipsism (of *any* kind, neither classical or methodological nor transcendental)—is something that one does not, and cannot, know how to justify further. Argumentation drops out as irrelevant. My refusal to be a solipsist may not, to be sure, lie beyond debate and justification *forever*. But at *this* point right *now* it may be the place where *I* stand firm, taking responsibility for where I stand. I can imagine no arguments which could shake my ultimately unargued non-solipsistic position. If all the people around me became members of the Solipsistic Party, I hope I would rather fail to understand them than join them. If I did join them, I would in an important sense become someone or something else.

My form of life is thus "pitched deeper than the level of the social" (Conant 1990: lxviii), even if I continue insisting on the irreducibility of the social against the reductive individualism of the solipsist. Yet, a kind of "hermeneutical solipsism" may emerge here, as my private moment of non-solipsistic existential commitment[25] might simply be incomprehensible to you, especially if you are not sympathetic to the pragmatic "will to believe" strategy I have adopted, and to all others as well. This is a feature of our human predicament. We have arrived at what might be called *the dialectics of non-solipsistic enlightenment*. At least it could be the case that we are unable to communicate our rejections of solipsism to others. Solipsism may not yet have been avoided, if one just says, as I have done, that one is not a solipsist. The solipsist could claim victory at the meta-level.

Indeed, the recognition that we "always already" live with other people—the questioning of solipsism through the "ultimate experiential motive" of a lived distance between our own self and those of others—still leaves us with our ineliminable subjectivity and solitude, with "the fact that the other is other than we are" (Ehman 1966: 22). Indeed, while the solipsism of the *Tractatus* has been called into question, even Wittgenstein's later, emphatically social and pragmatic philosophy of language has been interpreted idealistically, skeptically, and even quasi-solipsistically.[26]

In addition to Cavell's above-cited discussion of our private moments in the following of normative rules, several attempts have been made to approach Wittgenstein along these or related lines. Bernard Williams (1974) claimed in an influential paper that the later Wittgenstein was a transcendental idealist or even a "collective" or "aggregative" solipsist, with the transcendental "I" replaced in the later philosophy by a transcendental "we."[27] Shortly after him, Elizabeth Anscombe (1976) discussed "linguistic idealism" in relation to Wittgenstein.[28] Saul Kripke's (1982) skeptical reading of Wittgenstein's rule-following considerations is famous, though it remains controversial.[29] And while Jaakko Hintikka has argued against the solipsistic reading of the *Tractatus* (cf. Chapter 3), we find him talking about "cultural solipsism" in relation to the later, more relativistic, Wittgenstein (Hintikka and Hintikka 1986: 21). Thus, although Wittgenstein has often been taken to have delivered a death blow against the Cartesian philosophy of mind giving rise to solipsism as a philosophical problem, there is a sense in which the solipsism issue remains alive in the non-Cartesian framework he provides us with.[30]

Furthermore, Bell reminds us that it may be a mistake to construe the private language argument as an argument against the solipsism Wittgenstein earlier was tempted to accept. On the contrary, this argument is "an endorsement and development" of solipsism (Bell 1996: 168). Both the earlier solipsism, which "self-effacingly" coincides with realism, and the later private language argument radically question the Cartesian objectifying approach to the self. Both distinguish genuine subjectivity from what can be objectively, referentially, or scientifically discussed. A "movement out of the self into the world" (Bell 1996: 170) is present in Wittgenstein's early and late reflections on solipsism, Bell notes with an approving reference to Cavell.[31]

Another scholar who has argued that Wittgenstein did not give up solipsism in his later work but endorsed a novel, "grammatical" version of it is Wilhelm Vossenkuhl. He points out that the private language argument, instead of refuting solipsism, is only plausible and understandable against the background of solipsism (Vossenkuhl 1995: 183ff.; 1999: 215, 227).[32] Grammatical solipsism allows normal linguistic usage, for example, utterances like "There really is tooth-ache" instead of "Only I feel tooth-ache" (provided that it is always I that can feel a toothache); thus, solipsism in a way disappears while containing a kernel of truth in the sense that aches and other private sensations are indeed private (see Vossenkuhl 1999: 227). As Vossenkuhl reminds us, the solipsist is "no illusionist" but can, for example, be compassionate toward another human being who suffers: s/he can believe as much as we can that another suffers pain (Vossenkuhl 1999: 228; Vossenkuhl 2009: 104). This takes us, however, far from what is ordinarily called solipsism, merely toward something like the postulation of irreducible *qualia*:[33] "Each human being is a solipsist in the sense that s/he can say to no-one else what exactly that person thinks and feels. The meaning of feelings and thoughts is what we can communicate. However, the feelings and thoughts have—as qualia—an individual and psychical presence, about which we cannot say how it really looks" (Vossenkuhl 1999: 233, my translation; cf. Vossenkuhl 2009: 109).

Even so, solipsism in this sense, in Wittgenstein's late philosophy, makes room for the account of language as public and common (Vossenkuhl 1995: 188–89). "Grammatical solipsism" in a way opens up a public realm of language use (Vossenkuhl 2009: 111). Thus, as other scholars (e.g., Hintikka 1996) have pointed out as well, private experiences, insofar as anything meaningful can be said about them, must be spoken about in public, non-solipsistic language. This is *not* to deny that subjects do have such experiences. The meaning of our expressions is not tied to anything psychical to what lies behind them. Yet, Wittgenstein needs solipsism, or the "truth" of solipsism consisting in the privacy (and the resulting inexpressibility) of subjective experiences, in his very argument against the possibility of a private language. According to Vossenkuhl (1999: 242–43), he needs solipsism roughly in the sense in which Kant needs things in themselves, as a limiting concept, *Grenzbegriff*. Solipsism is *not* given up; it is not shown to be false or meaningless (nor, however, true or meaningful); it does not disappear from the picture, but still plays a role. There are still "solipsistic limits" in Wittgenstein's later philosophy—and it is precisely those limits that show the impossibility of a private language (Vossenkuhl 1995: 289).[34]

While Vossenkuhl recognizes the transcendental setting in which Wittgenstein operates, he draws no analogies between Wittgenstein's solipsism and Kantian transcendental idealism (see Vossenkuhl 1995: 222) and even claims that there is no Kantian transcendental idealism or subjectivism in the *Tractatus* (Vossenkuhl 2009: 98). Others, like Kannisto and Bell (and the present author), take this analogy more seriously. I believe Vossenkuhl's emphatically solipsistic reading of Wittgenstein could be strengthened by a more explicit Kantian conceptualization.

Whereas the leading "solipsistic interpreters" of the later Wittgenstein (Bell, Vossenkuhl) are careful to keep the relevant kind of solipsism primarily "grammatical," linguistic, or semantical, even a stronger, metaphysical solipsism has been read even into Wittgenstein's later thought. According to this proposal, made by Sebastian Lalla, even the late Wittgenstein understands solipsism metaphysically, emphasizing the "ontological singularity" of the solipsistic self and the necessary tie between this transcendental self and its (the) world (see Lalla 2002: 17, 52–53, 95ff., 116, and chapter 6 *passim*).[35] Lalla thus also reads Wittgenstein transcendentally, viewing the relation between the self and the world as transcendental (e.g., Lalla 2002: 64), but he seems to operate with a strongly metaphysical conception of transcendental philosophy which, unlike the Kantian one, does not seek to avoid essentialistic metaphysics (*Wesensmetaphysik*).

Indeed, solipsism, Lalla believes, ought to be seen as a part of such metaphysics (Lalla 2002: chapter 3). What makes Wittgenstein's later thought solipsistic, according to Lalla, is the insight that essential privacy in the use of language and concepts cannot be publicly accommodated: none of us can experience the private qualitative states of others (Lalla 2002: 117).[36] "The essential privacy of language lies in the fact that no-one knows whether the other *means* exactly what the speaker means," Lalla explains (Lalla 2002: 129, my translation). This view, I take it, explicates Cavell's notion of a "private moment." Wittgenstein, early and late, has little understanding for a "personalist" solipsism (Lalla 2002: 73), in which the solipsistic self is taken to be a person (in a more or less normal sense); yet, there is, Lalla argues, a kind of impersonal, transcendental privacy to be assumed as the basis of all linguistic meaning, however publicly communicated. This transcendental solipsism, early and late, pertains (ineffably, inexpressibly) to the preconditions of meaning. Only by respecting an inaccessible privacy of intentional meanings can we make sense of the idea of a pluralism of meanings (Lalla 2002: 158).

If these somewhat unorthodox interpretations of Wittgenstein are even partly on the right track, it turns out that a late-Wittgensteinian pragmatic philosophy, however strongly it emphasizes normative, public practices of language use, cannot be easily employed to just set solipsism aside—or, at least, that it is not obvious that solipsism can be set aside even in such an apparently non-solipsistic framework. This is an important dialectical result at this stage of our investigation of the potential arguments the anti-solipsist might employ. The seemingly non-solipsistic late-Wittgensteinian pragmatic strategy may have to rely on the very (transcendental) solipsism one had hoped it overcomes. Otherwise, it may not be able to account for the public communicability of linguistic meaning it seeks to secure. The private moments of an ontologically singular subject cannot be eliminated from our picture of the emergence of meaning.

So much, for the moment, for the idealistic and solipsistic overtones remaining in Wittgenstein's later philosophy. Again, I must note that the purpose of this discussion is not to determine whether Lalla's, Vossenkuhl's, or any other unorthodox interpreter's account of Wittgenstein is correct in a historical sense. Returning to more systematic considerations (closely related to the later Wittgenstein's conception of forms of life), it should be made clear that there is an idealistic element in the kind of pragmatism sketched earlier in this section, too. A "pragmatic realist" may urge that even the realistic position can be adopted only on the basis of and within a human practice—or, better, a family of practices. We must live and act in the world in order to be realists about the world. Hence, realism is possible only within a broader quasi-idealistic framework, based on the constitutive activity of the subject, which, in this case as in Wittgenstein's later philosophy, can be seen as plural and social. Now, since we can and should be regarded as responsible for our engagement in our human practices (in both an epistemological and an ethical sense), we are also responsible for the shape the world takes, ontologically, through them. We are responsible for the transcendental constitutive activity of our own (individual and social) subjectivity, even though we (or I) certainly did not "make" or construct the world in any literal sense.

This responsibility extends, most importantly, to the place we accord to other human subjects in the world. In Cavellian terms, we may say that we need to "acknowledge" other selves as well as the nonhuman, independent reality in which we all live. At the meta-level, our responsibility consists in the fact that concepts such as reality and existence are vital to our lives. Virtually all of our practices presuppose them, as we must, in a way or another, divide things into real and unreal (or fictitious), existent and nonexistent—even though this perhaps cannot be done in any privileged, noncontextual way. The pragmatic argument against solipsism says that solipsism does not adequately acknowledge this responsibility. In particular, there is no neutral place to stand, no coherent possibility of "transcending" the realism versus antirealism debate by being a transcendental solipsist.

The pragmatic argument against solipsism investigated in this section and in the previous one *is*, in a way, a transcendental argument, albeit one starting ultimately from our ethically loaded practices of living our lives together with other people in a shared world. If one wishes to formulate the argument by speaking strictly about *my* duties and responsibilities, I will not protest. The premises are, first, that normative (including ethical) relations to other human beings constitute a given, actual fact of our (or my) human form of life, that is, that thoroughgoing normative skepticism (including moral skepticism) is a nonstarter; and secondly, that this situation pragmatically requires realism (non-solipsism) as its condition of possibility. The conclusion, then, is that realism must be accepted as a pragmatic-transcendental condition of humanly unavoidable world-engagement. But let me make it clear that this pragmatic-transcendental argument does not *ground* our ethical relations to others in any such realism; rather, such an argument begins with ethics—and its profound *groundlessness*—moving then to the transcendental condition of its possibility, namely, realism (cf. Chapter 5). Any normatively structured form of life, any practice involving selves outside myself, presupposes realism (or at least non-solipsism) in a pragmatic-transcendental sense.[37]

However, this realism ought to be distinguished from stronger metaphysical realism. There is no given, "ready-made," pre-categorized world that would possess its own ontological structure without the contribution of human subjectivity. Instead, ontological schemes structuring the world are practice-laden, and thus also value-laden (cf. Pihlström 2009), developed and justified through pragmatic considerations. Our commitments to the reality of other people, material entities, or moral values serve different human purposes, and *this* is the justification we have for making such commitments. Solipsism cannot escape this pragmatic line of argument.

One may also formulate roughly the same view by saying that our human practices and the value-directed purposes inherent in them function as a transcendental background of ontological commitments, including the non-solipsistic commitment we should make. In this sense, the kind of pragmatism described here is not very different from Kantian transcendental idealism, according to which the world is transcendentally constituted on the basis of the subjective conditions of the mind. The main difference lies, of course, in the pragmatic assumption of the dynamic practice-embeddedness of the transcendental subject for whom the world as a world of objects is possible. In this sense, the picture offered here is closer to late-Wittgensteinian than to Kantian forms of idealism. The term "idealism" may be misleading, however, for, as we saw, pragmatic-transcendental arguments can be formulated on a (non-reductively) naturalized basis, referring to humanly natural forms of life. If one adopts a moderate conception of what idealism amounts to—for example, along the lines suggested by Allison (2004) in his interpretation of Kant's transcendental idealism—there is no need to resist the use of this term, however. (But insofar as pragmatic realism is possible only in an idealistic context, is it so different from transcendental solipsism, after all?)

Let me recapitulate the transcendental dialectic of solipsism developed here. The pragmatic argument outlined above focuses on what the solipsist *does*, or claims to do, that is, on how s/he engages in a practice of discussion and argumentation, and on whether indeed s/he can do this and whether her/his view is thus pragmatically (performatively) inconsistent. These pragmatic considerations constitute a quasi-transcendental argument against solipsism—though, again, we must not forget that the main argument *for* solipsism considered in Chapter 3 is transcendental, too, claiming that we are committed to the "truth" of solipsism merely by using language, as our ability to mean anything by our propositions presupposes the isomorphism of language, thought, and the world along the lines of the *Tractatus*, presupposing (no-self) solipsism.

Thus, the mere form of the argument is by no means decisive, as transcendental arguments can be presented both for and against solipsism. The pragmatic-transcendental argument sketched in this chapter starts from the idea that philosophizing is an activity we engage in with other human beings we must acknowledge. Yet, as we observed, our being committed to *this* view may at the meta-level bring solipsism back, because my duty to acknowledge my conversation partners in philosophical dialogue is mine. It is my task to give up solipsism (in my life), and as we will further see in the next chapter, this has crucial relevance to the way we need to think about ethics in relation to the solipsistic challenge.

A Realistic *Credo?*

I have in this chapter tried to let the voice of the pragmatic opponent of solipsism (the "pragmatic realist") be heard, without silencing the solipsist for good, though (and without being able to here systematically develop any comprehensive pragmatist position, of course). I have, in a "dialectical" manner, tried to speak for those who wish to be realists despite the irrefutability of solipsism, suggesting that the very attempt by the solipsist to engage in any argumentative exchange with their opponent can be taken to presuppose public normative criteria within an irreducibly social human practice—and hence non-solipsism. On the other hand, while this line of thought models Wittgenstein's private language argument, we have also seen that Wittgenstein can be read as affirming the relevance of solipsism: *I* need to choose to (continue to) follow whatever criteria *I* take to be governing the practices *I* still commit myself to.

Moreover, one might simply "really" want to be, and be, a solipsist; no argument forces one out of solipsism. This is not an option that most of us find appealing, but it is very difficult to argue against (transcendental) solipsism on the basis of the pragmatic considerations offered earlier. The argument that the solipsist cannot coherently say that her/his position coincides with realism is ineffective against the extreme solipsist who does not even care whether their view comes close to realism or not. The solipsist might not even care whether solipsism can be coherently expressed. They might not be interested in arguing with the realist; the critic might just be interpreted as a pathological figment of the solipsist's mind.

Finding themselves in such an *impasse*, some philosophers are prepared to admit that our commitment to the existence of a real external world is merely a nonrational (or arational) and unjustified *credo*. It is not based on any argument and is not intrinsically any more rational than solipsism. My example of a philosopher holding this kind of fideistic realism, which we might label *credo realism*, is Henri Lauener (who prefers to call himself a relativist or a pragmatist rather than a realist, though). He writes as follows:

> With the realists of various brands I share the conviction that there is a world existing independently of my consciousness in which we all live and act. Without such an assumption, talk about actions or talk about stimulation of our sense organs in physiology would simply not make sense. No proper proof of the "reality of the world" can be given within a philosophical system because such a proof should have the form of an *absolutely* external argument which would remain ineffable since any formulation requires relativization to a language. (Lauener 1992: 51–52)

Thus, according to Lauener, there is a reality I did not make, a reality "out there" independently of human intervention. But this commitment to "reality" is not an ordinary philosophical commitment. It does not belong to the discursive realm of rational philosophical debate and argumentation at all; it is merely "pretheoretical" and "intuitive."[38] Putnam seems to maintain a related view:

> I am not inclined to scoff at the idea of a noumenal ground behind the dualities of experience, even if all attempts to talk about it lead to antinomies . . . . Because one cannot talk about the transcendent or even deny its existence without paradox, one's attitude to it must, perhaps, be the concern of religion rather than of rational philosophy. (Putnam 1983: 226)[39]

Lauener and Putnam are certainly right in rejecting not only "proofs" of the external world but also the view that we could simply solve the issue of realism by assuming the existence of a noumenal "reality in itself," namely, an unconceptualized prime reality, which we would then "cut" or "slice" up by using our concepts and linguistic frameworks (cf. Niiniluoto 1999). We have no idea of what kind of an entity this singular noun, "reality" or "the world," would refer to. Putnam (1987: chapter 1) labels this rather cheap solution to the realism issue the "cookie cutter" metaphor: the world in itself is a huge noumenal dough, which we cut up into objects (or events, processes, or whatever) from our different points of view, by using different conceptual schemes or "cookie cutters." In this metaphor, it is still assumed that there *is* some underlying reality with its own ontological basic structure. After all, not only the cookies but also the dough of which they are made would have to possess their own basic structure, which undermines the idea of structuring the world from truly different perspectives; on the other hand, the idea of an *unstructured* noumenal jam just does not make very much sense.

However, if this idea of unconceptualized reality does not help us in making sense of realism, nor does it make sense of solipsism. The solipsist would have to construe her/his world as such a primary reality in a similar sense. It would be an underlying metaphysical primordiality, the only difference to the realist's world being that it would be essentially tied to my own subjectivity. Once we seriously and reflectively give up such an unconceptualized reality, we will be tempted to accept neither metaphysical realism nor solipsism. We will, with Kant, Wittgenstein, and the classical pragmatists, be led to give up the temptation to describe the essence of the world in any metaphysical way. This, in effect, is what the transcendental strategy in post-Kantian philosophy is all about.

It should be obvious that I am not happy with *credo realism*. There is a vital difference between the pragmatic non-solipsist "will to believe" briefly introduced earlier and a blind *credo* merely affirming realism. The philosopher truly engaging with the solipsism issue—the one for whom it genuinely matters—does not propose to dissolve difficult questions of ontological commitment by mere noncognitive, arational acts of faith. To modify Kant's phrase, it would be a scandal in philosophy, if all we could do were to accept the existence of the world on the basis of such a nondiscursive *credo*.

We might suggest that philosophers like Lauener and Putnam adopt, in the end, forms of realism that *are* indistinguishable from solipsism. For nothing prevents the solipsist from expressing her/his own *credo* in a similar way. The solipsist would just interpret the content of that *credo* differently. The idea of a world existing independently of consciousness would still be the solipsist's own (transcendental rather than empirical) idea, nothing more; s/he would go on talking about an independent reality as unhesitatingly as the realist would (cf. Todd 1968). What we need is a *reasoned* (even if defeasible and qualified) defense of the existence of a common, intersubjectively shareable world. But no such defense seems to be available to us in any neutral terms the solipsist would also have to be committed to.

When subscribing to a picture of the world in which there are real human agents engaging in their practices embedded in their natural and social environment, we make a genuine ontological commitment. To understand it as such requires that it must be possible to rationally discuss and assess it. By no means should we rely on a mere blind *credo* in maintaining that the world and other subjects exist. What we may rely on is our pragmatic need to believe in the reality of the external world. The "pragmatic realist" can thus accept such philosophical theses as justified, even though no ordinary empirical or scientific justification—let alone logical demonstration—is available.

Our non-solipsistic *credo* need not, then, be a nonphilosophical attitude; rather, it can be understood as philosophically (i.e., pragmatically) warranted and defensible—though, in the spirit of general fallibilism, we should not hope that it could ever be conclusively warranted. There is nothing wrong with such "pragmatic proofs"; to say that our conviction that there is an external reality out there is a *mere* pragmatic presupposition of all our activities is to flirt with the false contrast between something merely pragmatic and something absolutely and non-pragmatically secured. We should drop the word "merely."

The solipsism issue matters to us so much that we cannot just give up philosophical argumentation and dialogue on this problem. We should not, in my view, follow Lauener and Putnam in saying that "rational philosophy" is unable to deal with such a metaphysical issue. The problem in Lauener's view, as well as Wittgenstein's, is arguably the sharp separation between philosophy and ordinary nonphilosophical life (including its needs for a realistic *credo*). For a pragmatic philosopher there can be no such dichotomy. If a realistic commitment *is* needed in our life, it is something we must account for philosophically, albeit pragmatically. It must not be shut out of philosophy, since philosophy and "practical" life are inseparable.[40]

Taking the concerns of our practice-embedded existence seriously in philosophy may be regarded as a form of "existentialism." Even James's "will to believe" idea, tentatively employed against solipsism above, has been characterized as "existentialist" (Putnam 1992). Before concluding this chapter, I therefore need to add a few remarks on such a critique of solipsism in relation to existentialism. The central idea (already preliminarily formulated above) with which I wish to bring this discussion to a close and thereby introduce the next, ethically focused chapter is that the rejection of solipsism should be viewed as an existential, hence pragmatic, *choice*.

For James himself, avoiding solipsism was a major concern.[41] Charlene Haddock Seigfried, a perceptive James scholar, argues that one of the key aims of James's entire pragmatism was to avoid solipsism. "The solipsism of the stream of consciousness," the fact that "my consciousness never partakes yours," was, according to Seigfried (1990: 92), a "life-long obstacle" for him. The problem of solipsism—as also suggested earlier in this chapter—is settled, and can only be settled, with reference to our common human *praxis* (1990: 188). According to Seigfried, James offers us a concrete hermeneutical analysis of our practice-embedded being in the world (see 1990: 189ff.), an analysis helping us to get rid of the threat of solipsism. The "refutation" of solipsism can only be found in our "embodied action in the world" and the "phenomenal bodily communication" based thereupon (1990: 279). Here James's views come close to the phenomenology of embodiment later developed by Merleau-Ponty.[42]

As we have also seen, one of the key themes of Sartre's existentialism—like James's—was the problem of how to avoid solipsism. The Jamesian pragmatic subject closely resembles the Sartrean existentialist subject, despite the differences in the two philosophers' conceptual vocabulary. The individual "willing to believe" that solipsism is not true, or that we can make genuine, ethically significant decisions in our lives, is comparable to the Sartrean existentialist subject who freely chooses their values and adopts an autonomous ethical stance. Our fundamental goals, according to both thinkers, are to be constructed in the practical lives we live with others, through our inescapably historically contingent existence, amid real-life pain, sorrow, and suffering.

Unless one believes that some special experience (e.g., the Sartrean one of being looked at) directly, phenomenologically, convinces one of the reality of others (see Chapter 3), one must, in order to live as a non-solipsist, make an existential commitment, to will to believe that others are real. Such a commitment is always, ultimately, ethical, but it is not a blind *credo*.

Thus, from a Sartrean and from a pragmatic point of view, ethics, the construction of human values and the concretization of such values in our real-life existence, is a key to the rejection of solipsism. Consciousness is an activity of all human structuring of reality, but it is always embodied, already there in the world, among "other" beings.[43] The kind of consciousness we are entitled to consider truly human cannot be a consciousness for which the solipsistic hypothesis is a real possibility. There is no role for solipsism to play in the primordially intersubjective setting within which we, according to both James and Sartre, live, move, and have our being.

In contrast to Sartre's serious engagement with the possibility of solipsism, various poststructuralist accounts of the "decentered self" and the "death of subject" give up the very issue of solipsism (cf. Chapter 1). On the basis of what has been argued, these attempts must fail (see also Chapter 6). The Sartrean-cum-Jamesian path is more intimately in touch with our human condition, while it also in its own way both leads us to give up the problem itself (albeit not without struggle) and, from a slightly different perspective, reintroduces it.[44]

The worry that again immediately arises, however, is that the pragmatic-existentialist subject for whom the rejection of solipsism is an ethical, existential, "will to believe" commitment is at bottom an individual human being. Both Jamesian pragmatists and Sartrean existentialists focus on such an individual subject. If I follow them in arguing against solipsism, I must choose to be a non-solipsist as an individual subject, as a quasi-solipsist; moreover, I must, each and every time, make my choice *now*, as a quasi-temporal-solipsist—since, as Sartre taught us, we have to choose our lives again and again, all the time, always at *this* precise moment (a "private moment," as it were). As was already speculated, our individual ways of giving up solipsism may, therefore, be incomprehensible to others (or even to our own past and future selves), and the solipsist might not approve of their logic. The problem of solipsism might seem to reappear just when we thought we had left it behind—in our very rejection of solipsism itself, in the commitment that we, as ethically concerned pragmatic-existential subjects, are prepared to make in favor of realism. The normative criteria that lead us away from solipsism ultimately depend on our private approval and reapproval. Perceiving this, we are back in square one.

What these sketchy remarks on the possibility that solipsism might "come back" should lead us to is a serious consideration of the metaphilosophical relevance of our problem. Solipsism may not only teach us something about our subjectivity and intersubjectivity, but also about what we are actually doing when philosophizing—about solipsism or anything else. Philosophy, I might (have to) maintain, is ultimately *my* business. It is up to me to decide what *I* take to be an adequate philosophical picture or argument—adequate, that is, from the point of view of my life and experience. And since solipsism *could* be true, after all, only about me and for me, its rejection is also something that fundamentally concerns me in my existentialist solitude.

By demonstrating how the solipsism issue tends to come back to us I have also tried to problematize standard dichotomies between realism and idealism. The kind of pragmatic realist who argues transcendentally for the existence of other subjects and of objective reality operates from a point of view this book seeks to show to be less firm and less certain, more groundless, than is sometimes supposed. The pragmatic realist's voice, which we have heard in this chapter, is only one voice among many in our investigation of the problem of solipsism. No realist (not even the pragmatic realist) is safe from the impossibility of finally overcoming solipsism.

CHAPTER FIVE

The Relevance of Solipsism

This chapter finally focuses on the *ethical significance* of solipsism. I am not moving to this topic because I would believe the "theoretical" (metaphysical, epistemological) aspects of our problem to have been settled in the previous chapters. On the contrary, we need to examine solipsism ethically precisely because it has not been, and cannot be, purely theoretically resolved, nor dissolved. Ethics does not enter the picture only after the work of theoretical philosophy has been done; if our examination of solipsism shows anything, it shows that ethics is always already incorporated in a serious philosophical attempt to understand any issue of fundamental human importance. Ethics, as Levinas says, is a "first philosophy"—and this I take to be a profoundly pragmatist point at the meta-level (see Pihlström 2009, 2011, 2013).

Let me summarize the argumentative situation we now find ourselves in after the somewhat complex discussion of the previous chapter, in which I attempted to let both the voice of the solipsist and that of her/his critic become heard. I have suggested that solipsism, in its most interesting form, as (Wittgensteinian) transcendental solipsism, is not directly refutable, because the transcendental solipsist can always interpret the realist's world—whatever there is according to the realist—on the basis of solipsism, as an element of her/his world. However, in Chapter 4 we imagined a pragmatic critic of solipsism urging that even when presenting this counterargument—that is, the argument claiming that whatever the realist is committed to can always be accommodated by the solipsist—the solipsist is at a meta-level committed to engaging in a normatively governed human practice of argumentation and language use. The critic can claim that the solipsist is pragmatically inconsistent in claiming to engage in such a practice while at the same time reducing even that practice into her/his own private world.

At this point, the solipsist can again at the transcendental level claim to reinterpret and (re)accommodate the pragmatic realist's intersubjective and public practice of language use and argumentation into her/his own solipsistic world, once again insisting that the realist's world "extends no further" than the solipsist's. There is no decisive argumentative move for the non-solipsist, even the pragmatic realist appealing to the practice of argumentation and its inherently public normativity, to stop this oscillation between the two viewpoints. Therefore, the final resource the pragmatic realist—indeed, not just any realist but precisely the pragmatic realist—has is the ethical and "existential" choice analogous to William James's "will to believe." At some point we, as non-solipsists or pragmatic realists, just have to stop the oscillation. We just have to refuse to follow the solipsist to her/his endless reinterpretations of the realist's position in her/his own terms. This is a moment of pragmatic decision-making comparable to an existential choice—a choice, the solipsist will remind us, that needs to be made by *me* at a "private moment" of decision.

Consequently, it needs to be investigated more thoroughly what this pragmatic choice to respond to otherness in a way irreducible to the solipsistic world amounts to. This motivates the discussions of this final substantial chapter of the book, focusing on ethical responses to otherness, especially to the mortal and suffering other. Even here, however, we will see that the solipsism issue cannot be easily left aside, because the final ethical responsibility for making the "will to believe" leap out of the oscillation movement of the arguments pro and contra into a full acknowledgment of otherness will have to be mine.

Facing Otherness

Arguably, then, it is the ethical point of view, as already hinted several times in the previous chapters, that provides the most important motivation for considering the issue of solipsism.[1] This chapter will, partly by continuing the critique of solipsism begun in Chapter 4, seek to determine the relevance of the problem we are considering from this perspective.

The upshot of Chapter 4 was the idea that solipsism might (and perhaps can only) be avoided in a pragmatic "will to believe" style, through an active ethical and existential decision rendering one's life together with other people meaningful and responsible. It might be suggested that this approach only avoids ethical solipsism and leaves metaphysical or epistemological solipsism (albeit in a transcendental, or Tractarian, form) untouched. However, employing pragmatic argumentation here is to break the dualism between the epistemic/metaphysical and the ethical. If solipsism *is* ethically irresponsible (even in its transcendental form), then we have for this very reason good epistemic and metaphysical grounds for giving it up (cf. again Pihlström 2009). Ethics is deeply entangled with metaphysics. Yet, this argument can hardly convince the Wittgensteinian philosopher for whom ethics is the subject's (my) attitude to the world as a totality, *sub specie aeternitatis*. Such a philosopher will deliberately stick to the ethical-versus-epistemic distinction as strongly as s/he distinguishes between values and facts. Wittgenstein famously maintained in the *Tractatus* and other early writings that the world contains no values, nothing ethical (or aesthetic, for that matter), nothing "higher."

Wittgensteinian Ethics and Solipsism

It has been suggested by a number of commentators that the background that led Wittgenstein to the transcendentally solipsistic picture in the *Tractatus* was the ethical point of view shaping his entire thought. Margaret Urban Coyne (1982: 318–22), for one, argues that the individuation of the Wittgensteinian transcendental (nonpsychological) self takes place through values.[2] Only the connection between solipsism and ethics in Wittgenstein's thought properly articulates the world's being "mine"; this, again, leads to the coinciding of solipsism and realism. The perspectival character of the world, more precisely, resides in its value aspect—and this, on Coyne's reading, individuates me (and my world). No worldly fact could do the job.

In a similar fashion, Richard Brockhaus (1991: 292–93, 302, 330–31) argues that the ineffable, metaphysical subject, the "inner limit" of "my world" (and hence what the solipsist intends, correctly, to express but cannot express), is primarily "the *willing subject*," the bearer of all value, a subject (will) that "permeates" my world, even though "the world" (the totality of facts) is independent of my will. If this is right, Wittgenstein should be regarded not only as a transcendental solipsist but also, even more importantly, as an *ethical solipsist* in the *Tractatus*.[3] The most significant passage in this regard, §6.43, says that good or evil will cannot alter the facts of the world (i.e., what can be expressed in language) but only the "limits of the world," so that the world becomes "an altogether different world."[4] In the "Lecture on Ethics," Wittgenstein seems to maintain that one can only grasp the nature of value experiences on the basis of one's own case (Brockhaus 1991: 329)—(quasi-)solipsistically.

I must again emphasize that I will offer no historical interpretation of Wittgenstein, but I believe his attitude to ethical solipsism must be taken seriously. From a different philosophical standpoint, Thomas Nagel (1970, 1986, 1987) also insists that we have to confront the problem of avoiding solipsism in both theoretical and practical philosophy. According to Nagel (1970), overcoming the practical analogy of solipsism is necessary, if one wishes to make sense of the very possibility of altruistic behavior.[5]

In contrast, a fundamental idea behind Wittgenstein's ethical views is, as already noted, that the world itself contains nothing ethical. Facts, including facts about altruistic behavior, are by themselves contingent, simply what they are, and therefore ethically insignificant. A surprisingly similar position is held by scientific realists and naturalists—a very un-Wittgensteinian species in many respects—who regard the world as simply physical, ultimately captured in a value-neutral scientific description. Science itself must, according to such naturalists, also be seen as a natural part of reality, and our inquiries into scientific knowledge and theory formation must themselves be entirely naturalized.[6] Within such scientism, the subject of scientific knowledge seems to play a role analogous to the solipsist's transcendental subject: it becomes a limit of the world, not a part of it. Science itself is also a part of the natural world and thus an object of scientific knowledge; the knowing subject (the scientific community rather than any individual) is, however, excluded from the eventual ontology of science, since in the "scientific image" of the world there are only elementary particles, magnetic fields, and the like—no human persons or subjects. Solipsism (the solipsism of the scientific subject) indeed coincides with pure (scientific) realism here.

One problem here is that, from such a scientistic standpoint, a conception of the subject as a "limit" is hardly coherent: either the subject is naturalized as an element of the natural world or eliminated altogether. There is no proper place for a genuine subject of scientific knowledge at all in this account. An even clearer difference to Wittgenstein's views is that there is not and cannot be any ethics accommodated by such scientism. The world (science and other human practices included) is left morally cold and value-neutral. Scientific descriptions of values and valuations in, for example, evolutionary terms can hardly replace what is at issue in questions regarding genuine moral motivation. Science, in a word, does not describe ethical life (or the world as ethically problematic) at all. Wittgenstein (1921, 1965), while agreeing that there is no value *in* the world, found ethical (and aesthetic, as well as religious) value lying, mystically, outside life, language, and the world—and saw ethics, aesthetics, and religion as constituting a transcendental "limit" of life, language, and the world.[7]

A useful summary of Wittgenstein's attitude to ethics has been provided by Dale Jacquette (1997), who identifies two basic arguments of Wittgenstein's in the relevant texts. The first is based on what Jacquette takes to be the "Kantian thesis" in Wittgenstein, that is, that the "existence of ethics" essentially applies to every logically possible world, not only to the actual (contingent) world. In particular, the existence of ethics is independent of whether there are living beings in the world or not. Since value, in turn, is always "value for consciousness," a world uninhabited by living beings would be amoral. It follows that the world in itself is amoral, neither good nor evil; hence, ethics "transcends the natural world" (Jacquette 1997: 306–07). This argument is found problematic by Jacquette; however, we are more interested in the second argument he distinguishes, as it is more closely connected with the solipsism issue.

This is the argument based on the concept of the metaphysical subject. Wittgenstein argues, according to Jacquette, that ethics transcends the natural world because, first, "the metaphysical subject is a necessary condition for the instantiation of ethics in (ethical value of) the world," and secondly, the metaphysical subject transcends the natural world (Jacquette 1997: 313). Explicating in more detail this argument skeleton, Jacquette arrives at the conclusion that Wittgenstein's argument is impeccable and that the crucial premise, the claim that "the metaphysical subject as the source of ethical valuation is transcendent, and that the subject's transcendence is transmitted to subjective valuation and so to value," is plausible even when distinguished from the semantics of the *Tractatus* (Jacquette 1997: 316).

The result is a kind of quietism (although Jacquette does not use this term): ethics belongs to that which must be passed over into silence according to the final proposition of the *Tractatus*. There can be no (deep, interesting, non-vulgar) talk about ethics and value. As Jacquette puts it, "There is only the transcendence of ethical attitude and practice that colours the world of objective fact with ethical-aesthetic value in subjective experience grounded by the world-transcendent metaphysical subject" (Jacquette 1997: 320). Yet, this does not make ethics or value any less important; it does not imply "ethical nihilism,"[8] or any degradation of value, although it does imply a nontheoretical attitude to ethics (and aesthetics), urging us to stop constructing and defending ethical and metaethical theories (Jacquette 1997: 322–23). Even the solipsist, arguably, stands within an ethical framework of good and evil, at least insofar as her/his thought and imagination, and not just practical actions, can also be ethically evaluated (Watzka 2000: 82).

Jacquette (1997, 2002), like many others, speaks consistently about the "transcendence" of ethics and the metaphysical subject in Wittgenstein. We should, however, be careful with such terminology, especially within the Kantian tradition to which the terms "transcendent" and "transcendental" belong. Wittgenstein's (1921: §6.421) statement that ethics (along with religion and aesthetics) is *transcendental* should be taken seriously (cf. Watzka 2000: 100–01; Appelqvist 2013, 2016). Despite Wittgenstein's mystical bias, there is a sense in which ethics does *not*, according to him, lie "outside" the world (and life) in any literal sense (how could it, after all, as *nothing* can?). It lies, rather, at the limit of the world, for ethics, like religion and aesthetics, provides a view to the world as a whole, as valuable in some higher yet perspectively subject-related sense. In short, ethics is essentially about the subject's attitude to the world and life, constituting a condition for the possibility of the world, which is (for the subject) always a perspectivally structured world. This position is compatible with, or even required by (and arguably requires), transcendental solipsism: the subject, as a limit of the world, views the world as a limited totality under the aspect of ethical value. There is no *transcendence* involved, only *transcendentality*.[9] Wittgensteinian ethical solipsism construes "the ethical" as an inner feature of the (my) world limited by the transcendental subject (me).

This again indicates how solipsism "matters." I have argued, among other things, that if solipsism were true, it would be difficult to make sense of any normative engagement or human responsibility (see Chapter 4). This claim can now be properly extended to the ethical realm. Solipsism naturally implies that all evaluative propositions are *about me*, not about any external objects possessing some alleged value. Ethics is a matter of *my* world, or life, being a happy or unhappy one. As Felix Gmür (2000: 116) explains, emphasizing the connection between solipsism and Wittgenstein's aesthetics, the (un)happy life paradigmatically shown in art is always mine: "*My* life is *the* life, as happiness can manifest only in my life, as only I can live my life happily. Solipsism has its primordial form in art; the metaphysical solipsism with a vanishing 'I' [der Ich-tilgende, metaphysische Solipsismus] finds its paradigmatic expression in the aesthetic solipsism of the right worldview" (my translation). Any value there is in the world or outside it is, then, necessarily value *for me* (Watzka 2000: 96–97).

It is not impossible or inherently absurd to hold this view. Solipsism might be an easy solution to moral tragedies: if everything happens merely in "my world," I need not deeply worry about the suffering of others—except as an empirical state of affairs in this world of mine. Recalling the pragmatic assessment of solipsism in Chapter 4, we should note that this *is* a genuine pragmatic advantage.[10] But it begins to seem less advantageous once it is turned upside down: if I am a solipsist, all the suffering and evil there is in the empirical world is grounded in me. If I am a transcendental solipsist, I had better not forget that the things I find in the world constituted by myself are still empirically real. In our pragmatic consideration of solipsism, we have to carefully examine what kind of practical benefits, and from whose point of view, our solipsistic and non-solipsistic options yield.

Solipsism is a natural companion to Wittgensteinian ethical absolutism (clearly formulated in Wittgenstein's 1929 lecture), which we may find pragmatically unsatisfactory in this real world of fear, sorrow, and suffering—though it does contain profound reflections on what can be linguistically expressed in ethics. If I am a solipsist, I am the only one to be held truly responsible for suffering. But if I am (say) a pragmatic realist (in the sense of Chapter 4), I will have to urge, *contra* Wittgenstein, that ethics must not, and cannot, transcend the empirical, material, and temporal world. Moral action inevitably takes place *in* the world. In ethics, nothing is absolute, transcendent, or beyond our practice-laden language use and world-engagement; what is more, this very "worldliness" is itself a transcendental condition for the possibility of ethics as *we* know it in our ordinary lives laden with ethical problems. For ethical engagement to make sense, we *have to* be able to discuss ethics and value rationally in language (although there may be good reasons to follow Wittgenstein to his resistance to all traditional "theories" of ethics). *We* are not in a position to accept the Wittgensteinian thesis of the ineffability of ethics—any more than we are in a position to embrace ethical solipsism.[11]

Arguably, our non-solipsistic commitment to other subjects is, from a Wittgensteinian perspective, something that language cannot meaningfully express—any more than it can express solipsism itself.[12] Rather, it manifests itself in our life. We might, thus, argue that while the realist's world in a sense extends no further than the solipsist's, this possibility of preserving empirical realism within transcendental solipsism by no means supports solipsism, insofar as ethical considerations are seriously taken into account. If I am a realist, even if I had arrived at realism *via* solipsism (i.e., after having found them indistinguishable, as Wittgenstein suggests), I had better not be an "imperialist" realist (cf. Putnam 1983: 238)—provided that I wish to be an ethically responsible person and view my world in an ethical light. I had better be a real, yet pragmatic, realist and give up solipsism (as suggested in Chapter 4). But if we were genuinely convinced that solipsism coincides with realism, would it *matter* ethically whether we are solipsists or realists? Couldn't we just "leave everything as it is" and drop irrelevant metaphilosophical questions? Wouldn't this attitude amount to a Wittgensteinian therapeutical conception of philosophy par excellence? At least there seem to be no empirical differences in the outcome of our actions depending on our choice between solipsism and realism. There is, then, no immediately observable pragmatic difference between the two views.

The main, or only, difference is that one's attitude to the world as a whole may be fundamentally different, depending on whether one subscribes to (transcendental) solipsism or realism. Arguably, such fundamental attitudes *are* relevant to people's lives. Ethics, in the Wittgensteinian framework, is completely detached from the empirical world. Empirical events—even death, murder, or genocide, empirically considered—are, *qua* empirical, not ethical at all. They gain ethical significance only when evaluated *by me*, or my will. As this will is, for Wittgenstein, solipsistic, isn't there a significant difference to realism to be located here? We may argue in a modus tollens fashion: distinguishing between solipsism and realism does matter, ethically, in our lives (because human life is, prima facie at least, life with other people); hence, the thesis that solipsism and realism coincide is absurd—*for us*, given the kind of life we actually lead.

Such a difference between solipsism and realism in the ethical sphere is a transcendental, nonempirical difference; in this sense, ethics *is* transcendental. The difference cannot be simply captured with reference to something that takes place *in* the factual world, which, according to solipsism, is constituted by transcendental subjectivity. Yet, as I will show next, the "ethical responsibility" argument against solipsism, our insistence on acknowledging "the other" (or, more concretely, another person), does not take us beyond the solipsism issue, as it is still *me* who will have to take the responsibility for this acknowledgment. Locating the "pragmatic" difference between solipsism and realism in the ethical realm and admitting that ethics is "transcendental" may, after all, give the solipsist a major argumentative advantage at the meta-level. Possibly, the transcendental conception of ethics that makes possible our pragmatic, ethical argument against the solipsist's attitude to the world as a whole itself crucially depends on solipsism. By elaborating on this idea, I will argue that the solipsism issue is more intimately embedded in our ethical predicament than it might seem, however pragmatically we try to view our human situation.

Subjectivity and the Other

The solipsistic challenge concerns, above all, the subject—me—in the context of ethical thought and deliberation. We have seen that it is quite impossible to argumentatively refute solipsism for good. There is no neutral point from which we could determine whether solipsism is, ethically, a picture of *ultimate responsibility* (i.e., a sincere affirmation of the conviction that it is necessarily me with reference to whom anything whatsoever must be ethically assessed) or *utter irresponsibility*. The latter picture can be seen to be at work, perhaps, in Joseph Conrad's *Heart of Darkness*, where the quasi-solipsistic Kurtz in a horrifying way "accepts" the darkness of his soul.[13] The former, however, is the essence of the views developed by thinkers like Levinas and Sartre who insist that *I* am responsible for the other person and eventually for the entire world. The world rests upon *my* shoulders, ethically speaking. All moral responsibility there is, or can be, is mine. Isn't this account of ethical responsibility indistinguishable from (ethical) solipsism?

The possibility of solipsism teaches us a metaethical lesson about a certain *groundlessness*, or lack of foundations, in our human relations with other people and the world we live in. There is no metaphysical or epistemological guarantee to rely on. Ethics cannot be grounded in metaphysics (e.g., the philosophy of mind) or empirical scientific results (e.g., evolutionary psychology). We cannot but accept as "given" our duty of acknowledging other bodily, tangible, vulnerable, and historically contingent human beings (rather than immaterial minds), that is, of having an attitude toward them as "souls." This can be construed along Wittgensteinian lines,[14] or, alternatively, along phenomenological lines, emphasizing our being committed to a community of egos in a fundamental way.[15] But this givenness is not based on any fact of the matter that could be either scientifically or metaphysically determined. We need not (and cannot) *first* settle the solipsism issue theoretically in order to ground ethics on a firm basis; on the contrary, our ethical response to other human beings' experiences, especially their pain and suffering, is the inescapable background of any theoretical discussions of the reality of those experiences.

As David Cockburn emphasizes, the category of "human being" is fundamental in our thought.[16] There is no metaphysical argument available that could demonstrate that the object of our attitude toward a soul really exists; nor is such an argument needed. No such argument could show that there are other minds or other human beings out there that we *only then*—after having become theoretically convinced of their existence—ought to take into account ethically. Moral motivation, the acknowledgment of, and concern for, our fellow human beings does not need any more fundamental argument on the basis of which its legitimacy could be established. Such acknowledgment is itself a fundamental (albeit, in an important sense, non-foundational) bedrock of our life. This can be taken to be one of the key lessons of Wittgenstein's later philosophy. Indeed, as Peter Winch (1987: 147) argues, the "attitude" in Wittgenstein's "attitude towards a soul" ("eine Einstellung zur Seele") itself requires the concept of a soul; as the German "zur" suggests, the attitude here is inseparable from its object. I must already engage in a form of life in which others are considered "souls" in order to have this kind of an attitude; it is not an attitude I might just adopt or abandon at will (1987: 149).[17]

Emyr Vaughan Thomas illuminatingly discusses the changes in Wittgenstein's philosophy in this regard. The early Wittgenstein, inspired by Tolstoy, among other ethical and religious writers, admired "an inner capacity to be independent of the world through absorption in the present," which could liberate the self from anxiety and bring with it an experience of "absolute safety" (Thomas 1999: 198). As we have seen, the position of the *Tractatus* (and of the pre-Tractarian *Notebooks*) might even be interpreted as a temporal solipsism, or solipsism of the present moment, leading to an atemporal, timeless, view of the self and the world (which are the same, *now*, in the present).[18] However, even though its aims are deeply ethical, no genuinely ethical "selflessness" results, according to Thomas, from this solipsistic immersion in the present moment.[19] He concludes that the early Wittgenstein "failed to resolve the tension between his ethical impulse towards selflessness and a viable means of giving expression to it in his philosophical account" (Thomas 1999: 202), that is, that his position is, while "couched in terms of renunciation [of the self]," nevertheless "inextricably bound to a world-view involving a form of *self*-concern" and thus "ultimately self-directed" (Thomas 2001: 101).

However, Thomas (1999: 206–07) further argues that it is only in his later thought that Wittgenstein succeeds—this time by giving up the solitary self as a locus of ethical value, as an owner of the world. The selflessness receiving manifestation in Wittgenstein's later philosophy, in his conception of human beings, is "a more durable selflessness" than the solipsistic one of the early thought, "a selflessness no longer susceptible to collapse into a quasi-solipsistic absorption in the present" (1999: 208).[20] More generally, Thomas (2001: chapters 2 and 4) attempts to show that the kind of self-concern that remains in the early Wittgenstein's solipsistic version of self-renunciation is not inevitable in religious thought emphasizing self-renunciation.[21] Yet, it remains unclear whether the solipsistic overtones of the very project of self-renunciation can really be avoided in this manner. It seems that the giving up of the self must still be *someone's* activity—indeed, *mine*.

This reconfirms the point that a solipsistic dialectic is still at work even when we move from a Tractarian conception of subjectivity to Wittgenstein's later more pragmatic philosophy. Nevertheless, from the standpoint of scholars like Cockburn and Thomas, that is, our fundamental acknowledgment of other human beings and the ethical selflessness associated with such acknowledgment, we ought to admit (as an element of such acknowledgment) that no philosophical view emphasizing our intersubjective relations to other people will be able to provide a (or the) foundational philosophical framework for our rejection of solipsism. We do not *first* need a philosophical *theory* about reality, human interaction, subjectivity, the mind, language, and normativity. What we need is prior ethical concern for others in our life (an "ethical impulse," in Thomas's terms), in those fleeting moments of life which for us are the substance of the world. Theories are possible only when such life together with others already takes place. We may here speak about the limits of (pure) ontology: metaphysical theorizing about the nature of reality, about what exists, about other minds, or any other fundamental issue in the absence of an ethical perspective is seriously limited. The limits of my language are the limits of my world, if Wittgenstein is right, but the limits of my ethical responsibility are also the limits of my metaphysical seriousness.

Following Cavell and Cockburn in particular, we ought to recognize a certain amount of truth in skepticism about the external world and about other minds: there is no metaphysical security available. However, this finitude of our human ability to face another human being is not, as such, a *failure*; the kind of skepticism (or solipsism) involved here is very different from classical skeptical solipsism. Cavell (1979: 45ff., 241) maintains that Wittgenstein takes the skeptical thesis (about the world and other minds) as undeniable and maintains that our relation to "the world as a whole" and to others is not one of (certain) knowing; thus, we do not fail in our knowledge about these things, either.[22] Moreover, Cavell suggests that if the solipsist regards her/his view as a "solution" to the problem of other minds (or as an elimination of that problem), s/he must be disappointed: that problem is a problem *about me*, about my being an other mind to the others (1979: 442).

The finitude, groundlessness, and insecurity we encounter here are key elements of our life. The ethical point of view is irreducible; there is nothing metaphysical to rely on as a foundation of the duty of acknowledging another human soul. However, the price for this position is that there is no way of rationally (or at least conclusively) arguing that this really is a duty for us. Arguments in moral theory already presuppose that such a basic acknowledgment takes place. Some Wittgensteinian-inspired philosophers are even tempted to describe such acknowledgment as *mysterious*. "It is strange and sometimes it is mysterious, that other people can affect us as deeply as they do," Gaita (1991: 50) writes.[23] The duty—one's personal duty—to see another human being as a soul can perhaps only be described (or, better, shown rather than put to ordinary words) in religious texts, such as the parable of the Good Samaritan (Lk. 10:25-37) to which Winch (1987: chapter 11) draws our attention, emphasizing the indexicality of the question, "Who is my neighbour?" It is *me* for whom this is a relevant question; *I* have to ask who *my* neighbor is (1987: 155)—and thus we are back in ethical solipsism. That is, we have not left ethical solipsism aside even when we have taken the apparently non-solipsistic step of adopting an ethical attitude of acknowledgment toward our neighbors (whoever they are).

We have, through the idea of the mysteriousness of our acknowledgment of, and our personal duty of acknowledging, other human beings, arrived at a view relatively close to Levinas's account of the primacy of the ethical encounter with "the Other" (*l'Autrui*) and of ethics as a "first philosophy." It is the infinite other that comes first; according to Levinas, the fact of our living "faced" by other human beings is the most originary (or "pre-original") point where no theoretical-versus-ethical (or "is" versus "ought") distinction can even be drawn.[24]

It might seem that there is no problem of solipsism in Levinas's philosophy (to which we will return more closely in the next section), which begins from the other's otherness, rejecting any Cartesian assumption of a privileged self-representing subjectivity. Levinas is often thought of having crucially stepped beyond Husserl and the (methodologically) solipsistic approach dominating much of the phenomenological tradition.[25] Jacques (1982), in turn, attempts to go even beyond Levinas's affirmation of otherness by arguing that subjectivity and the personal identity of the self are transcendentally dependent on a network of communication, on a prior (transcendental) intersubjectivity—something that Husserl, because of his phenomenological method focusing on self-consciousness, never achieved (cf. Chapter 3). Jacques points out that "the approach to alterity taken by existential phenomenology is based on phenomenological premises that seem to me inadequate in principle to delimit the constitutive domain of intersubjectivity, once we set out to define it without privileging the ego at the expense of the *alter*" (Jacques 1982: 130–31). He seeks to provide a transcendental argument, which would "break once and for all with the philosophical narcissism of the ego" (Jacques 1982: 130), reminding us that interhuman relations "have the status of an ultimate reality," because without reference to such relations I could not even speak about solitude (Jacques 1982: 116).[26] My arguments in Chapter 4 above bear some resemblance to this line of thought.

The key point here, according to Jacques, is that even Levinas in a way endorses solipsism at the theoretical or rational level of investigation.[27] In a manner reminiscent of the early Wittgenstein and some of his commentators, particularly Pears (see, again, Chapter 3), Jacques argues that solipsism is meaningless:

> To say that I am the only one who speaks or thinks is not only wrong, but meaningless. How can I wonder whether my present experience is the only reality, as there is no such things as *my* experience, or even *my* world? The point is not whether or not we should accept the idea of solipsism, and then try (like Husserl) to overcome it, or (like Levinas) to resign ourselves to it, but whether or not we should agree to regard it as a problem. As soon as we accept the idea, it becomes impossible to put forward

any serious arguments against it. Therefore, we should refuse to regard it as a problem, because as a problem it is not real. Solipsism is an absurdity that is not even "significant." Speaking and thinking are just not the sort of things we can do on our own. (Jacques 1982: 160)

It seems to me that Jacques here forgets his otherwise admirable transcendental mode. He fails to perceive the transcendental reasons why Wittgenstein (and, I am tempted to think, Levinas) considered solipsism not only "significant" but also, in an important sense, correct. These reasons invoke not just the possibility of speaking and thinking but also the possibility of ethics as truly serious, as *my* responsibility for others in their mortality and fragility. Again, we cannot escape the conclusion that we have not left solipsism behind as soon as we begin to emphasize the ethical importance of other human beings.

In any event, no one, not even Jacques, can deny that it is still *me* for whom solipsism is, within the philosophical framework of irreducible intersubjectivity, a nonstarter. I am, as has become clear, proposing to view both solipsism and its negation as fundamental ethical choices. There is, however, an important asymmetry here: as a non-solipsist, I ought to assume a *responsibility* for my position (cf. Cavell 1979: 268, 312), that is, accept my bedrock, the piece of land where my spade is turned and where I stand firm, as *mine*. I should, moreover, be prepared to subordinate my position to a critical discussion, if I happen to find my bedrock unstable after all. Since there can be neither true responsibility nor criticism in a solipsistic world, this ethical move is not, I am tempted to think, possible for the solipsist. But now the solipsist can counter me by claiming that her/his sense of responsibility, of really accepting a position as one's own, is more genuine; even I, as a non-solipsist, cannot escape the "mineness" of responsibility.

Rejecting solipsism in the ethical realm, I have committed myself to a kind of (moral) realism, which I may take to be pragmatically justifiable (cf. Chapter 4). It should be clear, however, that solipsism does not amount to (or entail) moral indifferentism, nihilism, or amoralism. The solipsist can accept the genuine existence of values, provided that their existence is always (transcendentally) tied to subjective valuation. *Could* the solipsist adopt a completely nihilistic "theory" of morality? Perhaps they could, by claiming that it does not matter at all what kind of empirically real events take place within their world, not even whether that world—the only world there is—comes to an end or not. Such a position would regard *both* facts of the world *and* the world itself, as a totality, insignificant.

Wittgenstein's (1965) view was restricted to the former: facts of the world have no meaning or value in themselves, and the meaning or value of the world as a whole lies outside—or, better, at the limit of—the world (and language and life). Wittgenstein was certainly not a moral nihilist or indifferentist.[28] Indeed, he regarded suicide—the end of the world—as an "elementary sin." For a thoroughgoing nihilist, on the contrary, there would be no value or significance either in the world or outside it, or even "at the limit." For Wittgenstein, there seems to be some mystical value in the existence of something (the world) rather than nothing. *That* the world is is "mystical."

It *is*, perhaps, possible to adopt a nihilistic indifferentism in ethics. To do so would require not that one commits suicide but that one does not care whether to commit suicide or not and, correspondingly, that one does not care whether one, for example, kills or injures others or not. However, moral debate and reasoning must end somewhere (cf. Pihlström 2005). There is a point at which the pragmatic moral realist can, and should, only say to their opponent (e.g., a solipsist or a nihilist): "I am not going to follow you. I will stay where I am, continuing to acknowledge others, even you." The problem is whether they can consistently reply in this fashion: if a pragmatist insists on the duty of acknowledging even the nihilist, they may pragmatically contradict their own position. Is there a limit to acknowledgment, as there is a limit to argumentation (see Chapter 6), reached at some point within our practices of acknowledgment? These questions point toward a not easily penetrable complexity in our moral lives. I may have to admit that if I fail to acknowledge the solipsist as a genuine subject (because her/his view is utterly alien to me and I could never share it), I will in a sense accept that view, after all, that is, *live* the "truth" of the non-acknowledgment of otherness manifested in the solipsist's position. Paradoxically, in refusing to treat the solipsist as "one of us," I am in a constant danger of falling into solipsistic non-acknowledgment myself.

More technically, the very notion of otherness seems to become paradoxical when applied to the solipsism issue. The solipsist's otherness is extreme: s/he is an "other" to me, if anyone is, for s/he refuses to treat me (and others) as a genuine subject, as another. If the otherness relation were symmetrical, I should also be an "other" to the solipsist. This is impossible on the assumption of solipsism. For the solipsist, no one is truly an "other." Can I then even say that the solipsist is an "other" to me? The crux of the matter seems to be that the relation just is not symmetrical. The solipsist is "another" to me in a peculiar sense: I am not another self (nor anything else) to her/him. In fact, for Levinas, there is a fundamental asymmetry at the heart of ethical otherness: the ultimate responsibility for and to the other is *mine*, not *vice versa*. I cannot demand any symmetrical responsibility from the external other for myself. Is the solipsist, then, a Levinasian other, a true example of someone demanding responsibility from me?[29]

We may make a conceptual suggestion at this point, before moving on to further reflections on the significance of solipsism. If we, pragmatically and naturalistically, conceived of the human, practice-engaging self (*pace* Wittgenstein) not as a limit or boundary of the world but rather as belonging to the (natural and cultural) world inhabited by a community of human beings, we could still save an element of the "limit" conception by employing the notion of *inexhaustibility* in trying to make sense of our realistic attitude to both the world and the self. The world as well as the self as an element of it resemble the infinity of the Levinasian other by being, for us, inexhaustible: we can always approach them from new, previously unseen or even unimagined, viewpoints (both epistemically and ethically). There is always more to be found there than has actually been found, perspectives that have not previously been mine (or ours). What we need, then, is a pragmatic, responsible commitment to the reality of an inexhaustible world. The notion of inexhaustibility employed here is not only ontological and epistemological but also ethical, insofar as our ontological and epistemological responsibility is necessarily ethically structured.

However, even in switching the central metaphor from the metaphysical notion of a "limit" (of the world) to the more pragmatic and naturalist notion of "inexhaustibility" (in contrast to, say, unattainability or transcendence), we should bear in mind that in Wittgenstein's later philosophy there are no specifically ethical language games in which ethics could be discussed. Ethics still remains irreducible to any "natural history" of our language use, and hence inexpressible—perhaps even more so than in the early philosophy pointing toward mysticism. The later Wittgenstein says very little about ethics, and while Levinas constantly writes about ethics, for him, too, the truly ethical responsibility to and for the infinite (inexhaustible) other belongs to the realm of "saying," never to that of the "said."[30]

Perhaps we ought to construe the role of the ethical in Wittgenstein's later thought in the following way. There is no specifically ethical language game, because ethics, being the most important feature of our human being-in-the-world, is always already a structural characteristic of any language games we play. The ethical is rooted in our forms of life as deeply as our language itself is. It is as inexhaustible as our human world itself, that is, there is no perspective or framework in which it does not play any role at all. Its essence cannot be captured by means of any particular language use, any more than the "essence of the world" can. To employ Tractarian terminology, the ethical may *show* itself in our life and language (or any aspect of them); it need not, and cannot, be specifically discussed—as if it could be detached from the life in which it has its being. This is what it means to say that our moral selves are inexhaustible. Morality is so inextricably present in our existence that, no matter how deeply we dig into the basic commitments of our lives, we always encounter layers of ethical structures. To *discuss* ethics theoretically would, from the Wittgensteinian point of view, be to separate it from our human reality that would simply be inhuman in the absence of ethics. The ethical is already there in our adopting an attitude to the other person as an attitude to a soul, that is, in our groundless (but grounding) rejection of solipsism. Ethics, as in Levinas, comes first—before any more specific language games we play in various areas of life.

Still, even this insistence on the primacy and inexhaustibility of the ethical does not make the problem of solipsism go away. My infinite responsibility for the Levinasian other, for their death above my own, is, as already emphasized, *mine*. I am irreplaceable as the bearer of this inexhaustible responsibility. It is *me* for whom ethics is (or—ethically—ought to be), though ineffable, the primary, most important, thing that matters in life and language.[31] As the only genuine bearer of ethical responsibility (from my own point of view), I may still be—nay, I necessarily am—the only fully ethical subject there is. As Wittgenstein maintained, my will may still be the only ethical will there is, the only will capable of being morally evaluated. The idea that ethics is fundamentally about me, about what I ought to do in (or with) my life (potentially in *any* given situation of life), and that ethical significance should be found in my own actions as distinguished from those of others, has, as already noted, been defended by several philosophers influenced by Wittgenstein (cf. Winch 1972: 6, and especially chapters 8–11; Rhees 1999: chapter 9). The similarity between this view and existentialism is, it seems to me, striking. I am not claiming Wittgensteinian moral thinkers or existentialists to be solipsists, but there seems to be a solipsistic element embedded in their conviction that it is me and no one else who has to decide what ought to be done in a given situation, insofar as this decision has ethical significance. From an ethical point of view, *my* life is, according to these thinkers, the only life at stake when it comes to ethics. Moral evaluation only applies to me, and genuinely moral situations arise for me only. It is more than slightly paradoxical that the distinctive character of morality—its absolute and fundamental status in our lives—needs to be perceived through what is "true" in solipsism.

This quasi-solipsistic situation may inevitably be the case regarding my moral relations to all others and the rest of the world, even if ethics as the most significant part of my humanity were already there, right from the beginning, in my encounters with others whose existence is (and is acknowledged by me to be) independent of mine but who cannot bear *their* responsibility independently of me because of the (Levinasian-style) infinite responsibility *I* have for them (and for their responsibility). I will elaborate on this theme in the next section focusing on the concept of death, with further references to Levinas.

Solipsism and Death

Human suffering in the empirically real world, as viewed by the transcendental solipsist, *is* still empirically real, as real as any other events taking place in the world. For a transcendental solipsist who is an empirical realist, there are still other subjects in the world, although they exist *as* objects for her/him. These other subjects, or wills, may not act in accordance with my, the solipsistic subject's, will. The human bodies acting in the world, just like all other, nonhuman objects, are independent of my will, if we again follow Wittgenstein's transcendental solipsism. Thus, my solipsistic "freedom" or "power" is strictly limited to my viewing the world as a limited totality; I cannot change its facts at will. The transcendental solipsist may, presumably, even be an (empirical) determinist. S/he need not entertain any illusion about the power of her/his own will to exercise changes in the world. There is an analogy here: in *dreams* we often feel entirely powerless, governed by "external" factors, though we know (when awake) that dreams are subjective products of our own imagination. In short, the solipsist need not be able to control the world s/he "owns." The solipsist need not believe in free will in any standard sense.

Furthermore, even the solipsist cannot avoid entertaining the thought that one day s/he will be gone. The solipsist hardly is, *pace* Lafleur (1952: 527), immortal. Arguably, the craving for immortality so natural for humans is always in the first place mine; hence we are perhaps all to some extent solipsists simply by being concerned about our own mortality. But the distinction between the transcendental and the empirical is again needed. Empirically speaking, I can *now* say that when I die, the world will, empirically or factually, go on mostly as it did before my (the solipsist's) death, but at the transcendental level death is not an event in the world. The final, most pregnant, ethical and metaphilosophical dimension of our theme is the question of how the solipsist should (again ethically) consider matters of life and death and how we (non-solipsists) should understand the resources of philosophical reflection regarding these matters.

Death—Mine or the Other's?

As the brief comments on existentialism in Chapters 3 (in relation to phenomenology) and 4 (in relation to Jamesian pragmatism) suggest, death is one of the key existential issues related to solipsism. What is at stake here is, of course, *my own* death, the death toward which I am living my life, not death as a scientific concept objectively applicable to living organisms. Realistically, my death is merely one rather insignificant natural event in the world, an event whose inevitability may make my life seem absurd (cf. Nagel 1979,

1986). Solipsistically, my death is the end of the world, either with a bang or a whimper. None of these alternatives sounds promising. Solipsism may make life even more absurd than it otherwise seems, although its purpose may have been the opposite.

Brockhaus (1985: 261ff.) distinguishes between two notions of death in Wittgenstein's *Tractatus*: (i) the empirical, biological, death as a natural event in the world and (ii) the death of the metaphysical subject, that is, its disappearance, the end of the world. This distinction bears on Wittgenstein's conception of value, ethics, and happiness. Since all the objects there are in the world are "eternal" within the framework of experience whose form is given by the metaphysical subject, the disappearance of that subject must be seen as a kind of miracle. Hence, its existence is a miracle, too (1985: 262). The world as "my world" has a unity: there is an *ethical monism* underlying the Tractarian ontological pluralism of states of affairs. On Brockhaus's reading, "my world *can* wax and wane *tutti*, but only insofar as this waxing and waning is centered on, or due to, some change in the inner limit, the metaphysical subject" (1985: 266; see Pihlström 2016: chapter 4).

Brockhaus's interpretation is easily reconcilable with the transcendental reading of the *Tractatus* considered earlier; however, from the perspective of the kind of pragmatic naturalism and realism I sketched as an alternative to solipsism in Chapter 4, the Tractarian distinction between two kinds of death may seem superfluous. What is philosophically significant is, rather, the natural death, dying, and mortality of flesh-and-blood human beings in this empirical world. This is the death of the concrete other that we must, following Levinas, take seriously as the core of ethics. Natural death, its inevitability in our own lives as well as in the lives of others, is the source of ethics.[32]

A comparison between Wittgenstein and Levinas may at this point be illuminating. Wittgenstein's conception of ethical value may be interpreted as totalizing (and of course solipsistic), since it regards the world (which is mine) as valuable as a whole, as a totality of my life, viewed *sub specie aeternitatis*. Levinas's view, on the contrary, seeks to avoid any totalizing ethics, locating the ethical in the concrete face-to-face relation to the mortal and vulnerable other. Yet, the later Wittgenstein, with his emphasis on the "attitude towards a soul," comes closer to Levinas's face-to-face conception of the ethical relation, whereas Levinas, again, cannot get rid of the problem framework of solipsism, since in his view the infinite, pre-ontological and pre-totalizing responsibility for the other is inevitably *mine* and nobody else's (as suggested in the previous section). Who, here, is this "me," individuated not as an empirical object in the world but as the center of ethical responsibility?[33]

A distinction must be drawn between solipsistic and non-solipsistic philosophies of death. A comparison not only between Levinas and Wittgenstein but also between Levinas and Heidegger is relevant in this context. It is clear that the conception of death elaborated on in the *Tractatus* is solipsistic, even temporally solipsistic; for Heidegger, too, death is, in a comparable way, primarily mine—just like human existence or *Dasein* itself is. *Dasein*'s inevitable "mineness" is clear in *Sein und Zeit* (Heidegger 1927: §9), where Heidegger famously distinguishes between authenticity and inauthenticity. From the Heideggerian perspective, being-toward-death, *Sein-zum-Tode*, is *Dasein*'s ultimate mode of being, the existential project that (only) may make my life authentic.[34] When reflecting on death, I must, inevitably, focus on my own death, on death as the culmination of my existence, as the last (pseudo-)event of my being-in-the-world. Wittgenstein's solipsistic view of death is characterized by an aspiration to timelessness, to the eternity of the "now" (cf. Thomas 1999, 2001), and Heidegger's by an affirmation of the historicity of human existence, but the first-person perspective appears to be fundamentally the same. Despite Heidegger's critique of Husserl's methodological solipsism, he does not seem to be free from a basically similar "egological" approach, at least when he writes about death and *Dasein*'s mineness in *Sein und Zeit*.[35]

Levinas, on the contrary, at least tries to formulate a non-solipsistic philosophy of death by focusing on the other's death instead of mine: death must be conceived primarily as the death of another person, if this concept is to have any ethical significance:

> In its expression, in its mortality, the face before me summons me, calls for me, begs for me, as if the invisible death that must be faced by the Other, pure otherness, separated, in some way, from any whole, were my business. It is as if that invisible death, ignored by the Other, whom already it concerns by the nakedness of its face, were already "regarding" me prior to confronting me, and becoming the death that stares me in the face. The other man's death calls me into question, as if, by my possible future

indifference, I had become the accomplice of the death to which the other, who cannot see it, is exposed; and as if, even before vowing myself to him, I had to answer for this death of the other, and to accompany the Other in his mortal solitude. The Other becomes my neighbour precisely through the way the face summons me, calls for me, begs for me, and in so doing recalls my responsibility, and calls me into question. (Levinas 1989: 83; see also Levinas 1999: 24–25 and chapter 11)

Focusing on the death of the other also enables us to avoid solipsism of the present moment, since temporality itself is rendered possible (only) by my encounter with the other: "The very relationship with the other is the relationship with the future. It seems to me impossible to speak of time in a subject alone, or to speak of a purely personal duration" (Levinas 1999: 44).

Once again, however, the problem of solipsism returns.[36] Death, as mine, is from my point of view something infinite, *the end*; now, the same ought to be true about the death of the other in the Levinasian framework. Levinas describes how I am responsible for the other's death and how this responsibility for the other, as infinite, is *unshareable*. It is *me* who occupies someone else's place "with the *Da* of my *Dasein*" (Levinas 1989: 82); therefore, "I am inescapably responsible and consequently the unique and chosen one," "non-*interchangeable*," in the face of the other (Levinas 1989: 84; cf. 181). It is, in other words, the ego itself, *me*, that is "wrenched from its primordiality" through an encounter with another ego (Levinas 1998: 177). The other's mortality, the turning away from death as a solitary project characterized by mineness in a Heideggerian-Wittgensteinian sense, paradoxically leads to my being chosen as singularly responsible for the death of anyone else.

It is from this pre-original responsibility, from my need to respond to my right to be, to take someone else's place, that language itself— as a response to my being called into question—arises (Levinas 1989: 82). Seeking to move beyond Heidegger, Levinas ends up with singling out me, the ethical subject, as the unique and chosen one. He is, then, an ethical solipsist:[37] "The word *I* means *here I am*, answering for everything and for everyone" (Levinas 1989: 104); I, as a "self," am a "*sub-jectum*," "under the weight of the universe, responsible for everything" (Levinas 1989: 105). "The non-interchangeable par excellence, the I, the unique one, substitutes itself for others" (Levinas 1989: 106), and this substitution is my own in a profound sense, since I am "integrally or absolutely ego" and no one can substitute her-/himself for me, although I substitute myself for all (Levinas 1989: 115; see also 243). "I am unique and chosen"; "it is I, and no one else, who am hostage for the others" (Levinas 1989: 116). "I support the universe" (Levinas 1989: 123). "I'm uniquely chosen for responsibility" (Levinas 1987: 125, 158), ultimately in the sense sublimely expressed in the Babylonian Talmud: "The world was created for me!"—although this is something that "each [person] is obliged to say" (Levinas 1987: 118). It is, then, always and inevitably, me, a mortal individual, who ethically focuses on the other's death, and must do so, bearing responsibility, substituting myself for the other, and while each one of us "is obliged to say" the same thing, the obligation here and now applies, from my standpoint, to me only.[38]

Even though Levinas stands in a tradition transcending Cartesian skeptical or methodological solipsism—through Kant's and Husserl's egological accounts of transcendental subjectivity to Heidegger's critique of the Cartesian elements of Husserl's phenomenology—he cannot avoid some of the basic commitments of that tradition (which other critics of solipsism, like Heidegger, have not been able to avoid, either).[39] In his elaborations on my responsibility for the other, Levinas is, at least methodologically, an ethical solipsist. He turns toward my original responsibility just like Descartes turned toward the ego's (my) subjective cognition and the worry about its representing the way the external world is.[40] Levinas's ethical solipsism is transcendental in the sense that the solipsistic assumption about my being the primary locus of responsibility is made at a higher level than the mundane, empirical one at which other human beings are encountered. "My world" is primary to the other's (or, in a way, only I and no one else can have a world) at least in the sense that I have to be responsible for the other who is, necessarily, "a stranger in my world," someone for whom I must "make room" in my world or whom I must welcome "into my home," someone who "finds no other support besides me in my world" (Beavers 1995: 100–02). It is this unique responsibility that leads me to see "the world as uniquely for me"—for me to be able to say to the other, "Here I am." What I am facing here, by realizing such an infinite responsibility, is the solipsistic situation in which "my world" is essentially different from the rest of the world.

This is a highly peculiar form of solipsism, but a form of ethical solipsism nevertheless. True, I am afraid of "occupying in the *Da* of my *Dasein* someone else's place," and this fear comes to me "from the face of the other" (Levinas 1999: 23); but, if this is possible, isn't my *Dasein* again the primary core of reality, something that could have been, but is not, the *Dasein* of an other and now is, disturbingly, irreplaceably mine?[41] It is only me who can genuinely worry about occupying another's place; for anyone else, there is no such ethical worry available. Paradoxically, in deciding, ethically, to support the other and not to kill her/him, I make, transcendentally speaking, a solipsistic decision. Levinas's ethics of responsibility can take off the ground only if basic ethically solipsistic assumptions have already been made.

Another thinker not far from Levinas in this regard, Zygmunt Bauman (1992: 40–48), joins Levinas in focusing on one's ultimate ethical responsibility for the other. In particular, this means that a truly moral principle *can never* legitimate the death of another and *must always* require that my responsibility for the other extends to my duty to die for her/him, to offer my life as a "gift"—without necessarily wanting to do it, and especially without thinking that I am heroically sacrificing my life for some general value or ideology (1992: 200–10). Now, solipsism comes back, just like in Levinas, for it is again, equally irreplaceably, me whose moral responsibility it is to die for the other. I am not making this statement in order to attack either Levinas or Bauman. Rather, it is one of the metaphilosophically striking features of solipsism that it may help us understand human mortality, not only our own first-person perspective on death but also the relation between our being both mortal and ethically concerned about others' mortality, and thus help us to philosophize about death in an ethically significant way (cf. Pihlström 2016).

Søren Overgaard (2007: chapters 5 and 8) not only heavily criticizes solipsistic interpretations of Wittgenstein (even transcendental solipsism) but also perceptively notes the kind of solipsistic threats in Levinas's position identified here, while arguing for a thoroughly non-solipsistic conception of otherness in both phenomenology and Wittgenstein. Overgaard seems to join those who see a kind of truth in solipsism by emphasizing the fundamental first-person/third-person asymmetry, both epistemologically and ethically (2007: 7–8, 89–102, 152–53), but he reminds us that no solipsistic consequences follow. On the contrary, this asymmetry is necessary for there being others to me: "My inability to live the other's mental life is in fact a *precondition* of her existence for me as another" (2007: 96). We can always view the world only from our own perspective, "from *somewhere*," as finite, particular subjects (2007: 98–99), but this does not entail solipsism but its opposite.[42]

It is perhaps ultimately a terminological matter whether to call this appreciation of the fundamental asymmetry a "truth in solipsism" or the opposite of solipsism. No serious solipsistic interpreter of Wittgenstein (or Levinas) ever thought that any kind of classical solipsism would follow from this asymmetry. It seems to me that we can accept most of what Overgaard says about the status of others in Wittgenstein and the phenomenologists he compares Wittgenstein to (namely, Husserl, Sartre, and Levinas), as well as most of what he says about the infinite ethical responsibility that is mine according to Levinas, while maintaining that this movement of thought always returning to the basic asymmetry between me and others—especially relevant in the moral sphere—does express an underlying tendency of solipsism to "come back." This tendency itself could be regarded as transcendental solipsism. It is parallel to the above-examined return of solipsism in the disguise of our "private moments" of ethical decision to acknowledge the other (cf. Chapter 4). What is transcendental here is the unavoidability of our always returning to this fundamental difference between our own perspective and those of others, especially when we must take ethical responsibility for the mortal other, a responsibility we can never transfer to anyone else.[43]

Furthermore, we should not, when discussing death from the point of view of ethical solipsism, overlook the issue of *suicide*, which, according to Albert Camus's famous remark, is the single important problem in philosophy. For the young Wittgenstein of the *Notebooks*, suicide is an "elementary sin." Why? Since only the empirical facts of the (my) world disappear in suicide, couldn't even the act of suicide just be interpreted as an empirical event, albeit the last one? Presumably not: the death of the subject should be regarded as the disappearance of the conditions that make the empirical world possible. Hence, it is not a merely empirical event but also a transcendental one.

The distinctive character of Wittgenstein's account may lie in his trying to say, simultaneously, that empirical life and death, just as all empirical or factual events in the natural world, are ultimately trivial and that death is, despite its empirical triviality, something important or even sublime. Wittgenstein's solipsistic approach to death is nowhere more clearly visible than in his attitude to suicide. One may speculate that it is, as so often, Schopenhauer's (and to some extent Weininger's) influence on his early thought that was crucial here. From the Schopenhauerian perspective, suicide, as a rejection of my will, is only a rejection of *this particular* will and hence an "ultimate affirmation of the individual" instead of being a genuine liberation from the overall suffering caused by the noumenal will (Brockhaus 1991: 63).

A striking feature of Levinas's position, on the other hand, is his disinterest in suicide. There is nothing ethically significant in suicide, as only the death of the other, not my own death, is (albeit quasi-solipsistically) the locus of ultimate responsibility. "Suicide is a contradictory concept," Levinas (1989: 42) claims. Even so, the problem of solipsism will return, once again, as soon as I realize that *I* should not draw ethical attention to the notion of suicide and but focus on the death of the other instead.[44]

This may in fact be what Wittgenstein's notion of the "problem of life" (which of course includes the problem of death) comes down to: the impossibility of arguing, in a demonstrative way, against the solipsistic view of death (and, correspondingly, of life). An ethical perspective on death as the death of the other ought to be seen as a continuous challenge to me, a challenge of avoiding solipsism. Yet, again, it is me and me only to whom such a challenge is given, throughout my life. It appears that if *I* am really willing to lead an ethical life, to be responsible for what I do, I had better be an ethical solipsist. Paradoxically, while avoiding solipsism seems to be a pragmatic precondition of ethical relations to other people, to attempt a philosophical demonstration of the falsity of solipsism would be to act unethically in a profound sense.[45]

Death and Transcendental Solipsism— Pro and Contra

Let us continue our reflection on solipsism and death by examining an interesting contemporary debate. J. J. Valberg's theory of death and the self, heavily indebted to Wittgensteinian transcendental solipsism, has been interestingly criticized from a naturalistic point of view by Mark Johnston; the recent books by these two philosophers (Valberg 2007; Johnston 2010) are major contributions not only to the philosophy of death but also to the reassessment of transcendental solipsism.[46]

Valberg employs the notion of a *personal horizon* in his examination of death. It is, he tells us, "only by being 'at the center' of the personal horizon, of the horizon that is 'mine,' that something (a human being) is a 'subject'" (Valberg 2007: 11). This horizon, however, is, like the Wittgensteinian transcendental subject, "nothing *in itself*"; it is not among the many horizons there are but "*the* horizon" (Valberg 2007: 12; cf. 96–97, 185ff.), and *this* is the "truth in solipsism." This nothingness is a fundamental element of the transcendentality of the horizon. If the horizon were "something," a thing in the world, it would no longer be transcendental (though this is not exactly the way Valberg expresses his point). It would not play the constitutive role in making the world possible if it were itself an object or a place in the world.

Things get complicated when Valberg starts to speak about other horizons, all of them claiming "preeminence" for themselves (Valberg 2007: 129). "In regarding you as a metaphysical equal, I recognize your horizon as outside my horizon," he says (Valberg 2007: 144). But isn't this precisely what is problematic especially when we consider death and solipsism? Death "in the metaphysical sense" is the "cessation of the crucial subject matter, of my horizon," of "that from within which the world appears" (Valberg 2007: 178). Valberg argues that "the fact that I will die (in the metaphysical sense) leaves the totality I call 'the world' untouched," because "the fact of death concerns not the ceasing to be of anything *in* that totality, but the ceasing to be of THIS, the horizon of the totality" (Valberg 2007: 179).[47] It is right here, then, that solipsism is brought into this picture. My horizon's being "*the* horizon" makes it "mine" (Valberg 2007: 185). Therefore, the word "my" in these phrases cannot refer "possessively" to the human being I happen to be (Valberg 2007: 182). Valberg—much more explicitly than Wittgenstein—*endorses* solipsism, albeit in a deliberately paradoxical form claiming that "we" (all) know it to be true:

> In this way, we are all solipsists. What makes my horizon "mine" is that it is the horizon. . . . Solipsism is a solution to our problem. . . . I think we already know it to be true . . . but we

have to become open to what we know. We have, in other words, to discover philosophically this truth that we already know, the truth of solipsism. (Valberg 2007: 186)[48]

It is death that "puts us in touch with the truth of solipsism, our own solipsism, in a way that nothing else does" (Valberg 2007: 187). Here Valberg considers Wittgenstein's *Tractatus*, observing that Tractarian solipsism is concerned precisely with the "horizon or limit of the world" (Valberg 2007: 189).[49] He interprets the relevant sections of the *Tractatus* by saying that this horizon—that is, the "self of solipsism"—"is nothing in itself" in the sense that there is no increase in reality whatsoever due to its being internal to that self; the self of solipsism "adds nothing to the world, just as death takes away nothing from the world," though what it does take away is precisely the self of solipsism, the horizon, the limit (Valberg 2007: 198).

In Valberg's terms, death will eliminate all presence; there will be NOTHING. "The world will remain, but there will be NOTHING"—and this cannot be relativized into there being just "NOTHING for me," because "what death means to us" is not such relativized nothingness but absolute nothingness (Valberg 2007: 207). We do not, at death, just lose the world (on the contrary, the world will continue to exist without us, which is horrifying), but we lose the horizon enabling the world to appear—to be—at all. It is this NOTHINGNESS as a complete absence of anything that Valberg believes we inevitably find awful and incomprehensible (Valberg 2007: 215ff.). Death is not only dreadful but in a sense *impossible*, solipsistically understood (Valberg 2007: 227–28, 482–83). A temptingly easy solution would be to emphasize the mortal other at this point, urging us to take seriously the other's horizon and its existential fragility before our own, but we should remember (as we saw in relation to Levinas) the tendency of solipsism to return: if my horizon collapsed into NOTHINGNESS, I would no longer have the other, either, as someone to whom I would be infinitely responsible from within my horizon. The other needs (in Levinas's parlance, "summons") *me*, and thus my horizon. There are no metaphysical equals: "I alone face absolute NOTHINGNESS" (Valberg 2007: 232).

Only toward the end of his book does Valberg employ the concept of the transcendental self, which he identifies with the "horizonal self" (Valberg 2007: 403ff., especially 407). The absence of the transcendental self amounts to the absolute nothingness that death is. It is the transcendental self that has, and can have, no metaphysical equals. If it did, it would simply be an object in the world.

Johnston criticizes Valberg's views in his own attempt to deal with death and the self. He discusses—with references to both the *Tractatus* and Valberg—what he calls the "arena of presence" (his version of Valberg's "horizon"), at the center of which we seem to find ourselves. Unlike Valberg, he attacks solipsism—and the transcendental considerations of philosophers like Wittgenstein and Valberg generally. Yet, the death of a given human being that just happens to be me is different, he says, from my "ownmost" death. I cannot really imagine my ownmost death, as it is the disappearance of the "arena" (Johnston 2010: 168–69). The problem is that the transcendental subject cannot just "disappear" from the world like any object, or the empirical subject, can. The disappearance of the transcendental self is, again, the end of the world.

I am not convinced that Johnston sufficiently appreciates the transcendental consideration of the matter in the *Tractatus* and in Valberg's study. The transcendental subject—the center of the (my) arena of presence—is not an object of *any* kind, not even an intentional object, not a thing in the actual world or any possible world, and therefore its end is the end of the (or any) world. Only objects in the world, not the arena or the world-limiting and world-categorizing self, can have identity conditions. While Johnston's discussion comes close to the "no-self" solipsism of the *Tractatus*, it avoids (question-beggingly) transcendental solipsism.[50] Here Johnston seems to assume (unlike Valberg) that there *are* many arenas of presence, not just one (mine), and that there is a straightforward sense in which mine could disappear. The problem is whether one can even meaningfully *say* this, insofar as one starts from transcendental considerations.

Wittgenstein's argumentation is based on a transcendental examination of the necessary conditions for the possibility of meaning and representation; the result of such an examination is that the world can only be limited by me (my subjectivity) in order to be linguistically representable. In employing his vocabulary of "picking out" as applied to the *Tractatus* and its metaphysical or transcendental subject—or the arena—Johnston overlooks the distinctive features of a truly transcendental treatment of the matter. The subject of the arena cannot be "picked out" from among others.

Any picking out will inevitably take place, in Valberg's terms, within the (my) horizon. No horizon can be picked out; there is no meta-horizon within which to do that.

Nevertheless, one of Johnston's crucial ideas (preparing the ground for his overall thesis that in a sense "the good" may literally survive death, because they are not tied to their individual personal identities) is that the arena of presence and one's occupying it are *illusory*. We are in a way hallucinating that we are in the center of an arena of presence. We are dealing with merely intentional objects (Johnston 2010: 225).[51] Johnston concludes, "The real problem in principle with the idea of the resurrection of the self is that *not even God* could re-create this very arena of presence. (The same could be said of your arena of presence.) God could no more do that than he could re-create Macbeth's dagger or any other *mere* intentional object" (Johnston 2010: 222). Johnston further argues that the (Buddhist) doctrine of there being no persistent self (*anatta*) leads to the doctrine of *agape*, the commandment to take others' interests as one's own. The *unreality of the self*, allegedly demonstrated by the argument for the illusoriness of the arena of presence, leads to the observation that our identities are relational and relative, "Protean," and this in turn motivates (without logically entailing) the idea that we should take others' interests into account as our own—and that "the good" among us do. "A certain kind of hallucination—that of a container or arena—bounds *even our veridical experience of the world*," Johnston tells us, and therefore "our selves are ... creatures of the unreal" (Johnston 2010: 230–31). The self's importance thus vanishes.

The *agape* commands us to treat ourselves as if we were arbitrary others, "albeit one whose life one is called to live" (Johnston 2010: 236)—but now, who is this "one"? The transcendental subject all over again? Or the Levinasian ethical subject? I find Johnston's argument intriguing but flawed, because it commits the "naturalistic fallacy" common to non-transcendental philosophies of the self, presupposing a conception of the self (or its "arena") as an object in a world "ready-made" prior to and independently of the self. Johnston remains a metaphysical realist—though he does not seem to be able to get rid of the transcendental self, either, which leads to a tension at the center of his position.

Indeed, as Valberg (2007: 262) puts it, the "naturalizer"— in my terminology, the one viewing the self from a naturalist, metaphysically realistic standpoint[52]—"lacks, philosophically, a grasp of the horizonal conception of the self." Lacking such a grasp, we won't get far in the philosophy of death, nor anywhere else. A failure to appreciate the transcendental character of the subject existentially concerned with its mortality leads to absurdities such as the view that one's being able to die only "one's own death" is no more dramatic than one's being able to, say, have only "one's own haircut" or "one's own lunch" instead of (strictly speaking) anyone else's. In a trivial sense, those things are one's own, too; we all have our own lunches and haircuts rather than others'. But our deaths are our own in a much more pregnant sense—a sense calling for a transcendental, even solipsistic analysis (as we have seen). A failure to take seriously the transcendental dimension of the problem leads to the tendency to view everything—deaths, haircuts, lunches—on a par, as belonging to the same empirical world whose metaphysical structure is fixed independently of our subjective constitutive contribution. When that metaphysically realistic assumption is given up, a considerably enriched picture of the special significance of one's own mortality opens up.

While there are powerful arguments in transcendental philosophy, especially phenomenology and Wittgenstein, that can be employed to defend a transcendentally idealistic or solipsistic conception of the (mortal) subject, there is a reflexive problem that also needs to be addressed. Even the transcendental philosopher must—in order to take death seriously, ontologically and ethically—*view the subject (even the solipsistic subject) as genuinely mortal*. Otherwise the idea that by removing the subject we remove the world itself cannot be made sense of. Death must be a *genuine limit* to transcendental subjectivity. (If the transcendental self itself is a limit of the world, then death is, in a not easily articulated sense, the limit of a limit.) In other words, insofar as the transcendental self—far from being any transcendent, otherworldly metaphysical postulation—is an aspect of our own selfhood, of *me*, and insofar as mortality and the finitude it entails are necessary transcendental structures of my subjectivity, mortality and finitude must be necessary structures of the transcendental self, too.

Arguably, then, the subject, even *qua* transcendental, must be "natural" (material, embodied), because otherwise its mortality will be sacrificed. The question is whether a transcendental approach to solipsism, death, and mortality, seeking to critically overcome at least naïvely reductive naturalism, can recognize its own dependence on a certain kind of naturalism. This resembles not only the pragmatic counterargument to solipsism (in Chapter 4) but also the way in which phenomenological analyses of transcendental subjectivity are rooted in the "natural attitude" whose postulations the phenomenological method brackets. The phenomenologist studying subjectivity as something to which (to whom) the world as natural and objective is given, bracketing the positing of the natural world, including the subject as a natural part of the world, must in a sense begin from the natural attitude, seeking to overcome it from within.[53] The natural and the phenomenological (transcendental) attitudes are reciprocally contained in one another; neither is available to us without the other, and the "us" here—the subject to whom these attitudes are available and who must move from one to the other—needs to understand its own character as something (albeit as no "thing") that is paradoxically in constant movement between these two poles.

Similarly, when we seek to account for death transcendentally, we must understand ourselves as transcendental subjects to whom the world is given in a way that solipsistically disappears in death—yielding an end of the world in the sense that the very givenness of the world will be eliminated—and simultaneously as empirical parts of the world that are in such a fragile position as mere limits of the world precisely because of their (our) material, bodily vulnerable nature. If we do not take seriously this embodied vulnerability of the transcendental subject (i.e., the fact that bodily vulnerability is a transcendental feature of subjectivity, a necessary condition for the possibility of the kind of life we find ourselves living), we fail to take seriously a fundamental transcendental outcome of our inquiry, the solipsistic conception of death as the end of the world. This could be seen as one way of cashing out Wittgenstein's (1921: §5.64) remark on the "shrinking" solipsistic self's disappearing into the world (not from the world), yielding the coincidence of solipsism and realism analyzed in Chapter 3.

Valberg is concerned with the same interplay between the natural (bodily, dying) and the transcendental that I have emphasized:

> If right now my brain ceased to function, what would happen? There would be NOTHING. Would the Kantian "subject of the categories" survive the NOTHINGNESS that would be consequent upon the shutting down of my brain? Since its

being depends causally on certain things happening in my brain, the Kantian subject would cease to be. But here the subject of the categories appears as (in Kant's phrase) "an object of the categories," in particular, as an object of the category of causation. (Valberg 2007: 224)

The causal processes in the natural world leading up to my death would eliminate the world—and there would then be NOTHING, in Valberg's terms. Acknowledging this is to acknowledge the dependence of my transcendental subjectivity ("my horizon") on worldly natural facts. But it is also to acknowledge the impossibility of such facts being there in the absence of my (the) horizon, that is, the transcendental self. There is a tension here, or even a paradox—a specific death-related feature of the more general "paradox of subjectivity" (Carr 1999)—but one virtue of Valberg's discussion is that he locates the fundamental problem we have to deal with as long as we are willing to engage in a transcendental inquiry into the self and its mortality. We should avoid any straightforward realistic naturalization of death and subjectivity into mere objects in the world, but on the other hand we should observe that the transcendental worries regarding finitude and mortality emerging from within our mortal condition analyzed in terms of the solipsistic subject already presuppose our taking seriously the naturalistic prospect of the "shutting down of my brain." Transcendental subjectivity is a dimension of *our* subjectivity, which is the pragmatic natural subjectivity of a world-involving and world-engaging mortal creature—even for the transcendental solipsist.

Does the natural embeddedness of my subjectivity mean that metaphysical realism—understanding the subject as a part of the world after all, of a world that exists and possesses its "own" ontological structure independently of the subject—returns to the picture (in a way analogous to solipsism's tendency to return)? I do not think so. For it is not exactly metaphysical realism that returns. It is only a certain kind of realism compatible with solipsism that is needed, and that realism is sufficient for maintaining a (non-reductive) form of naturalism compatible with transcendental inquiry.

When the transcendental solipsistic self is challenged to recognize its own dependence on naturalism and thereby its disappearance into the world in a Wittgensteinian sense, it must do this by referring to the ineliminability of the transcendental self, though. It is still *me* who is challenged to distinguish between the perspectives on myself as a subject and as an object. In this sense, the transcendental self could be seen as a never-ending spiral: its reflexive reflection on its own paradoxical status as both transcendental and natural goes on forever. Death is, then, like an axis around which the spiral circulates. In its reflection on its own double status, the self inevitably reflects on its mortality—and on its inevitably solipsistic approach to that reflection.

The Suffering Other

After these evermore reflexively complex transcendental reflections, we may be reminded that death—banal, ordinary deaths—can be regarded as something evil, and are often caused by what can be described as evil actions. Now, despite the fact that a form of ethical solipsism may be necessary for the truly ethical responsibility of an individual self, it might be argued that the *problem of evil and suffering* (cf. Kivistö and Pihlström 2016; Pihlström 2014, 2020) cannot be accounted for by the solipsist in any adequate manner. It might seem to be right here—in our ethical response to suffering others, dependent on our being able to be good or evil—that solipsism finally collapses, even if it were admitted as a theoretical possibility.

The transcendental ethical solipsist, for whom my will is the only ethically relevant will, cannot say that other people, even those who, say, in the empirical world kill or torture innocent human beings, are evil, because ultimately s/he cannot morally evaluate others at all. Thus, s/he may not have any satisfactory perspective on the problem of evil. Nothing empirical can, for the solipsist, be ethically relevant, but the most striking cases of evil any philosophical account of evil and suffering must acknowledge are the well-known horrors of the empirical world and its history. Solipsism arguably prevents us from philosophically pursuing the problem of suffering at all, except in my own case. There would, in a word, be no distinction between good and evil in a solipsistic world, for anything I consider good or evil would ipso facto be so, with no external constraints.

Again, a distinction between transcendental and empirical evil might be useful. From the solipsist's perspective, we can ascribe the latter to anyone or anything in the empirical world whose limits are set by our transcendental subjectivity; it is the former kind of evil—the truly ethical kind of evil—that is available only to the solipsist her-/himself (i.e., me). It is only from my point of view that the world as a whole can appear as evil. For someone concerned with the *real* evil there is within the world this can hardly be sufficient. While perceptively drawing attention to my (and anyone's) personal responsibility for fighting evil, the (transcendentally) solipsistic approach to ethics does not enhance our understanding of or engagement with the phenomenon of evil as it becomes actual in our natural and social world. Yet, it is hard to find any conclusive argument against the solipsist even here—as we have seen throughout this study.

As emphasized in different ways by Wittgenstein and Levinas, among others, there is, and can be, no prior reason for us to be moral, nothing more ultimate than the ethical standpoint itself. It is my simple, unquestionable, unjustifiable duty to acknowledge others ethically.[54] But the problem in ethical solipsism is, of course, that there are no criteria for fulfilling this duty external to my judgment. As a solipsist, I may, of course, endorse any ethical criteria I wish, and they might be admirable: I may, for instance, decide to be a Kantian deontologist. But couldn't I just change or give up those criteria whenever I chose to? The critic of ethical solipsism asks, simply, whether a view according to which I can evaluate only myself ethically and only on the basis of criteria that I have chosen myself can be truly ethical at all.

Discussions of evil and suffering also lead us to consider *guilt*—in our own case, in particular, hence quasi-solipsistically (see Pihlström 2011). We are primordially, transcendentally, guilty for having taken the place of the other, as Levinas would put it. Another person, to whom we are infinitely responsible, might have lived instead of us (but did not). The argument against solipsism culminates here on the notion of existential responsibility. A simple argument could proceed as follows: If I were a solipsist, I could not be responsible in the sense required; that is, I could not be guilty of having violated someone else by my very existence.[55] But I am. Therefore, I cannot be a solipsist. Accordingly, solipsism is false (for me). Yet, once again, it is *me* who here sovereignly decides that solipsism is an ethical impossibility; moreover, the (ethical) solipsist could just refuse to accept the premise that guilt is impossible in a solipsistic setting. The solipsist can, indeed, have a conscience, too. After all, it is me who is guilty, and in this strong sense guilt is *only* applicable to me. We are not going to get rid of the problem even along this route.[56]

Indeed, guilt in its deepest ethical sense may be essentially tied to ethical solipsism. Dostoevsky famously reminded us—in *The Brothers Karamazov* and elsewhere—that while each of us is guilty for everyone's sins in front of all the others, I am more deeply guilty than anyone else. This comes very close to the Levinasian conception of my being singled out for infinite ethical responsibility. Insofar as I can, at this ultimate level of first-personal moral and metaphysical guilt, only examine my own guilty conscience, ethical solipsism prevails. My practically inevitable habit of also judging others morally might in fact be a further reason for guilt. This transcendental priority of first-personal guilt could possibly only be made sense of on the basis of transcendental ethical solipsism (see Pihlström 2011: chapter 3).

This position would also be more or less in accordance with Wittgenstein's view, as expressed in the *Tractatus*, that reward and punishment are ethically irrelevant, except insofar as they "reside in the action itself" (Wittgenstein 1921: §6.422)—that is, it is only my inner motivation or the state of my "soul" that ethically matters, and the resulting guilt or remorse. Indeed, a kind of ethical solipsism follows rather naturally from Wittgensteinian transcendental solipsism. If the transcendental subject, as the "limit of the world" (Wittgenstein 1921: §5.641), is solipsistic, then so must be the world that it limits and to which it brings good and evil through its *sub specie aeternitatis* attitude. Only the self—my transcendental self—can be good or evil, not the independent world. This, if anything, is ethical solipsism.

Both the ethical solipsist and the non-solipsist may agree that, from the unavoidable standpoint of my own life-toward-death, I can, or should at least try to, attach greater moral and emotional significance to the equally unavoidable sufferings and deaths of others. From a point of view that is my own and disappears when I do, I should, if I wish to be a responsible person, try to avoid privileging that very point of view. But the situation is, once again, delicate. Part of my respect for the other's suffering and death could result from the fact that the other *might* have been, and perhaps is or was, a solipsist (and, as such, another to me in a very strong sense). If so, their suffering deprives meaning from the world, and their death is the end of a world, whereas they do not (nor can they) pay symmetrical attention to my (future) death. Facing death, in short, seems to be a deeply solipsistic event, and the same may hold on a slightly more moderate scale for intense suffering. Death, at any rate, brings all human dialogue to a closure. Living toward death, we cannot help taking solipsism seriously, no matter how good reasons we have for regarding it as a fundamentally misguided view. Paradoxically, my responsibility to and for the other even extends to the possibility of her/his being, or having been, a solipsist. That person, instead of me, *might* have been the only genuine subject there was (and my inability to make sense of this possibility may be part of what the other's radical transcendence is, for me). After her/his death, the world could come to an end.[57]

We come back, finally, to the other side of the coin, as compared to the issue of death: the problem of the *meaning* or *significance* (or lack thereof) of human life. These issues are of course closely related, since it is the inevitability of death that is often regarded as depriving life of its meaning. Now, would a solipsistic life be maximally meaningful or meaningless? On the one hand, the solipsist's concerns would be the only ones there are, if the world were her/his own, that is, there would be nothing, meaningful or meaningless, to transcend her/him. On the other hand, this superiority to everything else might render the solipsist's life insignificant. The solipsist's death would indeed be the end of the world; *everything* would collapse along with it. There would be no goals to pursue beyond one's own, private ones, and death, ending all such pursuits, would render everything absurd.

Yet, even here there might be no crucial difference between the (ethical) solipsist and the realist, since human life in general, socially, culturally, and historically understood, could be regarded as absurd because of its inevitable finitude. There is nothing absolutely permanent for humankind as a whole any more than for the solipsist who only has private goals and purposes. Unless we believe in supernatural salvation, death will one day end it all, whether we are solipsists or realists. Death may even be a source of meaning (rather than an absurdity) in one's life, since it limits the life into a totality. Thus, mortality may be viewed as a transcendental condition for our being able to raise the question of the meaning of life (cf. Pihlström 2016). Certainly the solipsist, in comparison to the realist, is well placed here.

Yet if, in contrast to solipsism, we view the meaning of human life in a pragmatic way, in terms of our inescapable relations to others, also those surviving me (see, e.g., Scheffler 2013), we may be more easily able to avoid misery in the face of the absurdity of existence. Considering the problem of the meaning of life might thus provide some indirect support for non-solipsists, even though it is again futile to seek any final argumentative blow against the solipsist.

It has sometimes been suggested that the pursuit of an *authentic* (truly meaningful, significant) life could not take place in a solipsistic world. Authenticity may be considered inherently non-solipsistic. For example, Jacob Golomb (1995: chapter 5) seeks to show that the quest for authenticity in Heidegger (unlike, in his view, in Kierkegaard and Nietzsche) is not solipsistic; on the contrary, the concept of *Mitsein* ("being-together" with others) is a key element of that quest. But as there is no rational or theoretical argument in favor of authentic life—indeed, the very notion of such an argument would be paradoxical, as Golomb explains—there is, again, no proper argument against solipsism to be constructed on this basis. What we have to be satisfied with is something like the Jamesian "will to believe" strategy, which in this case amounts to a will to live, as "authentically" as possible, a non-solipsistic, ethically responsible life. This inconclusive, necessarily circular argument can, again, be reconstructed as a transcendental argument starting from the given facts of the life we actually live and proceeding to the conditions for the possibility of such a life. But it is certainly not a theoretical argument upon which one might base one's anti-solipsism.

While there is no "God's-Eye View" from which solipsism could be refuted, our metaphilosophical consideration of the issue in the ethical realm and in relation to profound questions of life and death has indirectly led us to appreciate a structural similarity between (naturalized and pragmatized) transcendental argumentation and pragmatic "will to believe" arguments. Both begin with the human condition—and there is no more fundamental place to begin. While there can be no final overcoming of the possibility of solipsism, ethically or otherwise, learning why this is so may open our eyes to fundamental features of the human condition. We have seen that the ethical solipsist can, albeit with considerable effort, try to accommodate the ethical and *weltanschaulichen* notions the moral (pragmatic) realist may find irreplaceable: mortality, responsibility for evil and suffering, guilt, significance, authenticity. Our true responsibility still lies in rejecting solipsism, ethically (and, perhaps, ethically solipsistically), even in the face of this argumentative *impasse*.[58]

The general result of this chapter is that as solipsism cannot be rejected argumentatively, the problem manifests fundamental importance in our treatment of central ethical concepts pertaining to our relations to other human beings. The analysis could be extended to a number of other concepts. Consider, finally, *empathy*, a prime example of an other-regarding attitude. It can be argued that the very possibility of empathy remains problematic, especially in its phenomenological analysis (cf. Stein 1989; see Chapter 3), due to the methodologically solipsistic starting point of the latter. Empathy can, as it were, never genuinely reach the other.[59] It remains *my* attitude to the other—an attitude toward a soul, to be sure, but still an attitude that *I* adopt. The same problem concerns Levinasian ethics of otherness, which, as we saw, sets the fundamental ethical demand of acknowledging the other to me, and me only. On the other hand, if empathy *is* taken to genuinely reach the other—if I can *really* feel the same emotions as the other, *share* the other's viewpoint[60]—there is the opposite danger of reducing the other to me. My empathy toward the other then renders the other "mine" in a quasi-solipsistic sense. I will capture the other. (The same holds for compassion, a notion close to empathy, at least if interpreted in the "*tat twam asi*" sense that Schopenhauer, for instance, favored.)

The worry thus is that genuine otherness may not be fully respected no matter how we philosophically understand the concept of empathy (or related concepts), and this can again be brought out by turning attention to the problem of solipsism. This is one crucial way in which solipsism matters—ethically and existentially. It always tends to come back, and it matters by reminding us that whatever we do, however we think about others—their suffering, vulnerability, and mortality, or their unique individuality as such—we only have our own capacities for moral reflection to rely on. We will never entirely escape the risk of either disregarding the other or swallowing the other into our own ethical project of living authentically, no matter how other-regarding we wish to be.

CHAPTER SIX

Concluding Remarks

Avoiding solipsism might be nothing less than our most important duty as philosophers—and as human beings. What I have tried to describe is the (ethical) experience that I *ought to* resist the tendency to slip into the easiness of being alone. This could in the end be regarded as a simple deontological "ought," and I just may have no further reasons for non-solipsism at such a fundamental level. At least *my* "philosophical temperament" (to use James's term) precludes solipsism, and it takes only a private moment of existential decision to judge solipsism unacceptable and immoral. This is where *my* spade is turned. Needless to say, by expressing my personal conviction in this way I inevitably make myself vulnerable to the charge of ethical solipsism. If anything, I have tried to urge that it is not easy to get rid of the problem.

I (and my reader) may have had an exhausting number of philosophical voices to listen to (both to criticize and to sympathize with) throughout this inquiry, but I hope the reader who has come this far has acquired an informative picture of the multifarious aspects of the issue we have considered. In this concluding chapter, I will present a rough summary of the arguments explored and make some general remarks on the nature, and especially limits, of philosophical argumentation generally, based on the problem of solipsism. I will, thus, conclude my discussion of the metaphilosophical aspects of solipsism. Again, it is from the ethical point of view that the threads of our inquiries ought to be finally pulled together.

A Summary of the Argument

I have established no philosophical *theses* regarding the truth or rational acceptability of solipsism. What would such theses be like? Have I been able to argue that there is a real world, including other human beings, independently of my experience? "Well, thanks a lot," someone might say, "I knew that already." To imagine that the outcome of this study ought to be a thesis concerning the truth or acceptability of solipsism (for example, "Solipsism is false," or "It is not very likely that solipsism is true") is to be utterly confused about what philosophical theses and arguments can be expected to be like. What I have attempted to do is to offer reasons for thinking about the solipsism issue in a certain specific way and for seeing how it matters to us. I have not attempted to answer the question, "Is solipsism true or false?" I am clearly not a solipsist, and I do not regard this as a very interesting question; rather, it may be meaningless, as Wittgenstein maintained. Instead, I have, focusing on transcendental solipsism and hence on the meaning—or lack thereof—of solipsism, rather than its truth, examined *how*—within what kind of conceptual frameworks, on the basis of which conditions, and from which point(s) of view—the solipsism issue could and should be discussed. I have arrived at some suggestions about the way in which it is (and about the ways it is not) a genuine problem, and I have indicated some ways it affects our dealings with other philosophical concepts and issues.

I hope, thus, to have made the following claims at least somewhat plausible:

(1) It is possible, and it may serve some philosophical interests, to distinguish between several different versions of solipsism. Some of these have a long history beginning (at least) with Descartes and extending through British empiricism, Kant, German idealism,[1] as well as the twentieth-century traditions of analytic philosophy and phenomenology to the Wittgensteinian themes that continue to haunt many contemporary philosophers.

(2) The Kantian-Wittgensteinian transcendental paradigm of solipsism is the most interesting and most problematic, although it is very difficult to determine what exactly

Wittgenstein's own views were (and I have *not* attempted to do that). A fundamental distinction, both historically and systematically, can be drawn between "classical" (non-transcendental, metaphysical and/or skeptical) and transcendental solipsism.

(3) There are reasons to think that even the transcendental solipsist (despite her/his empirical realism) cannot argue with anyone in the ordinary sense of the word. Yet, various human activities, including argumentation, can be solipsistically reinterpreted or reconceptualized. This is part of what it means to say that the problem of solipsism always seems to return.

(4) Nor can solipsism be directly refuted by means of traditional philosophical argumentation. In particular, the transcendental solipsist can always reinterpret the critic's argument from her/his own perspective, rendering it inefficient.

(5) The decision to reject solipsism can eventually only be made as an existential decision, on ethical grounds, echoing James's "will to believe," Wittgenstein's "attitude toward a soul," and Levinas's idea of the ethical primacy of the other. But again the problem returns, for it is me who has to decide (existentially) not to be a solipsist, to take a responsibility for another "soul" in their suffering and mortality. This return of the solipsism issue, the central and privileged position of the (ethical) subject, me, is especially clear in Levinas's writings on my infinite ethical responsibility and many "Wittgensteinian" moral philosophers' views on the absolutely personal character of ethical concerns.[2]

(6) The metaphilosophical moral to be drawn from this is the irreducibility of the ethical point of view even in metaphysical pursuits. No metaphysical or epistemological theorization can be independent of ethical considerations or serve as a foundation of ethics. The ethical perspective is inescapable and inexhaustible in the sense of being always already part of our engagement with the world we live in. Paradoxically, this is one indication of the way solipsism matters.

More historically speaking, the dialectics of modern philosophy that the issue of solipsism illuminates[3] can be described as follows (although I have by no means offered any choronology of the development of solipsism). First, the paradigm of the "philosophy of consciousness," beginning with Descartes's *cogito*, is opposed to the tradition of dogmatic metaphysics (in its ancient and medieval forms). Secondly, this paradigm is reinterpreted through Kant's, the German idealists', and Husserl's transcendental turn, which, however, is still partly based on underlying Cartesian ideas. Kant's affirmation of the unity of transcendental apperception makes transcendental solipsism an option in a way in which it was not an option for Descartes or his pre-Kantian followers and critics. Husserl's egological approach to the constitutional role of intentionality further confirms this possibility. Husserl remains a (Cartesian-cum-Kantian) methodological (yet transcendental) solipsist even in his late reflections on the transcendental structures of the lifeworld. While there are twists in the phenomenological tradition that make Husserl's solipsism seem inadequate and optional even from the phenomenological point of view (as argued by, for example, Heidegger, Merleau-Ponty, and Levinas), the transcendental framework of the solipsism issue reaches its maturity in phenomenology, on the one hand, and in Wittgenstein's early philosophy, on the other.

Thirdly, the very possibility of a phenomenologically construed transcendental solipsism as well as the paradigm of the philosophy of consciousness has been attacked by central twentieth-century figures: Heidegger, the later Wittgenstein, and the pragmatists, among others. The result, however, may be a kind of relativism or historicism, with a new form of transcendental solipsism emerging—a social or cultural solipsism, a solipsism "with a 'we' instead of an 'I'" (using, again, Putnam's apt wording). The social subject of language games or forms of life is substituted for the abstract ego at work in earlier formulations of transcendental solipsism.[4]

Fourthly, some leading contemporary philosophers have attempted to criticize this slippery slope to relativism and historicism; these are attempts that we have not been able to review in this inquiry, because even a partial consideration of the rather indigestible relativism literature would have led us astray. One of these attempts is the effort to formulate universally valid norms of argumentation and, in general, human communication in the discourse ethics and transcendental pragmatics (or "transcendental semiotics") of communication developed by Jürgen Habermas and Karl-Otto Apel.[5] The problem with such neo-Kantian approaches is that they may slide back to dogmatic, foundationalist assumptions, to "first philosophy" (cf. Pihlström 2003). Apel's view of the "ultimate foundation" of communication in the universally valid norms which provide necessary conditions for the possibility of any meaningful discourse is unappealing to most contemporary philosophers persuaded by naturalism in the philosophy of mind, language, and science. There is, to be sure, an ethical dimension in Apel's critique of both egological and relativist approaches in phenomenology, hermeneutics, and analytic philosophy, since the pursuit of universal validity is, in his view, eventually ethically grounded. But in the end, if we follow Apel's path, we cannot but return to square one, to a pre-transcendental point of departure. The very beginning of the philosophy of consciousness, which made solipsism seem plausible, was originally characterized by a critical attitude to dogmatic metaphysics.

Fifthly, since such a strong transcendental route is a dead end (though, I must repeat, this has not been demonstrated in the present study), it turns out to be rather attractive to view the rejection of solipsism as an unargued, fundamentally non-foundational and groundless ethical decision, never to be universally (dogmatically) validated by appeal to necessarily shared intersubjective norms or criteria—or by *any* purely theoretical argument, for that matter. This pragmatic, ethical approach recommended in Chapters 4 and 5 is still transcendental, since non-solipsism can be argued to be among the necessary (intersubjectively shared) conditions for the possibility of humanity as we know and experience it. Our engagement in our form(s) of life manifests non-solipsism. In short, in order to be fully human, we have to adopt an attitude toward souls in our relations to other people; this is constitutive of our form(s) of life. My relation to a Levinasian other reveals my ultimate responsibility as a subject. Yet, again, avoiding solipsism is *my* ethical responsibility. In this sense, the first-person perspective is more primary, more original—or even pre-originary in Levinas's sense—than the third-person perspective.

Accordingly, sixthly, despite the ethical primacy of the other, it is right here that the dialectics reaches its culmination: it is always, inevitably, *me* whose ultimate responsibility the groundlessness of ethical commitment highlights. If one believes with Levinas and Wittgenstein that one's responsibility to another soul is prior to all ethical theorization, to all representation, to ontology and epistemology, one has to take seriously the possibility of ethical solipsism. Avoiding solipsism ethically can, perhaps, in the end be only based on an ethically solipsistic decision to make room for the other "in my world," and on a subjective "will to believe" that one is able to do so.

This is the "dialectics of anti-solipsistic enlightenment." It may be true that my, or anyone's, genuine subjectivity—of the kind the solipsist (self-refutingly) claims to possess—is possible only in an intersubjective setting in which my responsibility for the other is always already in place, but, conversely, the emergence of that responsibility out of which my subjectivity can only arise already presupposes *me*, my "ipseity," as something equally firmly in place, something *to* which the other's face can silently state its demand of justice. Without the "first person," there is, in a word, no demand of justice, no otherness, no demand of the second or third person to be heard. Without a prior quasi-solipsistic affirmation of the primacy of the individual ego, there is no overcoming of the problem of solipsism on an intersubjectivist basis. I have to be there in order for anyone to be an "other" for me to be acknowledged. And this singles me out.

Solipsism and the Limits of Philosophical Argumentation

Solipsism then arises as a philosophical problem from the uniqueness of the first-person perspective, that is, my perspective on the world as an individual. From this standpoint, the ethical issues of life and death considered in Chapter 5 constitute both the most relevant motivation for solipsism and a key challenge to it. One of the metaphilosophical conclusions we reached in considering those issues is the inextricable entanglement of metaphysics and ethics. Our first-person perspective is always already ethically oriented. We have, thus, arrived at, if not a Levinasian "otherwise than being," at least the limits of ontology. Ontological theorizing will not solve the "problem of life." This Wittgensteinian problem can only be approached from an ethically loaded first-person point of view—mine.

Our ethical problem of avoiding solipsism also primarily arises from the first-person point of view. The paradox lying at the heart of my discussion throughout this book is precisely this: it is *my* duty as a responsible individual to avoid being a solipsist. It is from my private first-person point of view that I need to make the ethical decision to take the other into account, to avoid absolutizing my point of view as if it were the only one there is (though *from that point of view* it *is*, inevitably, the only relevant one, with no neighbors). Thus, whenever we emphasize human sociality in our insistence on the need to make the ethical and existential choice of avoiding solipsism, we rely on our first-person individual standpoint.

James (1907: chapter 1) maintained that individual *philosophical temperaments* guide our philosophical commitments—and ought to do so.[6] Jamesian philosophical temperaments and Wittgensteinian "private moments" ("This is what *I* do") are, moreover, closely related. The significance of these notions can be clearly seen in the context of the possibility of solipsism. *I* have to decide not to be a solipsist. Through that decision I partly define who I am. I pragmatically fix my identity as an individual involved in a community, a form of life.

We have learned that the realist, or the non-solipsist, cannot produce any conclusive demonstration of the falsity of solipsism. W. Donald Oliver, locating the seeds of solipsism in a Cartesian "privacy postulate,"[7] writes as follows:

> If solipsism . . . is meaningless or logically contradictory, then it is to the privacy postulate that we must look as the source of contradiction. It cannot be replied that it is only in the *use* of the privacy postulate to draw the solipsistic conclusion that the logical guilt lies, for the solipsistic conclusion is inherent in the postulate itself. Inherent only as a possibility, to be sure, but this is a possibility that can be excluded only by such psychological factors as the natural tendency to believe that there is an external world. If the privacy postulate has been advanced against our natural tendencies to believe, there is not, for those who hold it, any good reason for reintroducing what has once been rejected merely to save us from the solipsistic conclusion. (Oliver 1970: 38)

This tells us something about philosophical argumentation in general. Views like determinism, skepticism, relativism, and nihilism (whatever "postulates" they involve for individuals holding or opposing them) are analogous to solipsism in this respect. More generally, I am tempted to conclude that there is no interesting philosophical position which could demonstrate its truth by means of a direct, "neutral" argument acceptable to all parties to the dispute.

The possibility and irrefutability of solipsism enable us to see that this is the case. Argumentation is not omnipotent in philosophy. There are further considerations related to what we expect our philosophical views to say about, for instance, ourselves and the world we live in. Any philosophizing we engage in is inseparable from our task of knowing ourselves. We do not *want* to be solipsists—we *need* to reject solipsism—and there must be means of saying, beyond argument, why. But I have argued that such means must nevertheless be philosophical. *Pace* Robinson (1978) and many others, we need not be "unphilosophical" if we decide to stop somewhere between the extremes of solipsism and its opposite (whatever exactly that is). It is futile to demand a powerful argument silencing the opponent for good. Philosophical issues are never beyond further discussion. This, again, is what I have meant by the statement that solipsism tends to come back to the one who thinks about it deeply enough. Showing *how* it comes back is part of assessing the fundamental conceptual assumptions anti-solipsism involves.

One's rejection of solipsism may be based on a pragmatist metaphilosophy (cf. Chapter 4) urging that a continuous self-critical reflection on our starting points and background assumptions (Jamesian "philosophical temperaments") is our duty. Is *this* view compatible with solipsism? In a certain sense, it is: *self*-reflection, or reflexivity in philosophy, is certainly possible, even if there are no other selves.[8] But the very idea of *reflection* seems to presuppose a normative context of critical communication and, thus, other reflective subjects whose arguments are taken into account. The solipsist can be a self-critically reflective thinker only in a very limited sense. The solipsist can *say* that her/his reflections are as genuine as the realist's, though. But, again, to whom is *this* said?

Solipsism can be conceived of as an expression of what Putnam (1995: 75), referring to James and Wittgenstein (especially their writings on religion), calls the "limits of intersubjectivity" (cf. Watzka 2000: 161ff.). However, as in Kant's transcendental philosophy, the fact that there are, for us, such *limits* (of knowledge about other minds, of argumentative conversation with the solipsist, etc.) does not imply any human *failure* (of, for example, such knowledge or conversation) to cross those limits. Refuting solipsism, or coming to know that solipsism is wrong (whatever that might mean), is not something we are supposed to be able to do but actually fail to do (see Cavell 1979; Putnam 1994). Rather, we have to accept our human predicament, the non-foundational nature of our life, or what Cavell calls the "moral of skepticism." More precisely, this is not something we "have to" do but something we simply do.

This non-foundationality is closely connected with Cavell's idea of acknowledging, rather than knowing, other people. Solipsism is a very *inhuman* philosophy, but Cavell (as well as Putnam) has perceptively reminded us that it is a profoundly human tendency to try to reject, however desperately, one's humanity. Inhumanity remains a human possibility. Solipsism *might* be true (though it may also, with suitably drawn criteria of coherence, be incoherent), and some of us do have the temptation to think that a conceptual or transcendental version of it *cannot fail to be true*. We should acknowledge even those of our fellow humans who are unable to resist this human temptation toward inhumanity, continuing, nevertheless, to live our lives as anti-foundationalist non-solipsists.

Indeed, solipsism also, paradoxically, reminds us of human *diversity*. We are all unique and different. This is something that Hannah Arendt (certainly no theorist of solipsism) compellingly captured in her notion of *natality* (Arendt 1958): human beings are contingently born as distinct individuals with their own paths in the world, and they are uniquely able to bring something new into existence. This simple but vitally important idea can be compared, for example, to James's individualism or perhaps even to Wittgenstein's anti-Cartesian account of the self; moreover, according to Arendt's (1951) famous analysis of totalitarianism, it is precisely the aim of totalitarian regimes to destroy such individuality and uniqueness, rendering human beings superfluous as individuals.

Now, we might see the truth in/of solipsism as "cancelling itself out"—as it coincides with realism along Wittgensteinian lines— because when we seriously work our way through the solipsism issue, we may end up with a novel appreciation of the uniqueness of each human individual as an irreplaceable point of view on the world, analogous to Arendtian natality. The truth of solipsism thus leads us to the irreducible duty of acknowledging the unique individual other in her/his (Levinasian) otherness, as irreducible to me—and this includes the duty not to make the other superfluous in the way totalitarianism (as a kind of "collective solipsism") according to Arendt's analysis does. Yet, once again, this duty is *mine*, set from the unique individual perspective that *I* and no one else occupy. I am responsible for appreciating the diversity of human otherness. This is also why it matters to us *how* we work our way through solipsism to this appreciation of individual otherness.

The metaphilosophical moral of this final line of argument is the following. We do *not* (and should not) engage in philosophical reflection and inquiry merely, or even primarily, in order to arrive at a certain view or theory, such as the rather trivial-sounding one that we should acknowledge other human beings; rather, we do so in order to understand more deeply what it means for us to be committed to certain views (e.g., non-solipsism) in certain theoretical and practical contexts, that is, *how* we are committed to them in our lives. This meta-level understanding of how we (can) think about ourselves and others matters to us deeply, and *therefore* philosophy, even solipsism, matters.

On the other hand, while emphasizing the metaphilosophical relevance of solipsism—and its rejection—we should not entertain any illusion of engaging in a fully autonomous metaphilosophical investigation. Metaphilosophy is indistinguishable from "first-order" philosophy itself. The transcendental solipsist's allegedly neutral meta-level attempt to maintain the indistinguishability of solipsism and realism is, as we have seen, problematic in its ultimate failure of acknowledging the other (or any independent reality generally) in any other sense than as a construction, albeit a transcendental one, within "my world"; transcendental solipsism, hence, is not symmetrical regarding the self and the others, after all. Genuine otherness is already presupposed by our use of an ethical vocabulary invoking notions such as human dignity and acknowledgment, and it may be suggested that it is wrong to even try to develop an allegedly neutral meta-level theory that (at a transcendental level) reduces such other-involving vocabulary to solipsistic concepts. Now, if symmetry and neutrality are illusory for the transcendental solipsist, they should be acknowledged to be

CONCLUDING REMARKS

illusory for the non-solipsist (pragmatic realist) as well. Even when insisting on the metaphilosophical moral to be drawn from the solipsistic challenge, we cannot *remain* at the meta-level but must constantly engage in the first-order practices of acknowledgment we find transcendentally necessary for the possibility of any normative (ethical or epistemic) concept use. The philosopher must return to the cave.

One way of cashing out these reflections is to insist on solipsism as a *human* problem. The solipsism issue does not seem to arise at all in the context of postmodern or poststructuralist fragmentation of the subject (cf. Chapter 1). However, this observation can be turned into a modus tollens argument: *if* the solipsism issue does arise (in any sense, whenever we reflect on our relation to the world), *then* the postmodern fragmentation of the subject is itself problematic and cannot be taken seriously. The solipsistic issue, in brief, is a "humanistic" one. The solipsistic self, clearly, is not directly identifiable with a(ny) human self or subject, because in the transcendental context of inquiry it lacks specific identity criteria— being a "limit" of the world rather than a "thing"—but even so it is a notion we arrive at when examining our *self-understanding* as world-inhabiting and world-engaging creatures, that is, as human beings concerned with the human condition and the (humanly natural) "inhuman" attempts to overcome it. The struggle with solipsism is irrelevant for "antihumanists." Because solipsism is a serious philosophical concern, a concern that matters, and because it is necessarily humanistic, we may conclude that it is impossible to drop humanism as easily as some trendy posthumanists believe.

One of the ultimately humanistic insights of our discussion is that philosophical arguments regarding the "truth" of solipsism can bring us only so far. The non-solipsistic duty of taking a personal stand in acknowledging others is, pragmatically speaking, where my spade (and, hopefully, others' as well) is turned. This is what I say and do. Philosophizing may help us here precisely because it won't destroy our deepest human questions. (A theorization that did, or even attempted to, may be judged inhuman.) I sincerely hope my discussions of solipsism and related metaphilosophical issues have not destroyed any of those questions. I would have failed entirely, had my work silenced the solipsist for good. On the contrary, philosophy may help us live with the insecurity we almost inevitably feel after having observed that there is no knockdown argument against solipsism (or many other views we are unable to hold and still remain human) and that we must, therefore, rely on our own groundless, foundationless, ability to enter into responsible relations to others. Philosophy may, thus, teach us how to live with our seemingly unbearable uncertainties, even with our occasionally agonizing alienation from the world and our fellow human beings.

In this sense, in our continuing struggles with solipsism—and with the various ways in which it matters to us—our philosophizing is, at bottom, in Wittgenstein's (1998: 24) words, "work on oneself. On one's own conception. On how one sees things." When engaging in this work, we will never silence Wittgenstein's (1993: 258) question: "The solipsist flutters and flutters in the flyglass, strikes against the walls, flutters further. How can he be brought to rest?"

NOTES

Chapter One

1 While death will be discussed in this book, I will not *argue* that death matters to us; that's self-evident. However, by examining solipsism, the book will illuminate the very special way in which death and dying matter. See Pihlström (2016).
2 See Rogers (1970) on Storm, Duff and Marshall (1982) on Camus, Pettersson (1982), Guetti (2004), and Rudrun (2005) on Conrad, and Schurman (1987) on Beckett. See also Nuttall (1974).
3 See Sober (1995). Sorensen (1998) discusses solipsism in an evolutionary context; see also Ridge (2001). The term has even been used by socioeconomists (e.g., Linder 1992). Another unorthodox usage is Langton's (2009) discussion of pornography and "sexual solipsism." According to Langton, sexual oppression is "solipsism made real" (Langton 2009: 2).
4 Cf. Bonner (1994) and the essays in Neumer (2000).
5 It is not clear, however, that *I*, considering the solipsism issue, could coherently entertain the possibility that *someone else* might, for all I know, be the only genuine subject, that is, that solipsism might be true for someone who is *not me*. This would hardly qualify as solipsistic, because it would postulate a reality external to myself, albeit one not external to that other subject. But, conversely, also the rejection of solipsism must, insofar as it is me who rejects the view that the world is mine, begin from my "first person" standpoint. We will later be preoccupied with this puzzlement.
6 Cf. Hyslop (1995: chapters 1 and 3). He says: "There is an asymmetry between the knowledge we have of ourselves and the knowledge we have of others. We do not have and cannot have the relevant direct knowledge in the case of others. All theories of mind, therefore, depend on the evidence we have in our own case" (1995: 21). The problems of solipsism and other minds are distinct, because one could reject other minds while believing in nonmental reality. Though specific discussions concerning other minds are relevant to our topic, I cannot examine them in any detail.

7 One author rhetorically asks: "Would you want your daughter to marry a solipsist? Would you have wanted your mother to have been one? Should you want any less for your fellow man?" (Mitroff 1971: 391). It is known that Mrs. Ladd-Franklin once wrote to Bertrand Russell, confessing to be a solipsist and wondering why others had not embraced this—in her view reasonable—position. McGreal (1948) is one of the few philosophers advancing solipsism; his article may, however, have been a hoax (Ushenko 1948).
8 For informative overviews, see Rollins (1967), Borst (1992), Gabriel (1995), Vinci (1995), Craig (1998), and Thornton (2004).
9 This is, of course, a *philosophical* thesis; I am not concerned with *psychological* or "natural" solipsism, which Oliver (1970: 30) defines as "a rare condition to be found only in extreme cases of schizophrenia and childhood autism," characterized by a "withdrawal into a private world." Note also that it is more interesting to formulate solipsism as a thesis about the *dependence* of reality on me (my thought) than straightforwardly as the claim that all reality is *confined* to my mind (e.g., in the sense that the external world would be only "my dream").
10 Schopenhauer himself, although he wrote the book, *Die Welt als Wille und Vorstellung* (1844), was not a solipsist, at least not an ordinary one (see Chapter 3).
11 *Panpsychism*, the view that the world is fundamentally psychical or experiential (cf. Nagel 1979; Sprigge 1993; Pihlström 2008), need not be subjectivist, nor, therefore, solipsist.
12 The notion of categorization is central in the disputes over "metaphysical realism": does the world possess its own ontological or metaphysical structure (categorization), or are such structures imposed by us as language users? Cf. Pihlström (1996a, 2009).
13 Mary Shelley, the author of *Frankenstein*, wrote the dystopic novel *The Last Man* (1826), depicting the sole survivor of a pandemic. But the protagonist of *The Last Man* is not a solipsist, as he does not believe that the world depends on his mind.
14 Wittgenstein suggests in his lecture notes from 1930–33 that what solipsism says is not "learnt by experience" but is something that the solipsist couldn't imagine being otherwise (Wittgenstein 1993: 102–3).
15 If we combine the weakest versions of ontological and epistemological solipsism, we get a very liberal form of solipsism, according to which there is a mind-independent reality, though it can be known and categorized only with reference to my thoughts about it. It is probably better not to extend the meaning of "solipsism" to cover this case.
16 *If* foundationalism can be compatible with fallibilism, also the weak epistemological solipsist emphasizing the derivability of all knowledge from such "private" knowledge can be a fallibilist.

17 Kekes (1971: 44) says solipsism is "the spectre that scepticism raises," that is, the view that "there is no justification for accepting the presupposition that something exists outside of a solitary mind."
18 Cortens (2000: 93) introduces "referential solipsism": "no term in my vocabulary refers to anything besides my own sensory ideas" (cf. Todd 1968, on "analytical solipsism"). Hessell (2018) distinguishes between "traditional" and semantic solipsism.
19 In philosophy of language, "solipsistic semantics" may refer to the view that the assignment of meanings to representations does not presuppose the existence of any individuals (mental or physical) other than the thinker and their mental representations (LePore and Loewer 1986: 595–96). Yagisawa (1993: 213) defines "meaning solipsism" as the thesis that "it is metaphysically possible for a state to be a meaningful state without any other state being a meaningful state—that is, it is metaphysically possible for a state to be one and only one meaningful state."
20 Borst (1992: 487) simply says that the methodological solipsist "typically holds to solipsism as some sort of methodological strategy (either a method of inquiry or else a constructional programme)." The expression "psychological solipsism" has been used to denote the idea that only the agent her-/himself needs to be taken into account in psychological explanations (Maloney 1991). On psychiatric manifestations of solipsism in schizophrenia, see Humpston (2018).
21 Badenhop (2017) introduces the "moral solipsist" as someone who believes her-/himself to be the only *person* there is and therefore the only one to whom moral predicates and considerations apply.
22 A related position is characterized as "practical solipsism" by Nagel (1970: 114)—"an inability to draw fully-fledged practical conclusions about impersonally viewed situations." Beloff (1956: 546) defines "moral solipsism" as the equation, "x is good if, and only if, I approve x," where the "I" is the "I" of "a solipsism of the moment."
23 It might also be suggested that one may subscribe to "methodological ethical solipsism." If one holds this view, one always tries to act *as if* one were the only truly ethical subject there is.
24 Cf. Taylor (1995) on the sources of modern individualism in the epistemological idea of a punctual self justifying its beliefs to itself and the romantic ideal of self-realization. On "romantic solipsism," see also Maleuvre (2006: chapter 4).
25 Luntley's (1995) and Matthews's (1996) discussions of this theme are lucid; cf. Critchley and Dews (1996).
26 Although I will mention several classical and modern philosophers in Chapters 2 and 3, the central figures are Descartes, Kant, Schopenhauer, Husserl, Russell, and Wittgenstein.

27 Regarding the material chosen for investigation, it should be emphasized that many commentaries on Wittgenstein, Husserl, and some other philosophers are *primary* sources (not merely secondary ones) regarding the issue of solipsism, since the debate has largely taken place in interpretations of Wittgenstein and other classics.
28 Wittgenstein (1993: 225) asks: "Is it impossible to imagine a philosophy that would be the diametrical opposite of solipsism?" I will variously call the rejection of solipsism non-solipsism, realism, or (sometimes) pragmatic realism.

Chapter Two

1 Bell tries to show that Wittgenstein's version of solipsism should be taken seriously (see Chapter 3).
2 The authorship of the book is discussed in the "Preface" to Inchofer (1753).
3 See Schurman (1987: 154–55) and Gabriel (1995). von Hartmann (1877: 78) was one of the first to use "solipsism" in the sense of a rigorous form of subjective idealism.
4 What I have in mind here is not only Greek philosophy but also pre-philosophical literature. In his study on ethical ideas in Greek literature and society, Bernard Williams argues that the Homeric "shame culture" of archaic Greece invented the ethical notion of an "internalised other." Homeric and Sophoclean characters are pictured as acting out of necessity, as "experiencing a necessity to act in certain ways, a conviction that they must do certain things," in such a way that the source of this necessity is nothing external to them but "an internalised other whose view the agent can respect" and with which they can identify (Williams 1993: 103). This invention in a sense made ethical solipsism possible, because the ethically relevant "other" was taken to reside within oneself. The respect for the views of the internalized other is, Williams explains, self-respect, for the "other" arises from within oneself. Williams asks, "But if the other is identified in ethical terms, is he any longer playing any real role in these mental processes [of respect]? Has he any independent part in my psychology if he is constructed out of my own local materials? If he is imagined to react simply in terms of what I think is the right thing to do, surely he must cancel out: he is not an *other* at all" (Williams 1993: 84). According to Williams (Williams 1993: 98–99), even Plato offers us an "experiment in motivational solipsism" in his discussion, in the Republic, of the idea that the life of a just person,

even if isolated and misunderstood, is more worth living than the life of an unjust one.
5 According to Williams, the internalized other, though abstracted, generalized and idealized, "remains a genuine other" in the sense that it is "the embodiment of a real social expectation," and is thus "potentially somebody rather than nobody, and somebody other than me" (Williams 1993: 84, 103). The internalized other is not merely "a screen for one's own ethical ideas but is the locus of some genuine social expectations" (Williams 1993: 98).
6 Protagoras's doctrine has at least since Plato been considered self-refuting (indeed, it is from Plato's *Theaetetus* that we have inherited the conception of Protagoras as a relativist), but it has seldom been explicitly connected with solipsism. Burnyeat (1976: 191), however, considers the possible interpretation that the Protagorean thesis— that is, the claim, "Every judgment is true *for* the person whose judgment it is" (1976: 174)—might, in a solipsistic fashion, be true only in Protagoras's own world, others' (say, Socrates's) worlds being "incorporated" into his. Of course, there is nothing more to discuss, if Protagoras "simply asserts solipsistically that he, for his part, lives in a world in which this is so" (1976: 191). Even this, according to Burnyeat, is too generous for the self-refutingly relativist Protagoras (1976: 192). Gorgias is another sophist worth mentioning here. He notoriously thought that nothing exists, but also (quasi-solipsistically) that even if something did exist and even if we could know something about it, such knowledge could never be communicated.
7 Again, I do not wish to imply that Descartes was independent of prior traditions. A Cartesian-like "solipsistic evidence theory of truth" has been attributed to Augustine (Böhler 1984: 267). Some scholars resist the received view that Descartes introduced the idea of a "solipsistic self" into Western philosophy; according to Sorell (2001, 2005), he did no such thing. While my discussion of Descartes as an initiator of the modern issue of solipsism remains a caricature, we may legitimately speak about "Cartesian," as well as "Wittgensteinian," solipsism because these *are* standard notions in the literature.
8 This is a semantic rather than metaphysical doctrine, since Haack's "realisms" are mainly views about the nature of truth.
9 It might be suggested that Bell's demand only applies to transcendental solipsism (see Chapter 3).
10 See also, for example, Plaut (1962: 217–18). Thornton (2004: §1) also formulates a version of classical epistemological and skeptical solipsism by maintaining that "the foundations of solipsism lie at the heart of the view that the individual gets his own psychological concepts (thinking, willing, perceiving, and so forth) from 'his

own cases,' that is by abstraction from 'inner experience.'" This view, unlike solipsism proper, has been implicitly held by many philosophers since Descartes.

11 A more naturalistic definition, which nevertheless comes close to "classical solipsism," has been suggested by A. W. Moore (1996: 220). He defines a *world* as "any distribution of microphysical states across the whole of space-time," and singles out a part of the world which has "privileged evidential status for me," that is, "the biography of my brain." The solipsistic thesis (S) says that "any world that includes the biography of my brain is, for all I know, actual." A deeper skepticism is expressed by the modification (S*), which takes (S) to "the level of things in themselves": "For all I know, any 'noumenal' possibility that includes whatever sustains my subjective state is, for all I know, actual" (1996: 224). This "genuinely solipsistic thought" requires transcending the initial naturalistic framework, however. Moore speculates that solipsism might not have a coherent formulation at all (1996: 229–30). This topic is further discussed, with reference to (transcendental) idealism generally, in Moore (1997).

12 Gellner (1998) investigates how this argument was rooted in the Viennese sociocultural circumstances in which Wittgenstein's thought developed, also analyzing the sociocultural factors that made the position seem attractive.

13 Despite Nagel's concern with avoiding solipsism, it has been argued that his treatment of the problem of *qualia*—that is, of what it is "like" to be an organism of some kind, such as a bat, and to have a certain experiential point of view to the world—and especially his reliance on the notion of imagination in this context lead to a solipsistic strain in his philosophy (Wider 1990). Cf. the seminal paper "What Is It Like to Be a Bat?" in Nagel (1979). Nagel's other statements suggest that he understands the problem of solipsism along the lines of "conceptual solipsism" (Borst 1992). He describes solipsism as "the inability to make sense of the idea of real minds other than one's own" (Nagel 1986: 20), as a metaphysical view that "denies *sense* to the supposition that there are other persons besides oneself" (Nagel 1970: 104). While defending *qualia*, Nagel also pursues the "view from nowhere": "Not being a solipsist, I do not believe that the point of view from which I see the world is *the* perspective to reality. Mine is only one of the many points of view from which the world is seen" (Nagel 1986: 57; cf. Nagel 1970: 100ff.). This concern extends to the practical analogy of solipsism in ethics (Nagel 1970: 113–15, 145; 1986: chapter 8).

14 On the "brains in a vat" thought experiment, see, for example, Putnam (1981: chapter 1) and Tipton (1992).

15 See, for example, Stern (1947–48) and Rollins (1967). Stern believes he has shown, however, that the problem of solipsism is a pseudo-problem, since no subject can be determinately "alone" and "unique" in the solipsistic sense (Stern 1947–48: 686–87). For an essentially Cartesian treatment of the solipsism issue as the problem of whether we are justified in believing that there is an external world outside one's subjective consciousness (linked up with proving God's existence), see Dore (1989). The Cartesian problem is also taken seriously by Johnstone (1991), whose approach I will shortly comment upon.
16 On the "Cartesian assumptions" at work in the philosophy of mind, see, for example, Putnam (1994, 1999). For a substantial discussion of Descartes critical of the claim that his view of subjectivity is committed to a solipsistic self, see Sorell (2005).
17 However, the Leibnizian idea that each individual monad represents within it the entire universe (Leibniz 1714: §§60–62) is analogous to solipsism, too. Each monad, perceiving the universe from its own point of view, perceives "solipsistically" (Mondadori 1982), since there is no interaction among these metaphysical substances. Leibniz postulated a plurality of monads, but he did consider the possibility that only God and "me" (the soul) might exist (cf. Mondadori 1982: 41–42; and especially McRae 1982).
18 Some commentators do think that Berkeley's immaterialism leads to solipsism, though they tend to disagree on how and why this happens (cf. Grey 1952). There has been some debate over whether Berkeley should be interpreted as a solipsist; see, for example, the exchange between van Iten (1962, 1968) and Hausman (1968).
19 See the famous discussion in the *Treatise* (Hume 1739–40: Book I, Part IV, §VI). Hume's critique of the substantiality of the self is an important precursor of later views such as Sartre's or Wittgenstein's, in which the idea that consciousness can be found among the objects of the world is rejected (see Chapter 3). Husserl (1935: 97), however, implausibly claims that Hume ends up with solipsism. A distinction should be made between solipsism and Hume's "skeptical empiricism."
20 This term comes from Kolakowski (2001), who argues that "metaphysical horror" arises within a Cartesian framework but also from other perspectives (Platonism, Neoplatonism, Hegelianism). It pertains to the Cartesian ego as much as to the Hegelian Absolute: if "nothing really exists except myself," then I am "nothing," too (Kolakowski 2001: 23); if the Absolute is perfect, it is lifeless and cannot be described positively; it is, hence, "reduced, by its own perfection, to non-existence, and sinks into irrelevance" (Kolakowski

(2001): 42)—and the same happens to the ego, or the self, when viewed as a kind of solipsistic "absolute." The Cartesian ego, in particular, is "a kind of black hole," ineffable, "Nothing" (Kolakowski (2001): 73).

21 There is a peculiar "Dutch" version of solipsism not easily classified as a version of either analytic or Continental philosophy: the intuitionist mathematician L. E. J. Brouwer and his pupil Arend Heyting developed a version of solipsism as mystical experience. For Brouwer's reflections on "the sad world," the necessary "turning into the self," and mysticism, see his (1975: 1–10; cf. 480ff.). Placek (1999: 25–27, 86–89) argues that Brouwer should not be accused of a solipsistic denial of other minds: his view is methodological rather than metaphysical. Heyting's remarks on solipsism have been collected and translated into English by Franchella (1995), who notes that Brouwer distinguished between theoretical and practical solipsism: despite the theoretical impossibility of knowing the existence of other minds, one can have a "living experience" of other people (1995: 208–09). For Heyting, solipsism must be the beginning of all philosophy, since it is natural to believe that "we know primarily and for certain only our own representations" (1995: 217). The solipsist "sees other men, but she/he cannot reach them. Therefore, she/he can be described as a bee on a window-pane" (1995: 221). Yet, solipsism cannot consistently be a theory to be believed and communicated to others (1995: 218). Thus, Heyting's views naturally lead to Wittgensteinian considerations. Even Brouwer's position might be reinterpreted as a transcendental solipsism, for he employs something like the Kantian notion of a transcendental subject (Placek 1999: 89).

22 Russell (1948: 191–92) argues that dogmatic solipsism has no argument in its favor, since "it is just as difficult to disprove existence as to prove it." He thus focuses on solipsism as a brand of skepticism.

23 One might suggest that both ontological and epistemological (or, for that matter, semantic, methodological and ethical) versions of solipsism (cf. Chapter 1) may be adopted dogmatically or skeptically. It is, however, more natural to roughly equate epistemological solipsism with skeptical solipsism, as distinguished from any "dogmatic" position.

24 See, again, Chapter 3. Schachter (1997: 448–49) distinguishes between "agnostic solipsism" and "unicitous solipsism": the former is the view that we cannot defend the belief that there are other minds, whereas the latter claims that "my mind is *necessarily ontologically unique.*" Another dichotomy is the one between *type solipsism* and *token solipsism*: the latter says that "only he exists," while the former says that "only people of his type exist" (Sorensen 1998: 76).

On the distinction between the conceptual and the (Cartesian) skeptical versions of the problem of other minds, see Avramides (2001) and Vaaja (2015). Sorensen (2018) suggests that in an otherwise "mindless" world a mind capable of telepathy would have observational evidence for solipsism.

25 Independently of the formulations by Russell (or Wittgenstein), we might characterize the most extreme form of solipsism available as *dogmatic, ontological, conceptual, and "present moment"* solipsism, according to which it is inconceivable that there could be anything else than what is internal to my mind at this particular moment. This view says that the present contents of my thought are all the reality there could be.

26 The papers "A Defence of Common Sense" and "Proof of an External World" are reprinted in Moore (1959: chapters 2 and 7). Much of twentieth-century British epistemology, for example, A. J. Ayer's work, shares this tendency to discuss the problems of the external world and other minds under the rubric of skepticism (cf. Ayer 1956).

27 See especially Russell (1983: 10–14). The historical importance of the 1913 theory of knowledge is emphasized by Pears (1987–88, 1996): Russell's manuscript stimulated Wittgenstein's reflections on solipsism.

28 One of the best commentaries on Bradley's metaphysics is Sprigge (1993); cf. Candlish (2007).

29 An easy—too easy—argument against solipsism of the present moment would be obtained by realizing that enumerating *anything* takes time. The solipsist of the present moment denies the reality of time, accepting only present experiences; hence, s/he can hardly construct any "list" of the present "data," for any such data would already be past when the list had been completed. The solipsist thesis should, however, be taken in a conditional sense: *if* such a list could be constructed instantaneously, it would include only the experience had at that particular moment (i.e., now).

30 See also his discussion of "the limits of empiricism" (Russell 1948: 516–27).

31 Quinean empiricists might, with bold self-reflectiveness, insist that empiricism itself, when subordinated to an overarching naturalism, is an empirically (scientifically) testable theory of human knowledge-acquisition. Cf. Quine (1995).

32 For discussions of Russell's relation to solipsism, see, for example, Haack (1976: 237), and Jager (1972: 404–10).

33 In the United States, William James was the leading thinker preoccupied with solipsism in early twentieth century (cf. Chapters 4 and 5). Shook's (1998) bibliography of pragmatism lists several discussions of the relation between pragmatism and solipsism. Some critics charged

pragmatists, especially James but also Dewey, of solipsism (e.g., Bode 1905; Russell 1906; for a response, see Moore 1910: chapter 10). For James's replies, see his (1909, 1912). The British pragmatist (or "humanist") F. C. S. Schiller, in turn, argued that absolute idealism (e.g., Bradley's) leads to solipsism, since the formulation of solipsism only requires that *one* field of experience (e.g., the absolute's) is all-inclusive. Cf. Schiller (1907, 1912) and Schiller et al. (1923).

34 For a clarifying discussion of Santayana's philosophy, including his critique of solipsism, see Lachs (1987: chapters 7 and 9).

35 I will later elaborate on the idea that it is (perhaps only) because of the need for a somewhat arbitrary, yet philosophical, ethical commitment that we can and must stop our slide on the slippery slope.

36 In Johnstone's terms, one can adopt (1) "Internal World Solipsism" and be either (1a) a "Sensa Solipsist," claiming that "what exists is the private world of one's own sensations or representations," or (1b) a "Lingua-Sensa Solipsist," a "Wittgensteinian" representative of (1a). Alternatively, one may choose (2) "Observed World Solipsism," which comes in three varieties: (2a) "Ephemerata Solipsism," according to which "any portions of the world not actually perceived by oneself do not exist"; (2b) "Monopsyche Solipsism," a restriction of (2a) to the denial of other minds; and (2c) "Sense Data Solipsism," a radicalization of (2a) to the denial of the existence of unperceived properties and relations. Finally, there are four versions of (3) "Unreal World Solipsism": (3a) "Demoniac Solipsism," the Cartesian proposal that the world might be "a hoax conjured up by a demon"; (3b) "Phantasmata Solipsism," according to which the world is a "personal illusion"; (3c) "Oneirata Solipsism," which redefines the world as the solipsist's own dream; and (3d) "Non-Sensa Solipsism," which is something like (1a) except that the solipsist's private world is not constituted by sensations (Johnstone 1991: xvii; for characterizations of these, see Johnstone 1991: chapter 1).

37 Thus, epistemology, he says, should be "rationalized" rather than "naturalized." It is hard to follow him into the strong theses that the solipsistic challenge is "pancultural" (Johnstone 1991: 102), that there is (*pace* Wittgenstein) a role for "the private object in language" (Johnstone 1991: 181), and that solipsism can be formulated in a "private language" and even in "nonlinguistic modes of thinking" (Johnstone 1991: 207; see also 235). How could *any* thesis be formulated nonlinguistically?

38 Carnap (1967: §64) mentions Russell among the precursors of his autopsychological starting point. Haack (1977: 174–75) relates Carnap to an older tradition: the methodological solipsism of the *Aufbau* is, she claims, analogous to Kant's notion of the unity of

transcendental apperception. For more comprehensive treatments of the *Aufbau*, taking seriously Carnap's neo-Kantian background, see Richardson (1998) and Friedman (1999: chapters 5–6).

39 Ayer (1946: 171) says, "Just as I must define material things and my own self in terms of their empirical manifestations, so I must define other people in terms of their empirical manifestations—that is, in terms of the behaviour of their bodies, and ultimately in terms of sense-contents." Others here seem to be reduced to my sense-contents.

40 Even an empiricism such as Quine's could be regarded as methodologically solipsistic—despite its robust naturalism and scientific realism—since external objects are, for Quine, "posits" based on the stimulation of the sense organs of an individual physical organism. For Quine's reflections on the way in which his program amounts to a naturalization of Carnap's *Aufbau*, see Quine (1995). Quine's views may come close to "linguistic solipsism" (Roth 1987: 45, 63, 67, 71–72).

41 Putnam may have introduced the notion of methodological solipsism in its contemporary sense in "The Meaning of 'Meaning'" (see Putnam 1975: 220–21). Versions of methodological solipsism more recent than Carnap's have been developed by thinkers associated with the Chomsky/Fodor "language of thought" tradition in the philosophy of mind and language (Fodor 1975, 1980). Fodor (1980: 71) famously proposes methodological solipsism as a "research strategy" for cognitive psychology, reminding us that this is not "solipsism *tout court*." Lycan (1986: 247) defines methodological solipsism as "reliance in explaining behavior only on what is 'in the head.'" (See Woodfield 1982, particularly Bach 1982, distinguishing between "formal" and "conceptual" methodological solipsism, as well as Noonan 1981, 1985, 1986; Morris 1984; Marras 1985; Maloney 1985, 1991; Tuomela 1989; Rowlands 1991, 1995; McCulloch 1995: 176–77, 184–87.) Since Carnap is, for Putnam, the paradigmatic methodological solipsist, I will confine my discussion to his views.

42 Putnam's critique of both relativism and methodological solipsism is related to a critique of merely "immanent" (disquotational, minimalist, deflationary) theories of truth and associated "assertibility conditions" views of language. Such views lead, he argues, to a "methodological solipsism of the present instant." Cf. Putnam (1990: 107; 1994: 96, 275–76, 327).

43 Carnap (1967: §64) criticizes Mach because he does *not*, by Carnap's standards, start from the autopsychological, though Mach was of course a central predecessor of the neopositivism of the Vienna Circle.

44 It has also been argued that scientific evidence itself suggests that one can have no more immediate knowledge of one's own mind than

of other minds (Mitroff 1971). From a philosophical viewpoint, psychological evidence is, however, irrelevant.
45 Todd, rather than simply subscribing to analytical solipsism, aims to show that it is coherent (although it makes strong assumptions about, say, counterfactuals) and thus to raise it into the status of a serious candidate (Todd 1968: 317).
46 Among Putnam's late writings, the most sustained discussion of Carnap and methodological solipsism is Putnam (2012: chapter 22); while Putnam begins with a "deflationary" analysis of Wittgenstein's discussion of solipsism, his main aim seems to be an examination of Carnap and Reichenbach, and he argues that a solipsistic reconstruction of language along Carnapian lines risks the possibility of sharing a "moral world" (2012: 348).
47 Sober (1995: 557ff.) draws an analogy between solipsism and operationalism (or empiricism generally) in the philosophy of science: both are examples of "epistemic puritanism." "A solipsistic organism is like a scientist without a theory" (1995: 563).
48 Cf. Cockburn's (1990) critique. This first-person point of view is taken even by philosophers like Merleau-Ponty (1962), who extend the phenomenological approach to the material human body.
49 If a transcendental form of solipsism, such as Husserl's or Wittgenstein's (cf. Chapter 3) is put to a methodological use, for instance, in the investigation of the possibility of conscious experience or meaningful language, one may ask whether it will, as metaphysically neutral, be able to serve in its transcendental role. See, for example, Hanna's (2001) critique of Allison's (2004 [1983]) methodological interpretation of Kant's transcendental idealism.
50 On the pragmatic maxim, see, for example, Pihlström (2015). The classical references are Peirce's 1878 essay "How to Make Our Ideas Clear" (Peirce 1992-98, vol. 1) and James (1907: chapter 2). It should be noted, however, that from an ethical point of view the other should not be regarded as *too much* other, either. Other people, in order to be taken ethically seriously, should not collapse to myself, nor should they be totally alien to me. It is this need to find a middle ground, securing the other's genuine but not excessive otherness, that makes the solipsism issue ethically significant (see Chapter 5).

Chapter Three

1 This is not to say that there is no epistemological component involved; I just want to draw attention to the essential difference

between ("classical") epistemologically focused skeptical solipsism and the typically non-skeptical transcendental solipsism to which we now turn.
2. The transcendental solipsist might want to endorse strong ontological solipsism, but the viability of such an option depends on how exactly this position is interpreted. Metaphysical claims about the world "in itself" are rejected in transcendental philosophy; strong ontological solipsism appears to make such claims when stating the absolute dependence of all existence on the subject. Metaphysical statements from a "God's-Eye View" cannot be defended within properly transcendental solipsism.
3. An oft-cited passage, from the B-deduction, in which Kant explains what he means by the "original synthetic unity of apperception," reads as follows: "Das: *Ich denke*, muß alle meine Vorstellungen begleiten *können* . . . . Die mannigfaltigen Vorstellungen, die in einer gewissen Anschauung gegeben werden, würden nicht insgesamt *meine* Vorstellungen sein, wenn sie nicht insgesamt zu einem Selbstbewußtsein gehörten . . ." (Kant 1781/1787: B131–32).
4. According to Collins (1999), it is even misleading to call Kant an "idealist," because his views are so different from, say, Berkeley's. *This*, I think, is misleading. Kant surely is a father of modern idealism. Hanna (2001: 100) insists that Kant was an idealist—metaphysically, not just methodologically or epistemologically (as Allison and others claim)—but *not* a solipsist: "the representational contents generated by my cognitive capacities . . . are in principle also able to be generated by yours or anyone else's." See Beiser (2002: Part I) for a detailed account of Kant's idealism as critique of "subjectivism."
5. Insisting on the novelty of Kant's position in relation to, say, Descartes's is compatible with acknowledging that both Descartes and post-Cartesians like Leibniz were predecessors of Kant's notion of transcendental subjectivity.
6. When I cite Allison (2004) by providing the date of the first edition (1983), there is a specific reason to cite the earlier version.
7. Abela (2002: 107–13) argues that first-person reports on inner states have no epistemic priority over third-person ones, according to Kant, since without an interpreted, truth-constrained connection between us and the world there can be no correctness even in our beliefs about our own inner states. This transcendental argument bears some resemblance to Wittgenstein's private language argument.
8. Cf. again Hanna (2001). Even here, however, a (methodologically) solipsistic reading has been suggested: Schantz (2000: 167–68) argues that Kant's view of the "I think" as a formal condition of experience (as distinguished from the metaphysical idea criticized in

the paralogisms) is methodologically solipsistic, because it takes no account of the embodied nature of subjectivity. Wittgenstein (1993: 331) suggests the following: "The whole problem of solipsism arises from a situation like 'I'm looking at *this*.'—(You could define a solipsistic position by beginning every sentence with 'I think . . .'.)" See also Beiser (2002: 152).

9 Moore (1997: 125) claims that transcendental solipsism—an idealist doctrine he finds incoherent—can already be found in Kant, while Beiser (1998: 25–27) uses the phrase "Kantian solipsism" for reminding us that some early critics (e.g., Jacobi) charged Kantian idealism of solipsism (on Kant's idealism as defending realism, see Beiser 2002). Weissman (1993: 34, 194) sees solipsism as a result of the Kantian constructivist conception of transcendental "worldmaking," shared by, for example, pragmatists and Carnapian-Quinean empiricists. Insofar as such an interpretation is even partly accurate, the solipsism issue again turns out to be much more relevant to current philosophical concerns than one might prima facie think.

10 Cf., for example, Weininger (1905: 202); see Chapter 5. It has been argued that Kant proceeds solipsistically in his practical philosophy, relying on a solipsistic conception of reason, according to which the singular rational subject stands outside communicative relations to others. This approach is, presumably, in tension with Kant's ethical requirement of justice (Kuhlmann 1990); more recent Kantians like Apel and Habermas have therefore tried to detach Kantianism from the residues of solipsism (cf. Horster 1982). Kuhlmann (2017) sees the tradition of transcendental argumentation in post-Kantian philosophy as committed to "methodical solipsism." For a reading of Kant's defense of reason as inherently social and historical, see O'Neill (1989).

11 Hegel's complicated philosophy cannot be considered here. While his notion of the "absolute spirit" is comparable to the solitary solipsistic ego, its historical and socioculturally developing nature precludes any easy solipsistic reading.

12 Fichte's early, pre-*Wissenschaftslehre* writings are also available in Fichte (1988). See Beiser (2002: Part II) for a thoroughgoing examination of Fichte's idealism in relation to Kant's.

13 The latter number refers to Fichte's *Gesamtausgabe* (1834–46).

14 Kant did not approve of Fichte's *Wissenschaftslehre*, but his late notes, published as *Opus postumum*, where he writes about the "*Selbstsetzungslehre*," give the impression that an idea of self-positing is at work in his transcendental philosophy, too. He reflects: "I am an object of myself and of my representations. That there is something else outside me is my own product. I make myself. . . . We make

everything ourselves" (Kant 1993: 189). The "I am" is "a *verbum* by which I posit myself" (Kant 1993: 191). Transcendental idealism is in *Opus postumum* characterized by Kant as the view that "the world is only in me" (Kant 1993: 195). This formulation of idealism does sound solipsistic: "The position of something outside me, itself first commences in me, in the forms of space and time, in which I myself posit the objects of outer and inner sense, and which, therefore, are infinite positings" (Kant 1993: 195). For more comprehensive reflections on the relation between Kant and Fichte, see Beiser (2002).

15 Lachs (1987: 199), while regarding Fichte's view that "the activities of the self are the paradigm of creative activity" as his "fundamental unjustified assumption" in the vindication of idealism, notes that Fichte—nonsensically, in Lachs's view—regarded idealism (or, rather, solipsism) as a demand of morality: the possibility of morality depends on the "primacy of the ego" and on the ego's independence of any outward determination by material objects; hence, in order to be a person, one must be an idealist (1987: 201–2).

16 Cf. the translators' 1970 preface to Fichte (1794–95: xv). The fact that the Fichtean self cannot be individuated or personalized reminds us of Wittgensteinian solipsism: the solipsistic ego also loses its identifiability. Cf. also Beiser (2002: 273ff.).

17 Kant (1993: 248) says (emphases in the original): "**Religion is conscientiousness** (*mihi hoc religioni*). The holiness of the acceptance [*Zusage*] and the truthfulness of what man must confess to himself. Confess to yourself. To have religion, the concept of God is not required (still less the postulate: 'There is a God')." However, the place of the *Opus postumum* in the Kantian corpus is problematic; one should not too much rely on it in interpretation (but see Beiser 2002: Part I, chapter 10).

18 For the development of the terms "egoism" and "solipsism," see Gabriel (1995). In the eighteenth and early nineteenth centuries, these words used to mean the reverse than they now do—also in Kant and in Schopenhauer.

19 Cf. Janaway (1989: 148–50), Atwell (1995: 95–96), and Young (2005: 69–70). Atwell (1995: 95) explains that Schopenhauer does *not*, by "theoretical egoism," mean solipsism, if the latter is defined as the doctrine that "there are no minds other than my own" or that "I can never know for certain that there are other minds." Theoretical egoism should be understood as the view that "denies reality (i.e., will) to everything other than my own body."

20 A highly important historical issue to be mentioned here is Schopenhauer's influence on Wittgenstein's early philosophy (cf. Hacker 1986; Janaway 1989; Brockhaus 1991; Glock 1999). As

in Wittgenstein, the approach Schopenhauer proposes regarding solipsism is therapeutic rather than argumentative.
21 Other currents of solipsistic thought can also be distinguished in nineteenth-century German philosophy, where one finds, for example, a minor trend represented by Max Stirner in his *Der Einzige und sein Eigenthum* (1845), a work defending a "materialist solipsism," that is, practical egoism, liberalism, and anarchism under the slogan, "*Ich hab' mein' Sach' auf Nichts gestellt*." He makes the implications of this view very clear (1845: 8): "Meine Sache ist weder das Göttliche noch das Menschliche, ist nicht das Wahre, Gute, Rechte, Freie u.s.w., sondern allein das *Meinige*, und sie ist keine allgemeine, sondern ist—*einzig* wie Ich einzig bin. Mir geht nichts über Mich!" Cf. Kast (1998).
22 Cf. the Hintikkas' reading of Wittgenstein as a "phenomenologist" (Hintikka and Hintikka 1986; Hintikka 1996); see Park (1998).
23 Husserl's pupil Edith Stein wrote in 1917 a dissertation on *empathy*, distinguishing empathy from outer perception (Stein 1989: 6–7): empathy is "a kind of act of perceiving . . . *sui generis*" (Stein 1989: 11). A link to solipsism is clear (as in phenomenology generally) when Stein points out that "the appearance of the world," though not the appearing world itself, is "dependent on individual consciousness" (Stein 1989: 64). She argues, however, that I can cross the boundaries of my individuality and go beyond "the world as it appears to me" via empathy, which is the basis of intersubjective experience and, hence, also a condition for the possibility of knowledge of the outer world (Stein 1989). Her view appears non-solipsistic when she writes, "By empathy with differently composed personal structures we become clear on what we are not, what we are more or less than others" (Stein 1989: 116). Nevertheless, "the foreign person is constituted in empathically experienced acts" (Stein 1989: 109) and, therefore, in a way depends on *my* empathetic experiences. Therefore, it remains an open question whether empathy in Stein's sense genuinely reaches the other subject. Jacques (1982: 133) argues that phenomenological investigations of empathy are solipsistic, for they inevitably concern the other's meaning *for me*.
24 In addition to his major works relevant to our topic (e.g., Husserl 1931), Husserl's voluminous posthumously published writings on the phenomenology of intersubjectivity cannot be studied here. By emphasizing the presence of the solipsism issue in Husserlian phenomenology, I am not trying to refute the non-solipsistic readings of Husserl on intersubjectivity; I will only explain why it seems to me that solipsism easily comes back even in intersubjectivist developments of transcendental phenomenology. This dialectical structure will prove relevant later (Chapter 5).

25 English translation: "When I, the meditating I, reduce myself to my absolute transcendental ego by phenomenological *epoché* do I not become solus ipse; and do I not remain that, as long as I carry on a consistent self-explication under the name phenomenology? Should not a phenomenology that proposed to solve the problems of Objective being, and to present itself actually as philosophy, be branded therefore as transcendental solipsism?"

26 English translation: "only a subordinate stage philosophically," and "must first be delimited for purposes of method, in order that the problems of transcendental intersubjectivity, as problems belonging to a higher level, may be correctly stated and attacked."

27 English translation: "the experiencing intentionality of my ego."

28 English translation: "The illusion of a solipsism is dissolved, even though the proposition that everything existing for me must derive its existential sense exclusively from me myself, from my sphere of consciousness, retains its validity and fundamental importance."

29 Husserl's conception of the possibility of intersubjectivity is discussed, for example, by Mohanty (1989), and especially Zahavi (1996, 2001, 2003, 2005, 2012); cf. Smith and Smith (1995) and Philipse (1995) for an analysis of Husserl's transcendental idealism. A most illuminating treatment of Husserl's place in the transcendental tradition is Carr's (1999) interpretation of what he calls "the paradox of subjectivity": according to Husserl (and Carr), the self must be described as both empirical (in the world) and transcendental (as a subject to whom the world is given). Arguably, Husserl does not have the classical skeptical problem of solipsism but does have the problem of transcendental (or transcendentally reinterpreted methodological) solipsism. Overgaard (2002) defends a non-Cartesian, transcendental reading of Husser's *epoché* and the "solipsistic reduction"; for Overgaard's excellent discussion of intersubjectivity and otherness in phenomenology, see his (2007).

30 However, Zahavi's account of Kant's understanding of transcendental subjectivity as an "isolated ego" (Zahavi 1996: 236) is problematic. We should not speak about a "classical Cartesian-Kantian subject-philosophy" (Zahavi 1996: 242; cf. Zahavi 2001), not even to contrast it with Husserl's intersubjective account of the subject, since Descartes's and Kant's concepts of the subject are fundamentally different: the former postulated a substantial, metaphysical self, whereas the latter regarded the "I think" as a formal principle. Compare Mohanty's (1985, 1989) account of the possibility of phenomenological transcendental philosophy. Mohanty defines the concept of transcendental subjectivity as "the field in which all mundane concepts have their origin" and which cannot, therefore, itself be described in mundane terms (Mohanty 1985: xxiv).

31 English translation: "constituted purely within me, the meditating ego, purely by virtue of sources belonging to my intentionality."
32 See also Römpp (1992) on the significance of the problem of overcoming solipsism through a phenomenological investigation of intersubjectivity in Husserl. Carr (1987: chapter 2) argues that Husserl's problem of solipsism (in the *Cartesian Meditations*) is non-Cartesian and non-skeptical: the problem is to give a phenomenological grounding of the very concept of an *alter ego*, not to justify the view that others exist (1987: 49–50). The question is, thus, "*how* the others exist"—for me—that is, we are dealing with the problem of making "phenomenological sense" of other egos (1987: 50). More specifically, the problem is how anything that is not an object (*Gegenstand*) but another subject can be given to me (1987: 52–53); Husserl's "solution," according to Carr, is that "the alter ego is not posited *outside* my own experience; rather, he is *brought into* the sphere of my own experience through the broadening of the concept of experience" (1987: 60). This is, though non-Cartesian, also clearly solipsistic in a transcendental sense. See also Heinämaa (2012) on the intersubjective phenomenology of embodiment.
33 This is noted by Merleau-Ponty (1962: 60) and more recent scholars (e.g., Baldwin 1988: 37). Jacques (1982: 132), arguing that Husserlian phenomenology is committed to solipsism, notes that even *Krisis* is solipsistic: the other person is "constituted with a meaning that refers back to myself." Solipsism postulates "the *only* logically and transcendentally possible center," subjective consciousness; this transcendental solipsism is not avoided by admitting that my "concrete self" is not privileged (1982: 133).
34 According to Apel (1998), this is the main defect of Husserl's philosophy. Phenomenology lies firmly in the paradigm of the "philosophy of consciousness" and begins from a first-person perspective.
35 Some scholars, for example, Steeves (1998), find the account of *Cartesian Meditations* sufficient for a satisfactory phenomenology of intersubjectivity, as the Husserlian approach leads to the recognition that I am always fundamentally constituted as a member of a community in which there are other selves besides my own. Even here, however, otherness is constituted through *my* performing the transcendental phenomenological reduction and observing that the other cannot be bracketed *tout court*. Hence, solipsism is overcome only from a first-person point of view. See, however, Luft and Overgaard (2012) and Zahavi (2012) for more recent interpretations of phenomenology for which solipsism does not seem to be a major concern.

36 The Wittgensteinian identification of the world and (my) life is relevant here.
37 Yet, as Park explains, the solipsism that phenomenology—Wittgenstein's or Husserl's—cannot avoid is methodological rather than metaphysical or skeptical: the existence of other subjects is not "in fact" doubted, though the starting point is the first-person perspective (Park 1998: 66). It is debatable whether Husserlian phenomenology should be compared to the kind of methodological solipsism considered in Chapter 2 (cf. the dispute between Baldwin 1988 and Bell 1988). I prefer to call the methodological solipsism at issue here transcendental.
38 See, for example, Natanson (1981), Wider (1991, 1995), and Fretz (1992). Generally, one might claim that existentialists (perhaps beginning with Kierkegaard) are methodological solipsists: the starting point is always the individual subject, me—albeit in a non-Cartesian sense. At least some existentialists, perhaps Kierkegaard and Sartre in particular, could also be regarded as methodological ethical solipsists. Their ethical positions might be interpreted as requirements to act as if one were the only subject in the (ethical) world, that is, to act as a model to the entire humankind. (Cf. Chapter 5.)
39 That Sartre, as well as Husserl, remains within an essentially solipsistic framework, beginning from a private self, has been noted by several commentators. Cf., for example, Ehman (1966); Wider (1995) emphasizes the transcendental nature of Sartre's "idealism."
40 Cf. Mulhall (1996) and Glendinning (1998); the latter explicitly connects Heidegger's work with skepticism about other minds, speaking of "existential solipsism."
41 See Levine (2013) for a detailed discussion of the extent to which Wittgenstein was indebted to Russell even in his reflections on solipsism in the *Tractatus*; cf. Tejedor (2015: chapter 2) for Wittgenstein's disinterest in Russellian epistemologized solipsism.
42 The availability of Wittgenstein's philosophy remains a major scholarly question. This book is not a historical study; rather, I am treating Wittgenstein as a key point of departure in reflecting on a systematic philosophical question. My references to both Wittgenstein's own work and interpretive literature (used here as primary sources regarding our problem) are mostly limited to explicit discussions of solipsism. On the relevance of the *Nachlass* regarding the solipsism issue, cf. Stern (1996: 449–50). An interesting reference by Wittgenstein, in *Geheime Tagebücher* (February 8, 1914), to the need to judge one's life and one's philosophical views "by their compatibility with the 'strictly solipsistic point of view'" is discussed by Glock (1999: 446); see Wittgenstein (1992: 228–29); cf. Janik

(2001). Among introductions to Wittgenstein, Vossenkuhl (1995) is among the few in which solipsism is taken seriously as a major topic. Lalla (2002) deals specifically with the solipsism issue in Wittgenstein; I will return to his work in Chapter 4.

43 See especially Stenius (1960), Kannisto (1986), and Appelqvist (2012, 2013, 2016). As a scholarly issue, this remains unsettled. The thesis of Wittgenstein's Kantianism has been forcefully resisted: see, for example, Wallgren (2006); cf. Sullivan (1996) for a non-Kantian reading of solipsism in the *Tractatus*. There is, of course, the meta-level problem of whether we can read *any* doctrines into the *Tractatus*. The view that Wittgenstein is an ironist offering therapy for his readers instead of any ineffable metaphysical insights is developed by many scholars (e.g., Cora Diamond and James Conant) in Crary and Read (2000). As Diamond (1992: 1320) puts it, solipsism is *not* "an unspeakable truth"; rather, Wittgenstein uses the discussion of solipsism for the ethical purposes of his book. We need not decide this issue concerning the status of solipsism in the *Tractatus*. Even if the therapeutical readings of Wittgenstein were correct, the solipsism issue would be alive in the secondary literature. For a discussion of Wittgenstein's solipsism based on the Diamond-Conant interpretation of the *Tractatus*, see Kremer (2004); cf. Floyd (1998) and Chapter 5. For a thoroughgoing critique of Diamond's and her allies' reading of Wittgenstein, see Hacker (2001); cf. also, for example, Hessell (2018). *If* there are ineffable truths in the *Tractatus*, these clearly include the "truth" of solipsism (Hacker 2001: 100, 149–50); yet, according to Hacker, the later Wittgenstein shows solipsism to be "thoroughgoing muddle" (Hacker 2001: 167).

44 Hintikka (1958) and Anscombe (1959: 167) disagreed about the correct translation of §5.62. Later scholarship has shown that Hintikka was right: the phrase "Sprache die allein ich verstehe" refers to the only language I understand (i.e., *the* language), not to a language only I understand. McGuinness (2001: 8) speaks of the "language which *alone* I understand," emphasizing that although privacy is not at issue, the reference to language here is a reference to *the* language, the only language there is.

45 This link to Russell must be problematized, insofar as we view Wittgenstein's transcendental solipsism as fundamentally different from Russell's concern with Cartesian-like skeptical solipsism. In addition to Pears's writings, see McGuinness (2001: 2–3), Levine (2013), and Tejedor (2015).

46 I am not trying to determine whether the Hintikkas' phenomenological reading is plausible, and I will not offer any interpretation of my own of the status—logical or metaphysical—of Wittgenstein's "objects."

47 Accordingly, contemporary discussions of classical metaphysical and/or skeptical solipsism are obviously irrelevant from the Wittgensteinian perspective, though Hessell (2018) supposes Wittgenstein endorses "traditional" solipsism in the *Tractatus*.
48 There is no such problem of identifying the ego in Cartesian treatments of solipsism (Johnstone 1991: 197).
49 This dilemma has also been discussed by Puhl (1999: 42–47), who, like Pears, offers an anti-solipsistic (therapeutic) reading.
50 See also Overgaard (2007: chapter 5) for an analysis of how Wittgenstein, already in the *Tractatus* (and of course in the later work) rejects solipsism while appreciating the insight that there is a fundamental asymmetry between the first-person and the third-person perspectives; according to Overgaard, no solipsism follows from this asymmetry (here his view resembles Pears's). We will in Chapter 4 return to the elements of solipsism left in the later Wittgenstein; Overgaard's interpretation of Wittgenstein (and Levinas) will be commented on in Chapter 5.
51 Pears (1996: 128ff.) also considers the solipsist's concept of "pointing" and Wittgenstein's (later) critique of the solipsist's treatment of sensation types as analogous to her/his use of the concept of ego. See also here Pears (1993, 1998). For a summary of Pears's interpretation, see Child (1996). Child construes Pears's Wittgenstein's charge against the solipsist as a dilemma: either solipsism identifies the subject as a particular human being, in which case it is self-defeating, since the identification requires an ordinary physical world, or the solipsistic self "is spread over the whole world," in which case the theory is empty, collapsing to realism (Child 1996: 138). He claims that Pears leaves unexplained why anyone would want to be a solipsist, namely, where the solipsistic motivation comes from, and argues that Wittgenstein thought the temptation to solipsism arises from a misconstrual of the (genuine) first-/third-person asymmetry (Child 1996: 139ff.).
52 Pears (1987–88, vol. 1: 175) thinks that "Notes for Lectures on 'Private Experience' and 'Sense-data'" (in Wittgenstein 1993) is "the most profound discussion of solipsism in Wittgenstein's writings."
53 On the continuity of the themes of the private language argument in Wittgenstein's early and late thought (from a somewhat different angle), see Diamond (2000).
54 Cf. also Mounce (1981: chapter 9). Mounce (1997: 9–10) rejects construals of Wittgenstein's "solipsism" as a result of Schopenhauer's influence.
55 We should credit Pears also for his work on the influence of Russell's (1913) epistemology on Wittgenstein's (critique of) solipsism. According to Vossenkuhl (1995: 191), Russell's notion of solipsism is "vulgar" whereas Wittgenstein's is "critical" (but see Levine 2013).

Candlish (2007: 120) claims that Bradley was closer to Wittgenstein than to Russell regarding solipsism.
56 Choudhury (1953) also speaks of a transcendental form of solipsism, but in a way different from Wittgenstein. According to Choudhury, transcendental solipsism construes empirical reality (including temporality) as a "dream" of a higher, God-like self.
57 "Die Wahrheit des Solipsismus zeigt sich in der reinen Sprachlichkeit alles Verstehbaren.... Alles Sagbare und alles Denkbare liegt diesseits der Grenze [der Sprache], in *meiner* Sprache und damit in *meiner* Welt" (Vossenkuhl 1999: 220; cf. Vossenkuhl 1995: chapter 7).
58 See also Glock (1999: 447): "Any representation of the world occurs from a perspective which is *uniquely mine*. But since it is logically impossible that it should occur from any other perspective, this fact cannot be expressed in a meaningful bipolar proposition." It should be clear, though, that Wittgenstein is not asserting any "facts"; accordingly, transcendental idealism and even solipsism can still, *pace* Pears, be his preferred view although the solipsistic subject cannot be identified or "particularized" (see Tang 2011: 602, 606; Hessell 2018). Schroeder (2006: 93) also rejects Pears's interpretation as implausible, because Wittgenstein does claim solipsism to be true or even "entirely correct"; however, Schroeder problematically also claims transcendental idealism to be "absent" from the *Tractatus* (2006: 96).
59 Pears is right about the unidentifiability of the solipsistic metaphysical ego which is the locus of ethical value. But this unidentifiability is what should be expected. The relation between the unsayable "truth" of solipsism and Wittgenstein's conception of ethics has been well captured in Brockhaus's (1991: chapters 9–10) interpretation. He says (1991: 321–22): "If we could supply criteria for identity of the metaphysical ego ..., then our claim would necessarily be about something in the world, and thus would fail to be a possible candidate for the bearer of value. But ... there is no strain of Cartesian-Russellian scepticism in Wittgenstein; *that* there is a willing subject which is the bearer of value is ... 'bedrock.' This immediate consciousness of the criterionless uniqueness of the metaphysical ego lies at the roots of Wittgenstein's admiration for Pascal and Kierkegaard ...." Wittgenstein's "mysticism," then, "involves not only 'awe before the unconditioned,' awareness of the absolutely primitive position of Objects with their internal relations, but also the corresponding consciousness of the total uniqueness of the metaphysical subject" (1991: 322–23).
60 Most commentators discussing Wittgenstein's temporal solipsism (e.g., Coffa 1991; Hintikka 1996; Park 1998) fail to deal with his ethical views. Moore (1959: 311) tells us that Wittgenstein had confessed to have been tempted to say, "All that is real is the experience

of the present moment," or "All that is certain is the experience of the present moment" (quoted in Hintikka 1996: 243). Even though Hintikka is one of those who reject the standard solipsistic readings of the *Tractatus*, he reads Wittgenstein as maintaining that what solipsism of the present moment (i.e., not merely ordinary solipsism) means is "quite correct," though unstatable (Hintikka 1996: 249). Had Wittgenstein been explicit, he would have noted a parallel between "I" and "now": just as there is only one I and only one world, there is only one "now" (Hintikka 1996: 261). Hence, my experience now exhausts the world, according to the temporal solipsist. Presumably, the temporal solipsist suffers (or benefits?) from the unidentifiability of the "now" as much as from the unidentifiability of the ego, if Pears's argument is taken seriously. For a peculiar defense of a kind of temporal solipsism (egocentric presentism), see Hare (2009).

61 Vossenkuhl (1999: 222), however, problematically disentangles Wittgenstein's solipsism from any Kantian transcendental "subjectivism" or "idealism." Lalla (2002), in turn, endorses a solipsistic reading of Wittgenstein but argues that his solipsism is not merely grammatical or linguistic but metaphysical. (Cf. Chapter 4.)

62 Even Cook's (1994, 2000) empiricist reading, according to which solipsism is an unstable intermediary stage between unacceptable idealism and Wittgenstein's brand of phenomenalism, that is, "neutral monism" (which, for him, is "pure realism"), might enjoy some supporting evidence. In Cook's view, Wittgenstein maintained that neutral monism *à la* Mach (rather than, say, G. E. Moore's "realism") helps us avoid solipsism (Cook 1994: xvii, 7–8, 72, 121); a combination of empiricism, phenomenalism, and behaviorism was, according to Cook (2000: 14–15, 26–27), the only escape from solipsism by Wittgenstein's lights.

63 For a version of such (broadly) "new Wittgensteinian" criticism, directed against the attempt (by Williams 1974) to interpret both the early and the later Wittgenstein as a transcendental idealist, see Mulhall (2008). According to Mulhall (and his Wittgenstein), the distinction between idealism and realism is empty (Mulhall (2008): 388); moreover, the attempt (by Williams) to read transcendental idealism into the later Wittgenstein depends on the problematic prior assumption that there are elements of, for example, relativism and constructivism in the later Wittgenstein (Mulhall (2008): 394ff.). Mulhall, in my view, refuses to acknowledge the variety of the ways in which transcendental idealism can be developed without any prior philosophical commitment to, say, any given and fixed limits of language. For a therapeutic reading of Tractarian solipsism in relation to the confused problem of skepticism, see McManus (2004b).

Furthermore, as perceptive a reader of Wittgenstein as Putnam (2012: 342) offers a "deflationary" account of Tractarian solipsism, according to which transcendental idealism (and thus also solipsism) is, for Wittgenstein, "unintelligible nonsense."

64 The "I cannot have made the universe" line of argument against the solipsist was also explicitly formulated by Lafleur (1952) and has been proposed by many others as well.

65 Hacker (1986: 103) points out that the transcendental solipsist does not deny the (occasional) truth of propositions like "A has toothache" and "The tree is shedding its leaves"; s/he does not claim that the proposition "I am the only person who exists" is true (cf. Vossenkuhl 1995, 1999). Bell (1988: 53–58; 1990: 156–57) argues that Husserl's phenomenology is comparable to Kant's and Wittgenstein's views as a combination of transcendental solipsism and empirical realism.

66 Admittedly, the transcendental picture of the subject and the world here is far removed from Kant's, in which time as a form of pure intuition is a transcendental condition for the possibility of experience.

67 In solipsism of the present moment, it is, however, problematic to claim that the subject is embedded in a temporal world (of its own). The transcendental embeddedness must take place in an atemporal setting.

68 Wider seems to join Pears et al. by regarding Wittgenstein's (and Sartre's) solipsism as merely apparent. Like Wider, Carr (1999) classifies both Wittgenstein and Sartre as belonging to the "transcendental tradition" with Kant, Husserl, and the early Heidegger. These philosophers deal with the "paradox of subjectivity," distinguishing between the empirical subject (in the world) and the transcendental subject. Allison (2004 [1983]: 283–93; 1996: 65–66) has argued that a conception of subjectivity closely resembling Wittgenstein's may have been Kant's own, as the Kantian transcendental "I" is not an object of any kind, neither phenomenal nor noumenal. Kant's and Wittgenstein's affinities regarding the "I" should not be exaggerated, though, as Wittgenstein's linguistified transcendental idealism (solipsism) differs from Kant's faculty psychology. Yet, Johnstone (1991: 122), for one, fails to pay attention to the transcendental character of Wittgensteinian solipsism in claiming that since one's visual field is "simply a certain region of the world," it has, *contra* Wittgenstein, "neighbors." His claim that the Humean mind resembles the "neighborless assembly of sensations of Wittgenstein's solipsist" (1991: 122) is inaccurate, as there is no transcendental ego in Hume. The idea that the solipsist's mind would simply be a region of the world, for which the solipsist claims a privileged status, is thoroughly implausible. Jager (1972: 406) compares Russell's views with Wittgenstein's, speaking about a

"solipsism without a subject" even in Russell's case, though Russell did not focus on the intelligibility of solipsism (without a subject) in Wittgenstein's transcendental way. Allen (2018), in turn, compares the Tractarian subject to a "singularity" in the logical space.

69 In addition to Kannisto (1986) (et al.), see the discussions of the Tractarian self and the "truth" of solipsism in Anscombe (1959: chapter 13), Coyne (1982), Brockhaus (1985), Hacker (1986: chapter 4), Bouveresse (1987: chapter 1), Coffa (1991: chapter 13), Stern (1995: chapter 3), Watzka (2000), Jacquette (2002), Lalla (2002), Vossenkuhl (2009), Levine (2013), Appelqvist (2013, 2016), Tejedor (2015: chapters 2–3), Allen (2018), and Hessell (2018).

70 Cf. also Bell (1996: 167–68), Vossenkuhl (1999), and Gmür (2000: chapter 4). The brief remarks on solipsism available in the recently published notes of Wittgenstein's 1933 Cambridge lectures by G. E. Moore are also relevant to precisely this issue. Wittgenstein is reported to have suggested that solipsism is "right" if it merely says that "I have tooth-ache" is "on quite a different level from" third-person attributions of toothache, while being "absurd" if it claims that I (the solipsist) have something the other does not have (Wittgenstein 2016: 284 [8:24]). There is nothing—such as an experience, a visual field, or anything identifiable—that the solipsist possesses and others do not possess. As a "statement of fact," the solipsist's claim, "Only my experience is real," is, then, "absurd" (Wittgenstein 2016: 273 [8:6]); what ought to be said, according to Wittgenstein, is that the "visual field is nothing that belongs to any person" (Wittgenstein 2016: 271 [8:2]).

71 "Postmodern" repudiations of the Cartesian (or Enlightenment) notion of an autonomous thinking and representing subject are not far from this view, after all, though Wittgenstein's transcendental concerns must be carefully distinguished from mere Humean-like skepticism about the substantiality of the self.

72 For this and other relevant references to Schopenhauer, see Hacker (1986: 88, 94, 96). Cf. Griffiths (1974), Janik (1985: chapter 2), Worthington (1988), Brockhaus (1991), and Glock (1999). Janik (1985: 45) believes that Schopenhauer's thought culminates in a "mystical solipsism," which, in Wittgenstein, results in an identification of "the noumenal will" with my will (1985: 47). See, however, Janaway's (1989: chapter 13), Mounce's (1997) and Linhe's (2002) reservations regarding the relevance of the Schopenhauerian background to Wittgenstein's alleged solipsism. Janaway (1989: 324) joins the non-solipsist interpreters of Wittgenstein, taking the coinciding of solipsism and realism to mean that "solipsism is an apparent philosophical position which undermines itself when one attempts to state it—and hence not

the kind of position to which Wittgenstein could have conceived himself to be adhering." On this reading, "all others are equally" the transcendental subject I am, since there cannot be any empirical individuation of this subject (1989: 324–25; see also 329). Solipsism, if meaningfully statable, would have to consider the "I" a "factual entity" in the world, which it cannot do (1989: 330). Nevertheless, Wittgenstein *is* (in the *Tractatus*) a kind of Schopenhauerian (and thus, on Janaway's assessment, not particularly original), for he regards "the world of objects for the subject" as equivalent to "the world of objects" (Janaway 1989: 330). In addition to Schopenhauer, Otto Weininger has been mentioned as a source of Wittgenstein's solipsism (Janik 1985, 2001: chapters 2 and 3; Haller 1988: chapter 6; McGuinness 2001: 4–5; Schroeder 2006: 11–12; cf. Weininger 1905: 196, 202).

73 Cf. again Chapter 4. We should not forget that the Tractarian solipsism is meaning theoretically motivated. On Kannisto's reading, as the meaning of a name is, in the *Tractatus*, a phenomenal thing, solipsism follows from the combination of the phenomenality of the Tractarian objects and the referential theory of meaning (Kannisto 1986: 144; cf. Miller 1980).

74 Still, the *Blue Book* argues that there are both subjective and objective "uses" of the pronoun "I" (and its relatives, such as "my" and "mine") (see Wittgenstein 1958: 66; cf. Sluga 1996: 334–35).

75 Nor should we think that any *metaphysical* "theory" could solve the problem of the self. Wittgenstein's solipsism as an element of his wish to (dis)solve the "problem of life" by avoiding metaphysical speculation about the world is discussed by Worthington (1988). McGuinness (2001: 10), however, offers the following metaphysical (though also anti-Cartesian) reconceptualization of the solipsism of the *Tractatus*: "Everyone is, and I in particular am, a measure of the world.... The point is that language has a centre, and when I speak or think, I am that centre. I alone—but the same would be true of anyone else. When I speak or think, it is the world-soul, die *Weltseele*, speaking, but so it is whoever speaks." But from my point of view (insofar as I am a solipsist), this *Weltseele* is me. It is true for me, and for me only, that the same in a sense holds for others, too; I cannot adopt the point of view of the other from which s/he can be identified with the world soul. These very words—the talk about the world soul, and so on—also receive whatever significance they have from my standing at the center of language.

76 Here, again, realism and solipsism "coincide." Bell (1996: 161) proposes the label "self-effacing solipsism."

77 This is denied by Russell (1912), though—but we may leave Russell's non-transcendental approach aside.

Chapter Four

1 But wouldn't he, in this case, be me? According to the solipsist, there is little sense in the idea that another subject, God for instance, would be the only subject there is. If there *is* only one subject, the center of everything, that subject must be me.
2 This problem is, for Hyslop (1995: 7ff.), an epistemological one concerning justification, not a "conceptual" one, since we can form the concept of others' having experiences as soon as we reject naive empiricism about meaning. For a study of the problem of other minds from a Wittgensteinian perspective focusing on the conceptual rather than the epistemic issue, see Vaaja (2015).
3 Since the problem of other minds, though related to our concerns, is distinct from the issue of solipsism, I will not discuss it specifically any further. For a classical treatment of the issue, see Wisdom (1965); cf. Sagal and Borg (1993) and Hyslop (1995); for more recent discussion, see Avramides (2001) and Vaaja (2015). For Wittgensteinian approaches to the reality of other human beings, see Vesey (1974a), Dilman (1974), Cockburn (1990), Gaita (2000, 2004), and Litwack (2009); cf. Chapter 5.
4 On transcendental philosophy and transcendental arguments, cf., e.g., Pihlström (2003), as well as contributions to Stern (1999) and Gava and Stern (2016).
5 Findlay (1984: 21, 115) also speculates that there might be a connection between Wittgenstein's temptation to solipsism and his "egocentric predicament."
6 Cf. the exchange between Srzednicki (1972) and Tlumak (1976) on the possibility of arguing transcendentally against solipsism. Hyslop (1995: chapter 9) also claims that Strawson fails to avoid the problem of other minds, while Johnstone (1991: chapters 5 and 8) rejects "parasitism arguments" against skeptical solipsism, namely, arguments claiming solipsism to be a violation of certain presuppositions of meaning, language use, or inquiry. He admits, though, that what he calls "Sensa Solipsism" (i.e., the view that "what exists is the private world of one's own sensations or representations"; see 1991: xvii) can be shown to "self-destruct" by means of a transcendental (parasitism) argument (1991: 112–13).
7 McGreal (1948: 180) refers to Occam in his defense of solipsism as a "simple and believable" hypothesis, but Ushenko (1948: 508) is suspicious of this.
8 It is not, however, "internal realism" exactly in Putnam's (1981, 1990) sense.

9 Kekes (1971) believes that solipsism can be refuted by appealing to the existence of rule-governed language, which is incompatible with the idea that only a solitary mind exists. Earlier, Lafleur (1952) suggested that the distinction between truth and falsity cannot be maintained on a solipsistic basis and that the claim that solipsism is true thus refutes itself. These critiques hardly apply to the transcendental version of solipsism.

10 Cf. also, e.g., Oliver (1970). Hacker (1986: chapter 8) discusses Wittgenstein's later "refutation" of solipsism on these grounds. Recalling that Wittgenstein's (1953: I, §309) famous fly in the flybottle was originally the solipsist (1953: 215), he concludes that Wittgenstein's early idea of solipsism and realism coinciding actually describes his *later* position relatively well, since the ostensive gesture and statements like "This is seen," when genuine, point to the world (1953: 243–44).

11 Allen's (1993: 138) argument, developed in a Wittgensteinian context, is relevant here: "The solipsist is right to doubt the significance of a reference to something strictly incommensurable with 'his own' experience, but wrong to think his title to subjectivity comes to him originally or by nature . . . . The notion of a private subject with private mental states is on a par with that of a private commodity with a private price, or money 'only I myself' can spend. Like commodities and prices, subjects and subjectivity do not exist apart from the signs of subjectivity in the intersubjective exchange of speech and reply. Take away the language-game, abstract from an intersubjective regard for the body and the signs it emits, ignore history, and bracket social practice, and *what it is like* (subjective similarity and difference) is as indeterminate as the time on the sun." Here, the anti-solipsistic argumentation is comparable to the argument from the unidentifiability of the solipsistic ego. Similarly, the phenomenologist may arrive at the insight that the phenomenological *epoché*, the bracketing of the external world, never leaves me with just *my* experiences, or my "sphere of ownness," since this would already require another subject to individuate *me*. There is no loneliness or isolation in abstraction from an intersubjective world (Steeves 1998: 17–20; Overgaard 2002).

12 Oliver (1970: 34) is puzzled about the possibility of making such a leap: "Natural solipsism [i.e., total autism] may be the real thing, but it remains an enigma to us. Philosophical solipsism is a kind of hoax . . . because what is required to make it a meaningful hypothesis is what it would destroy were it an actuality. In short, solipsism is an impossible possibility, a possibility that, if actualized, would render meaningless that which makes it seem to us a meaningful hypothesis."

13 The Hintikkas construe Wittgenstein's change of mind as a transition from a phenomenological basic language (whose objects are objects of acquaintance) to a physicalistic, everyday one. This change marks the boundary between the pre- and post-1929 Wittgensteins (Hintikka and Hintikka 1986: chapters 6–7; cf. Hintikka 1996; Park 1998; and Pears 1987–88).
14 We saw in Chapter 3 that Pears (1987–88, 1996, 2001) denies that even the *Tractatus* is a solipsistic work.
15 Hacker (1986: chapter 9), Pears (1987–88: chapters 13–15), and Diamond (2000) provide some of the best discussions of this argument. On the relevance of the solipsism issue to the private language argument in Wittgenstein's later work, see also Lalla (2002); I will get back to Lalla's views shortly.
16 I have dealt with the tradition of pragmatism in relation to the issue of realism and transcendental argumentation at some length in Pihlström (2003, 2013).
17 This could be seen as a basic line of thought in *On Certainty* (Wittgenstein 1969).
18 Cf., however, Putnam (1994, 1995); see also Pihlström (2003).
19 One might think that it is difficult to find any analogy to Kant, the father of transcendental philosophy, here. However, even Kant seems to think that the "vindication" of human reason must be irreducibly *public*; reason cannot be solipsistically vindicated. This is discussed in the Transcendental Doctrine of Method in the *Critique of Pure Reason*; cf. O'Neill (1989) for an illuminating commentary. Thornton's (2004: §7) argument against the coherence of solipsism is analogously transcendental: a solipsism we could so much as think must be formulated in language; hence, solipsism presupposes what it denies, namely, "the existence of the public, shared, intersubjective world" necessarily needed for language to be possible. (Thornton does not explicitly deal with transcendental solipsism, though.)
20 This is of course just a very simple characterization of pragmatism. For more details, see, for example, the essays in Pihlström (2015).
21 See Wittgenstein (1953: II, iv). Cf. Cavell (1979: 84, and especially 329ff). Saying that our relation to the existence of the world, including other people, is a relation to something "acknowledged," "accepted," or "received" enables us to express the depth of that relation as compared to (mere) knowledge (Cavell 1981: 133; also 106–07). This is a theme Cavell finds not only in Wittgenstein but also in Emerson and Thoreau, and even in Kant. He adds, however, that if an attitude toward a soul is possible, then "soul-blindness" also is (Cavell 1979: 378). For Putnam's references to Cavell's notion of acknowledgment, see further Putnam (1992: 75, 177–78).

22 Sluga (1996: 344, 353), discussing the ethical motivation of Wittgenstein's anti-theoretical attitude to the self, draws attention to Schopenhauer's claim that we must reject the individuality of the human self, if we wish to achieve an unselfish ethic. The passage he refers to (Schopenhauer 1969 [1844], vol. 1: §68 [378ff.]) contains the idea that one should "regard the endless sufferings of all lives as his own" and "take upon himself the pain of the whole world." See also Young (2005: 180–86). I will return to this theme and its ramifications with ethical solipsism in Chapter 5.

23 Cavell (1979: 36) says, "I find my general intuition of Wittgenstein's view of language to be the reverse of the idea many philosophers seem compelled to argue against in him: it is felt that Wittgenstein's view makes language too public, that it cannot do justice to the control I have over what I say, to the innerness of my meaning. But my wonder ... is rather how he can arrive at the completed and unshakable edifice of shared language from within such apparently fragile and intimate moments—private moments—as our separate counts and out-calls of phenomena, which are after all hardly more than our interpretations of what occurs, and with no assurance of conventions to back them up." Lear (1998: 266–69) also draws attention to the idea of "inner experience" in Wittgenstein, suggesting that it is a transcendental condition of our subjectivity that we have a non-observational access to our lives from an internal perspective. This applies to me as an individual and to us as the "subject" of a form of life.

24 See Putnam's discussion in his (1987: 85ff.).

25 Is this, by the way, a "moment" of time in the sense of solipsism of the present moment?

26 Thus, Wittgenstein's later philosophy—if interpreted as a further development of transcendental philosophy—despite its focus on public language games and rule-following, can be argued to be compatible with transcendental solipsism against which no "private language argument" would be effective. According to Cavell (1979: 369–70), the "fantasy" of a private language fails to capture the sense in which "we are endlessly separate, for *no* reason"—to express *how* private we (as individuals or as a culture, or form of life) are, metaphysically and practically.

27 On the analogy between the transcendental subject and the "we" of Wittgenstein's later philosophy, see Lear (1998: chapters 11 and 12). With Lear, I find Malcolm's (1982) reply to Williams, claiming that there is "no tendency towards any form of idealism" in Wittgenstein's later philosophy, unconvincing. There *is* an element of idealism or even solipsism in the way in which *our* world gets structured through

our language games and forms of life. The perspectival character of our world-engagement is still present in the later Wittgenstein, *pace* Malcolm's claim that "aggregative solipsism" is a contradiction in terms (1982: 261). Mulhall (2008), however, criticizes even the view that the early Wittgenstein is a transcendental idealist. It should, furthermore, be noted that Wittgenstein's later philosophy is full of insights—and tensions—regarding our ability to understand "others" and their forms of life quite independently of the issue of (transcendental) solipsism; see, for example, Sandis's (2012, 2015) fascinating discussions.

28 This interpretation is sociologized and thus, to some extent, naturalized by Bloor (1996); see also Dilman (2004).

29 According to Kripke, Wittgenstein provides a "skeptical solution" to the "skeptical paradox" of rule-following; the issue of other minds is, moreover, analogous to that paradox (see the postscript to Kripke 1982). Kripke has been powerfully criticized by Putnam (1994), Hyslop (1995), and Lear (1998: chapter 12), among many others.

30 On Wittgenstein as a transcendental idealist even in his later thought, see also Lear (1998); cf. Pihlström (2003). Findlay (1984: 221) speculates that Wittgenstein's "extreme 'publicism'" in the *Investigations* may reflect "the secret working of his never abandoned, ultimate solipsism." In Findlay's view, however, the idea that the criteria of meaning of interpersonal speech among "talking and listening animals" which are "in the one world public to them all" would be (transcendentally) "private to a single, empty self" is irrelevant and unmentionable (see 1984: 123, 228). The idealistic interpretation is also manifested in the thesis that language games are, in later Wittgenstein, "truly the measure of all things" (Hintikka and Hintikka 1986: 196). In addition to idealism, the issues of relativism and understanding alien cultures have been explored in the Wittgensteinian tradition associated with such philosophers as (e.g.) Winch, Malcolm, Rhees, and Hertzberg. Although solipsism is seldom explicitly treated in these discussions, we should not overlook the analogy between solipsism and (radical) cultural relativism. Putnam, among many critics of relativism, has argued that relativism resembles solipsism as an (imagined) transcendental stance with the transcendental ego being replaced by a community engaging in a form of life incomprehensible "from the outside." (Similar remarks may apply to the notion of a "transcendental 'we'" in Husserl's phenomenology of intersubjectivity; cf. Husserl 1931: §49 [110].) Putnam often refers to solipsism rhetorically, for example, when he (1981: 216) reminds us that we are not caught in our "solipsistic hells" but are invited into a "human dialogue." Against radical

relativism, he repeatedly claims that it becomes indistinguishable from a "solipsism with a 'we' instead of an 'I'" (Putnam 1990, 1992, 1994).

31 Should we call this movement solipsistic? Interestingly, both Pears, who reads Wittgenstein non-solipsistically, and Bell, who reads him solipsistically, see a fundamental continuity between the Tractarian reflections on solipsism and the private language argument (see also Diamond 2000).

32 See Gmür's (2000: 116–19) discussion of how this grammatical solipsism "practically" coincides with realism; cf. Watzka's (2000: 133ff.) reflections on the idea that the solipsist, even in the *Investigations*, is "right" to the extent that sense impressions *are* private. Watzka goes as far as to say that the "metaphysician" of the *Investigations* and of the *Blue Book* is the solipsist (2000: 20). Vossenkuhl (1995: 317) even notes that Wittgenstein was "a practicing solipsist" in his method of writing philosophy as a kind of self-examination.

33 Cf. here the comment on the solipsistic tendencies of Nagel's (1979, 1986) views on *qualia* (in Chapter 2). See also, again, the remark by Wittgenstein (in 1933) about solipsism being "right" in the sense that the claims concerning my having toothache and another person having toothache are "on quite a different level" (Wittgenstein 2016: 284 [8:24]).

34 Vossenkuhl (1999: 242–43) concludes that solipsism resembles the Kantian *Ding an sich* in its limiting role. (See also Vossenkuhl 1995: 190.) Still, it is somewhat doubtful whether solipsism could be a view that "everyone" holds. It is tempting to think, again, that solipsism, if true, could be true, or could even be coherently maintained, by me only. The truth of the solipsistic insight, if there is any, could concern only me; for others, this could (from my point of view) only be a false insight.

35 For Lalla's argument against Vossenkuhl, see Lalla (2002: 130ff.).

36 The private language argument, on Lalla's interpretation, addresses the essential difference between public and private languages, instead of the impossibility of the latter (Lalla 2002: 110–11). Attempts to "harmonize" public and private languages cannot succeed. One of Lalla's (Lalla 2002: 126) key references is the following characterization of an "intersubjectively relevant solipsism" by Wittgenstein (1953: I, §272): "Das Wesentliche am privaten Erlebnis ist eigentlich nicht, daß Jeder sein eigenes Exemplar besitzt, sondern daß keiner weiß, ob der Andere auch *dies* hat, oder etwas anderes." Unfortunately Overgaard's (2007) insightful defense of a non-solipsistic account of Wittgenstein fails to engage with Lalla's reading.

37 The kind of moral realism and the related realism about other minds defended (transcendentally) by the pragmatist should be made much clearer than is possible here (see Pihlström 2003, 2005, 2009). The pragmatic realist obviously believes in the genuine reality of other people—in their reality as subjects, centers of experience and valuation, to be taken seriously in the ethical assessment of our actions. Such a realist may postulate other subjects on the basis of the kind of pragmatic-transcendental argument explored above. S/he may also maintain, for instance, that valuational judgments have truth-values, that is, are true or false depending on how (humanly constructed) normative reality (particularly one's relations to other subjects) is arranged.

38 Nor does the transcendental solipsist need to think that the special position of the solipsistic ego or its relation to its (the only) world needs argumentative justification. Lalla (2002: 70–71) speaks about "ungrounded facticity" (*unbegründeten Faktizität*), pointing out that it is nonsensical to ask for a "justification" of the solipsistic (transcendental) self.

39 This quietism, if it may be so called, can be seen as derived from Wittgenstein himself: "The proposition that only the present experience has reality appears to contain the last consequence of solipsism. And in a sense that is so; only what it is able to say amounts to just as little as can be said by solipsism.—For what belongs to the essence of the world simply *cannot* be said. And philosophy, if it were to say anything, would have to describe the essence of the world" (Wittgenstein 1975: §54 [85]).

40 In contrast, Lalla (2002: 141) points out, referring to Wittgenstein's *Blue Book*, that there are no commonsensical answers to a philosophical problem and that, accordingly, a kind of unintelligibility is an essential element of solipsism. (It is not an accident, or a mere contingent fact, that solipsism, in the transcendental sense, cannot be meaningfully expressed. It is a philosophical background assumption of whatever can be expressed.) By insisting on the inseparability of philosophical questions and practical life, I by no means wish to deny that solipsism is first and foremost a philosophical problem, far removed from daily concerns. What its practical relevance amounts to is its potentially emergence in relation to any practical activity, including linguistic activity, we ordinarily engage in.

41 It has been claimed (e.g., Bode 1905) that James's radical empiricism leads to solipsism. James's response is contained in his (1912); cf. Pihlström (2008: chapter 5). On James's worries about the problem of other minds, see DeArmey (1982); for an insightful discussion of how

James in his radical empiricism sought to escape from "congeries of solipsism," see Putnam and Putnam (2017: 153–54, 355–59).
42 I discuss James's concerns with solipsism in a more scholarly fashion in Pihlström (2008: chapter 5). As this book does not focus on pragmatism or James, I leave those issues out of the present discussion.
43 O'Brien (1996: 191–92) refers to Merleau-Ponty's phenomenology of the body as an example of the rejection of a merely perceptual model of self-representation (a key premise in Wittgenstein's critique of the representability of the self). She argues, however, that though Merleau-Ponty deals with a "thoroughly situated self," his view on the body is close to Wittgenstein's view on the self: I do not observe my body, and my body is not merely one external object among others (cf. Merleau-Ponty 1962: 91–92). Still, O'Brien (1996: 192) makes a pragmatist point by insisting that, *pace* Merleau-Ponty, "we experience our bodies through experiencing the world—through handling things, examining them and walking around them." This emphasis on reflexivity—our experiencing ourselves *as* experiencing ourselves and the world outside ourselves—can, furthermore, be accommodated within a naturalized transcendentalist framework.
44 The topic of *love* is one of the curiosities of Sartre's phenomenological and existentialist analysis. One might speculate that any solipsistic philosophy of love is as paradoxical as Sartre's existentialist conception of the subject in general. The lover desires the object of her/his love as a free subject, capable of a genuine act of love from their own part. Simultaneously, s/he reduces the other into a mere object of her/his own love and desire. How could a solipsist expect love from anyone—or could the solipsist come back, even here? For a reflection on the relation between solipsism and love in a Kantian context, and on love (as well as friendship) as "an escape from solipsism," see Langton (1997, 2009: chapters 14–15).

Chapter Five

1 This is, of course, not an entirely novel idea. Clark (1964) argues that the choice between "absolutist" and "solipsist" epistemologies—which, according to Kremer (1960) to whom Clark replies, both beg the question—may be understood as a moral choice.
2 Recall that the identifiability of the ego is, according to Pears (1987–88), of primary importance in the *Tractatus*. However, the

"individuation" of the self through values, or ethics, is different from the kind of identification Pears finds problematic; surely, the self cannot be individuated as an object in the world.

3 In addition to the *Tractatus*, Wittgenstein's main texts on ethics include his early notebook remarks (Wittgenstein 1961), his 1929 "Lecture on Ethics" (Wittgenstein 1965), and his conversations with Friedrich Waissman in 1929–30 (Wittgenstein 1967b). On Wittgenstein's ethical background in the Viennese cultural life, cf. also Janik and Toulmin (1973), Janik (1985, 2001), and Gellner (1998). Janik (2001: 84) describes how our "culture of narcissism" was anticipated in *fin de siècle* Vienna: subjective intensity emerged as an "ultimate criterion of truth."

4 Hintikka and Hintikka (1986: 68) controversially suggest a Moorean (and "Bloomsburyan") background for this view: "If [the] immediate objects of Moorean valuable experiences ['aesthetic enjoyment' and 'pleasures of personal affection']—the emotional cousins of Russell's and Moore's sense-data—are among Wittgenstein's objects in the *Tractatus*, it will be literally true that the world (the totality of objects) of a person who has valuable experiences is different from that of a person who does not."

5 Nagel seems to claim that any actions based on merely subjective (instead of objective, impersonal, or altruistic) reasons commit the subject to solipsism. For a sustained critical discussion, see Sturgeon (1974); cf. Nagel (1986: 159).

6 Quine's naturalized epistemology is the paradigmatic example here; see, for example, Quine (1995). Stroll (2000: 186) describes Quine as a "practical solipsist," but this characterizes his philosophical style rather than his position.

7 For illuminating discussions, see Watzka (2000), and Appelqvist (2013, 2016); cf. also Kremer (2004).

8 Solipsism is sometimes taken to be close to (ethical) nihilism. Duff and Marshall (1982) argue that Albert Camus moved from a solipsistic-nihilistic view expressed in *The Outsider* (1942) to a moral position affirming the importance of a community of human beings in the existentialist hero's rebellion against the absurdity of existence. The world of Meursault, the protagonist of *The Outsider*, is solipsistic, because he has no understanding of the dimension of other people's lives (or, for that matter, his own) that is "informed by values, emotions and interests," failing to "recognise the reality of other people" and even "his own reality as a person" (Duff and Marshall 1982: 120). This world "approximates to a genuinely nihilistic world, empty of meaning and value" (Duff and Marshall 1982: 120), and Meursault is even close to being a solipsist of the

present moment, for he only reacts to immediate stimuli coming from his present environment (Duff and Marshall 1982: 119–20). Arguably, no moral "rebellion" is possible in such a world. Hence, the "solipsistic nihilism" that finds expression in Meursault's character is "transcended towards a moral understanding of the world" in Camus's later period; this, in effect, is a recognition of truly *human* (communal) life (Duff and Marshall 1982: 130).

9   Linhe's (1996: 26, 40–42) discussion is also misleading, since he assumes that Wittgenstein places ethics and the metaphysical subject in a transcendent otherworldly "domain." Brockhaus (1991), in contrast, reminds us that no otherworldliness should be read into Wittgenstein's ethical views. The status of ethics as in a sense both transcendental and transcendent is interestingly discussed by Stokhof (2002): far from belonging to an ontologically transcendent realm, ethics is an inner feature of the world (my world, the world as identified with my life), and thus a transcendental precondition of the world. Stokhof argues that Wittgenstein develops a logical (as distinguished from ontological) notion of transcendence (Stokhof 2002: chapter 4, especially 235–38). I discuss Stokhof's reading in Pihlström (2011: chapter 5). For Wittgenstein as a "moral solipsist," see also Schroeder (2006: 101–04).

10 McGreal (1948: 180) says, "To understand phenomenal creatures as illusory persons, and yet to deal with them as though they were real—that is the secret of happy solipsism!" This is reminiscent of Hans Vaihinger's fictionalist philosophy of "as if" (*als ob*).

11 This "impure" picture of morality as relying on natural human needs and concerns is associated with the pragmatists' moral philosophies. I have discussed the connection between James's apparently non-Kantian ethics and Kantian deontology in Pihlström (2008, 2013); for an explicitly transcendental investigation of pragmatic moral realism, see Pihlström (2005). Cf. also Kivistö and Pihlström (2016: chapter 5) and Pihlström (2020).

12 This feature of the *Tractatus* is not explicitly discussed in Kannisto (1986). Kannisto examines Wittgenstein's attitude to ethics only in some of his Finnish writings.

13 For a discussion of *Heart of Darkness* as a description of "utter solitude" and "ultimate loneliness," see Pettersson (1982: 81–84). Rudrun (2005) also interestingly explores Kurtz's solipsism in the novel; on the basis of his analysis, it could be suggested that an attempt (such as Marlow's) to know and understand another self (Kurtz) might teach a lesson about the "truth in solipsism." Guetti (2004: 263–64) explicitly compares Kurtz's solipsism to Wittgenstein's Tractarian remarks.

14 As developed by, e.g., Winch (1972, 1987), Dilman (1974), Cavell (1979), Cockburn (1990), Gaita (2000, 2004), and Phillips (1992). Cf. Wittgenstein (1953: II, iv); see several essays in Vesey (1974b). On the later Wittgenstein's conception of the "soul," see also von Savigny and Scholz (1995) and von Savigny (1996).

15 Steeves (1998: 8n) puts it clearly: "An ethic need not to [sic] be 'founded,' for the ethical world *is* our world, appearing to us at every moment" (Cf. 1998: 62ff.).

16 Nagel's attitude to (metaphysical) solipsism is relevant here: "I regard [solipsism] as a position to be taken seriously; what is correct in it, I believe, is that if one begins with the sole idea of oneself and one's own experiences as a model, one may not have sufficient material to extrapolate to a significant notion of other selves and their experiences. . . . The avoidance of solipsism requires that the *conception* of other persons like oneself (not necessarily the belief that there are any) be included in the idea of one's own experiences from the beginning. . . . What is important is that we are not solipsists, and that the rejection of solipsism involves a capacity to view ourselves and our circumstances impersonally" (Nagel 1970: 106).

17 Our attitude to other human beings may, however, be both sympathetic and unsympathetic, and there is no reason to deny that the latter kind of reaction can be, and often is, a case of an attitude toward a soul (see Phillips 1992: 240, 255).

18 Thomas (1999: 201) refers to Rilke's poems here, observing that the poet "can achieve a sense of being unharmed by the vicissitudes and sufferings which threaten" by being "absorbed in the timeless present, looking neither to the past nor the future." Other classics in whose works Thomas (2001: chapter 3) finds the roots of Wittgenstein's "*Weltbild* of self-concern" include, e.g., Kant and Schopenhauer (2001: 76, 86–87). This worldview is characterized by "an obsessive seeking to give to the self a sense of independence in confronting an impersonal universe" (2001: 77), and the culmination of this seeking is suicide (as in Weininger's case). On solipsism of the present moment, see also, e.g., Dovel (2007: 44–58).

19 As Glock (1999: 449) puts it, "Either the world in itself is totally deprived of individuality, in which case I cannot find myself in it; or I can find myself in it, in which case I somehow extend my concept of self to the world as a whole, which would turn altruism into a gigantic form of egoism." According to Glock, Wittgenstein's transcendental solipsism is based on the recognition of this Schopenhauerian difficulty (1999: 449).

20 Kremer (2004) claims, however, that this kind of ethical selflessness *is* already achieved in the *Tractatus*, since the work should be read as

a therapeutical attempt to show the nonsensicality of metaphysical notions like the (transcendental) subject, the "owner" of the world. Kremer joins the resolute therapeutical interpreters (cf. again Crary and Read 2000), for whom Tractarian nonsense (including the solipsistic conception of the subject as the bearer of value) is simply nonsense. While I am construing the Tractarian picture of ethics in a transcendental fashion, Kremer is right in claiming that Wittgenstein's work belongs to the tradition of mystical thought. Religious mysticism is a heterogeneous tradition with the aspiration for selflessness as an ethical ideal as a pervasive feature. But whether this be Christian, Buddhist, Wittgensteinian, or a combination of various sources, the question remains whether the "unselfing" process still amounts to something like (methodological) ethical solipsism: it is always *me* whose self ought to be "emptied" in favor of a truly ethical life.

21 "I would urge that the concept of self-renunciation is fundamental [in Christianity, in religion in general] in that it determines the nature of what can count as the self's religiously authentic relation to God. As such, it determines one's understanding of the concept 'God' itself" (Thomas 2001: 123).

22 For a multifarious set of responses to the Cavellian theme of skepticism in Wittgenstein, see McManus (2004a).

23 On the need to acknowledge even extreme evildoers as our fellow human beings, and on the mysteriousness of such acknowledgment, see Gaita (2000). For Gaita's reflections on Wittgenstein's remark about having an attitude toward a soul and for his denial that such an attitude constitutes propositional knowledge of "other minds," see (Gaita 2000: chapter 10); cf. Winch (1987: chapters 10–12). Kannisto has pointed out, in conversation, that it is hardly a coincidence that Wittgenstein employs *pain* as a typical example regarding solipsism and the reality of others' experiences. The pain of the other is an irreducible moral category, and using it as a philosophical example makes Wittgenstein's reflections on other minds ethically relevant from the beginning. For a highly relevant discussion, see Read (2010).

24 Levinas's seminal work on this theme is *Totalité et infini* (1971); see also Levinas (1989). For reflections on Levinas's thought relevant to our topic, cf., e.g., Peperzak (1995), Beavers (1995), Critchley and Bernasconi (2002), and Morgan (2007). Crowell (1999), in turn, appeals to Levinas in his assessment of the development of transcendental philosophy, while Morgan (2007) is one of the most detailed studies on Levinas situating him in the transcendental tradition, also noting similarities to Cavellian acknowledgment and other Wittgensteinian themes (e.g., Morgan 2007: 76–78).

25 This, as well as the way in which Levinas's work belongs to the Husserlian tradition, is well expressed in a collection of his essays on Husserl (Levinas 1998). In a 1940 paper dealing with Husserl, Levinas says that the Husserlian subject is posited as a "monad" and that intersubjectivity, too, is constituted on a solipsistic basis (Levinas 1998: 82–83). This "solipsism" does not deny the existence of others, but the subject can, in principle, be considered "as if it were alone" (Levinas 1998: 83). Thus, "the possibility of solipsism" remains in Husserlian phenomenology (Levinas 1998: 85; cf. Chapter 3).

26 For an argument questioning the efficacy of transcendental arguments as attempted refutations of the imagined figure of a "moral solipsist," see Badenhop (2017).

27 Quoting a statement from *Totalité et infini* ("Solipsism is neither an aberration nor a sophism, it is the very structure of reason"), Jacques (1982: 139–42) criticizes what he takes to be Levinas's inadequate recognition of otherness. In his view, Levinas faces a tension between an accurate ethical description of otherness and "a metaphysics that sees the condition of all beings as one of separation and radical exteriority" (1982: 141). "If the absolute solitude of each being in its own existence is primary, as it is for Levinas," he claims, "then any relation, any movement toward the other can only arise from the depths of that solitude" (1982: 142).

28 Still, Cavell (1979: 361) construes the outcome of the private language argument thus: "I think one moral of the *Investigations* as a whole can be drawn as follows: The fact, and the state, of your (inner) life cannot take its importance from anything special in it. However far you have gone with it, you will find that what is common is there before you are. The state of your life may be, and may be all that is, worth your infinite interest. But then that can only exist along with a complete disinterest toward it. The soul is impersonal."

29 Levinas (1989: 48) writes, "The Other as Other is not only an alter ego: the Other is what I myself am not. The Other is this, not because of the Other's character, or physiognomy, or psychology, but because of the Other's very alterity." If the solipsist is construed as a Levinasian other, this must not be based on her/his (someone's) contingently being a solipsist. The issue is not psychological but—I would again like to say—transcendental. "The transcendental *I* in its nakedness comes from the awakening by and for the other," Levinas (1999: 98) says. Cf. Morgan (2007).

30 See the various formulations of this distinction in Levinas (1989).

31 The late-Wittgensteinian picture of language as based on public human actions and forms of life seems clearly anti-solipsistic: our language games rest on our *trust* in other language users (see

Wittgenstein 1969: §§ 508–09; Putnam 1992: 177–78; cf. Hertzberg 1994). We must acknowledge other people without any guarantees (Putnam 1992: 178). The price, however, is the persistence of the issue of solipsism. It is *me* whose task it is to trust others, to build up our common language on the uncertain grounds (Cavellian "private moments") of trust. It is, more generally, *me* for whom an "approach" to others is necessary in the first place: "I need an 'approach' to others, not for myself. My view of others is an attitude towards them, as souls, but I do not, symmetrically, approach myself this way. I do not have an attitude towards myself, that I have a soul. . . . There is a problem about others, not about myself" (Hyslop 1995: 124). So, the asymmetry between me and the others remains, quasi-solipsistically, even if and perhaps especially when I non-solipsistically acknowledge the others' reality and trustworthiness.

32 Gellner's reading of Wittgenstein is in many ways superficial, but he succeeds in formulating a crucial ethical point against Wittgenstein's conception of death: "If death is not an event in life, then at any rate it would seem that the death of others would be a part of life. But the *Tractatus* appears to be an autistic work in which there simply are no others. . . . If there are no *others*, then indeed, death cannot be a part of life. For the author of the *Tractatus*, evidently this was so" (Gellner 1998: 63).

33 See Pihlström (2016) for a more comprehensive Wittgensteinian-Levinasian reflection on the topic of this section.

34 See also several essays in Malpas and Solomon (1998). Solomon (1998) questions our tendency to over-celebrate death and mortality by forgetting their social dimension. Bauman (1992: 3ff., 15, 18, 34, 50–51, 130, 142) provides a powerful analysis of the ultimate subjectivity (mineness) of death, that is, the idea that my death (and my death only) is not an event but something unexperienceable and utterly lonely. Bauman's descriptions of postmodernity and the eternity of every present (1992: 168, 199) are actually close to solipsism of the present moment.

35 See, however, Leman-Stefanovic (1987) for an attempt to take seriously the "ontological significance" of the "ontic" event of another's death in a Heideggerian setting.

36 This, in my view, indicates the depth of Levinas's position. His being caught in the web of solipsism through the notion of one's infinite personal responsibility is far more subtle than the relatively simple rejection of solipsistic conceptions of death by, e.g., Elias (1982). Still, focusing on the personal, solipsistic nature of death as mine should by no means prevent us from recognizing the social, socio-anthropological, historical (etc.) conditions or contexts in which

the notion of death is inevitably situated—including the notion of death as something fundamentally personal or solipsistic. The transcendental solipsist, for whom death is first and foremost my concern, can easily be an empirical realist about mortal matters.

37 The same critique applies, mutatis mutandis, to other phenomenological theories of intersubjective morality, such as Steeves's (1998), which is close to a Levinasian position.

38 See also Levinas (1999: 5, 24–25, 27, 30). I am responsible even for the Other's responsibility: "To be oneself, otherwise than being, to be dis-interested, is to bear the wretchedness and bankruptcy of the other, and even the responsibility that the other can have for me. To be oneself, the state of being a hostage, is always to have one degree of responsibility more, the responsibility for the responsibility of the other" (Levinas 1989: 107). See also (Levinas 1989: 226): "I always have, myself, one responsibility more than anyone else, since I am responsible, in addition, for his [the other's] responsibility. And if he is responsible for my responsibility, I remain responsible for the responsibility he has for my responsibility." (Cf. further Levinas 1989: 245–46; Levinas 1999: 105–06.) Things get complicated, however, when one adds Levinas's concept of God to the picture. God, for him, is "other than the other," "other otherwise, other with an alterity prior to the alterity of the other, prior to the ethical bond with another and different from every neighbour" (Levinas 1989: 179). Could I meaningfully be said to be responsible even for the responsibility of such an extremely, unspeakably, other? Another problem is that even though I always have one responsibility more than the other, my responsibility originates in the other. If this is correct, could I ever be responsible for killing the other? In the act of killing, the conditions for the possibility of responsibility seem to be taken away.

39 One should also mention Schopenhauer here. A quasi-solipsist conception of ethics is, I think, presupposed by those who follow Schopenhauer (and his oriental sources) and locate the beginning of ethics in the *compassion* that arises when "I see the suffering of others to be, on the transphenomenal level, *my* suffering" (Brockhaus 1991: 58). Isn't it solipsistic to assert, *tat twam asi* ("this art thou")? (Cf. Schopenhauer 1969 [1844], vol. 1: 370–74).

40 Beavers situates Levinas in the Cartesian tradition: Levinas shares with Descartes, among other things, a view of "the finite mind turned inside out by the idea of infinity" (Beavers 1995: 2). At least in *Totalité et infini* (Levinas 1971), the revelation of the other person as the beginning of ethics presupposes that the "egoistic self" is already established, since the other calls my egoism into question (Beavers 1995: 69). Something that does not exist can hardly be called into

question. Beavers seeks to reconcile Levinasian concreteness and Kantian universalism, for Kantian ethics can be said to articulate the Levinasian position "within the horizons of reason" (Beavers 1995: 122). But, again, the framework of solipsism is not left behind: "[The] Kantian theory is justified precisely at the moment when the call to responsibility is answered by *my* concrete moral response" (Beavers 1995: 127; see also 130).

41 Levinas (1999: 28) also writes, "The *I* is the very crisis of the being of a being . . . in the human . . ., because, being myself, I already ask myself whether my being is justified, whether the *Da* of my *Dasein* is not already the usurpation of someone's place." See also (1999: 164).

42 Overgaard's account of Wittgenstein and Levinas is set in the context of his intersubjectivist reading of Husserl (see Chapter 3). In Husserlian terms, he says, "It is precisely because I am the *Ur-Ich*, that is, because I stay firmly rooted in my own subjective life, in my own perspective, that there can be others for me" (Overgaard 2007: 102).

43 Regarding Levinas, Overgaard (2007: 156) in my view problematically views ethics, though it makes an infinite demand on me, only one consideration among others: "*Within* the ethical order, or from an exclusively ethical viewpoint, I am infinitely responsible. However, human life makes many other claims on me . . . so that ethics becomes one voice among many. [Levinas] is not claiming that one may lead a full human life by heeding to this voice alone." This is undoubtedly true, but doesn't the infinity of the ethical duty and its overridingness precisely make it tragically impossible to "lead a full human life" with any kind of good conscience? In my view, Overgaard here downgrades the absoluteness of the ethical "must."

44 On the other hand, would one's stepping to one's own death instead of the other be a suicide?

45 This is a conclusion actually emerging from the work of one of Wittgenstein's unduly neglected background figures, Weininger, who claimed ethics to presuppose solipsism and considered attempts to avoid solipsism hypocritical. According to Schroeder (2016: 12), Weininger indeed represented "moral solipsism," which Wittgenstein inherited from him.

46 I am referring to these contributions briefly and inconclusively; I cannot do justice to the richness of their discussions. See, however, Pihlström (2016) for some elaboration.

47 The absence of what Valberg calls THIS is NOTHINGNESS, there being no horizon. Puzzlingly, even then, the world "would still be there, just as it is," but "it would not be present" (Valberg 2007: 180). A Wittgensteinian-like interplay between solipsism and realism seems to be at work here.

48 See also Valberg (2007: 484). Elsewhere, he points out that becoming open to the truth of solipsism is making a philosophical discovery (2007: 205), responding to a challenge of self-understanding (cf. 2007: 234).
49 Valberg notes (2007: 186) that this is very different from the naive epistemological solipsism that philosophers like Russell addressed.
50 Cf. the critical discussion by Johnston (2010: 182–85) of the *Tractatus* and of Valberg.
51 However, in a Wittgensteinian vein, the idea of dealing with objects, intentional or not, here is misleading.
52 Obviously to be distinguished from the non-reductive pragmatic naturalism invoked in the transcendental non-solipsistic argumentation of Chapter 4.
53 This paradoxical character of human subjectivity is analyzed in a transcendental manner in Carr (1999). For further discussions, see again Pihlström (2016: chapter 3).
54 Unless one already is concerned with morality, the question "why be moral?" cannot even arise. See Pihlström (2005).
55 The intricate relation between subjectivity and guilt is expressed by Levinas (1989: 102) as follows: "The more I return to myself, the more I divest myself, under the traumatic effect of persecution, of my freedom as a constituted, wilful, imperialist subject, the more I discover myself to be responsible; the more just I am, the more guilty I am. I am 'in myself' through the others." Dostoevsky's works, especially *The Brothers of Karamazov*, are extremely rich sources in this regard.
56 Cruz (2001: 201–02) distinguishes between guilt, which he thinks can be solipsistic, or intrasubjective, and responsibility, which he takes to be necessarily intersubjective. Given our discussion of Levinas's notion of infinite responsibility, we may question this dichotomy.
57 This is, again, a paradoxical formulation. Another person can be a solipsist in their philosophical views, but isn't it necessarily true that if solipsism is correct, then the only one who can be right about it is me? As the (potential) subject of solipsism, I am without equals. That is, it may be impossible or conceptually incoherent for me to believe that there is only one subject and that subject is someone else than me (and that, hence, I am only an object for that subject). The possibility of someone else's being a solipsist (and solipsism being true) would introduce an unacceptable degree of contingency into the subject. While I wish to direct attention to the possibility of ethical responsibility in the face of the (philosophical) solipsist's death, I admit that even the idea that it might have been the case that that person was the only genuine subject may not make sense at all (for me

or anyone else entertaining this idea). But then again, to whom in the end do these remarks make sense?

58 Another way of approaching the ethical rejection of solipsism would be to investigate the possibility that ethical solipsism might eventually entail ontological solipsism. I cannot see big promises in this direction, however. It is useful to define ethical solipsism in an ontologically weak manner, accommodating the possibility that the solipsist might not literally deny the existence of others but might be concerned solely with the ethical quality of one's own life. Alternatively, one might hold that ethical solipsism entails only a weak form of ontological solipsism, according to which the structure of the world (in this case, especially the ethically relevant relations between human beings), rather than its existence as such, depends on my constitutive activity.

59 On the need to go "beyond empathy" in phenomenological investigations of intersubjectivity, see Zahavi (2005: 163ff.).

60 It could be claimed that we live not only in a culture of narcissism but also in a culture of *sharing*, even obsessive sharing: many of us share their lives with others in the social media, engage in "economies of sharing," and consume empowering self-help in which experiences and life-narratives are constantly shared (indeed, "thanks for sharing" is a phrase not only heard at rehabilitation clinics but also in consultation business and leadership training sessions). This phenomenon may be a welcome corrective move against the exclusive emphasis on individual possessions not shared with others (i.e., the culture of traditional capitalism). It may, however, obscure the fact that *not everything can be shared*. This "transcendental fact," as we might call it, can be emphasized in terms of solipsism; this is again one of the ways in which solipsism contains a "truth." We cannot just abandon our privacy and individuality, or share everything, and solipsism may remind us about this.

Chapter Six

1 On German idealism—from Kant through Fichte to Hegel's, Schelling's, and others' absolute idealism (cf. Chapter 3)—as a campaign against "subjectivism" and for the reality of the external world, see Beiser's (2002) monumental study (which does not explicitly deal with solipsism, though). German idealism is one example of a major philosophical tradition that would deserve considerably more detailed attention from the perspective of the solipsism issue.

2 Among the commentators comparing Wittgensteinian and Levinasian approaches, Overgaard (2007: chapter 8) is particularly valuable. See also Kivistö and Pihlström (2016) as well as Pihlström (2020).
3 Minar (1998) investigates the later Wittgenstein's treatment of the "dialectic" of solipsism. Instead of presenting any demonstrative refutation of solipsism, Wittgenstein "proceeds dialectically, tracing a path toward solipsism through a particular reading of certain features of the grammar of the first person and providing us with resources for resisting the temptations that beckon us to start down this path" (Minar 1998: 330). I hope to have been able to show that the dialectic works to the other direction, too. Minar also acknowledges this: having argued that, for Wittgenstein, "accepting that nothing in the world guarantees that I always make sense is part of what it is to have a world," and that facing this fact instead of fleeing from it (as the solipsist does) "is part of owning up to my responsibility for saying what I mean," he notes that the solipsist does produce an image of my confinement in my world in such a way that "*his* sense of limits, *his* construction of them, is responsible" (Minar 1998: 351).
4 Apparently harmless but in reality extremely dangerous forms of cultural solipsism may actually matter much more than we might initially think. Read (2010: 600–01) argues that the kind of "enlarged" solipsism of what he calls "communalism" was at work in the Nazis' refusal to acknowledge the common humanity of all human beings— and that Wittgenstein's *Philosophical Investigations* (as a "war book") argues against such communalisms, and for the acknowledgment of other human beings, in its rejection of a private language and in examining pain as the paradigmatic case of relating to others. Solipsism, Read says, "*can be seen as a kind of extreme version of racism*" (2010: 609; original emphasis).
5 Cf. especially Apel (1998). Apel's work is particularly useful in tracing the development of the methodologically solipsistic "philosophy of consciousness" and its criticisms.
6 I have above frequently illustrated the conflicts around solipsism by employing James's notion of a philosophical temperament.
7 This postulates the privacy of mental content. Oliver (1970: 34ff.) argues that the privacy postulate is one of the assumptions underlying modern philosophy. (However, Oliver's discussion is confined to classical, rather than transcendental, solipsism.)
8 Accordingly, Cavell's (1979) insistence on the problem of self-knowledge as a fundamental issue in philosophy might again be accommodated by the solipsist.

REFERENCES

Abela, P. (2002), *Kant's Empirical Realism*, Oxford: Clarendon Press.
Allen, B. (1993), *Truth in Philosophy*, Cambridge, MA: Harvard University Press, 1995.
Allen, M. C. (2018), "The Metaphysical Subject and Logical Space: Solipsism and Singularity in the Tractatus," *Open Philosophy* 1: 277–89.
Allison, H. E. (1996), *Idealism and Freedom: Essays on Kant's Theoretical and Practical Philosophy*, Cambridge: Cambridge University Press.
Allison, H. E. (2004), *Kant's Transcendental Idealism: An Interpretation and Defense – Revised and Enlarged Edition*, New Haven, CT: Yale University Press (1st ed. 1983).
Anscombe, G. E. M. (1959), *An Introduction to Wittgenstein's Tractatus*, London: Hutchinson University Library.
Anscombe, G. E. M. (1976), "The Question of Linguistic Idealism," in J. Hintikka (ed.), *Essays on Wittgenstein in Honour of G.H. von Wright*, Acta Philosophica Fennica 28, Amsterdam: North Holland Publishing Co., 188–215.
Apel, K.-O. (1998), *From a Transcendental-Semiotic Point of View*, ed. M. Papastephanou, Manchester: Manchester University Press.
Appelqvist, H. (2012), "Apocalypse Now: Wittgenstein's Early Remarks on Immortality and the Problem of Life," *History of Philosophy Quarterly* 29: 195–210.
Appelqvist, H. (2013), "Why Does Wittgenstein Say that Ethics and Aesthetics Are One and the Same?," in P. Sullivan and M. Potter (eds.), *Wittgenstein's Tractatus: History and Interpretation*, Oxford: Oxford University Press, 40–58.
Appelqvist, H. (2016), "On Wittgenstein's Kantian Solution to the Problem of Philosophy," *The British Journal for the History of Philosophy* 24: 697–719.
Arendt, H. (1951), *The Origins of Totalitarianism*, Chicago: The University of Chicago Press.
Arendt, H. (1958), *The Human Condition*, Chicago: The University of Chicago Press.

Atwell, J. E. (1995), *Schopenhauer on the Character of the World: The Metaphysics of Will*, Berkeley: University of California Press.
Avramides, A. (2001), *Other Minds*, London: Routledge.
Ayer, A. J. (1946), *Language, Truth and Logic*, Harmondsworth: Penguin Books, 1986.
Ayer, A. J. (1956), *The Problem of Knowledge*, Harmondsworth: Penguin Books.
Bach, K. (1982), "*De re* Belief and Methodological Solipsism," in A. Woodfield (ed.), *Thought and Object: Essays on Intentionality*, Oxford: Clarendon Press, 121–51.
Badenhop, D. (2017), "Still Lonely: The Moral Solipsist after Transcendental Argumentation," in J. P. Brune, R. Stern, and M. H. Werner (eds.), *Transcendental Arguments in Moral Theory*, Berlin: Gruyter, 87–105.
Baldwin, T. (1988), "Phenomenology, Solipsism and Egocentric Thought," *The Aristotelian Society, Supplement* 62: 27–43.
Bauman, Z. (1992), *Mortality, Immortality and Other Life Strategies*, Cambridge: Polity.
Beavers, A. F. (1995), *Levinas beyond the Horizons of Cartesianism: An Inquiry into the Metaphysics of Morals*, New York: Peter Lang.
Beiser, F. C. (1998), "The Context and Problematic of Post-Kantian Philosophy," in S. Critchley and W. R. Schroeder (eds.), *A Companion to Continental Philosophy*, Malden, MA: Blackwell, 1999, 21–34.
Beiser, F. C. (2002), *German Idealism: The Struggle against Subjectivism 1781–1801*, Cambridge, MA: Harvard University Press.
Beiser, F. C. (2006), "Moral Faith and the Highest Good," in P. Guyer (ed.), *The Cambridge Companion to Kant and Modern Philosophy*, Cambridge: Cambridge University Press, 588–629.
Bell, D. (1988), "Phenomenology, Solipsism and Egocentric Thought," *The Aristotelian Society, Supplement* 62: 45–60.
Bell, D. (1990), *Husserl*, London: Routledge.
Bell, D. (1996), "Solipsism and Subjectivity," *European Journal of Philosophy* 4: 155–74.
Beloff, J. (1956), "Facts, Values, and Moral Solipsism," *The Journal of Philosophy* 53: 541–49.
Berkeley, G. (1710, 1713), *Philosophical Works Including the Works on Vision*, ed. M. R. Ayers, London: Everyman, 1975. (Contains *A Treatise Concerning the Principles of Human Knowledge* [1710] and *Three Dialogues between Hylas and Philonous* [1713]).
Bloor, D. (1996), "The Question of Linguistic Idealism Revisited," in H. Sluga and D. G. Stern (eds.), *The Cambridge Companion to Wittgenstein*, Cambridge: Cambridge University Press, 354–82.
Bode, B. H. (1905), "'Pure Experience' and the External World," *The Journal of Philosophy* 2: 128–33.

Böhler, D. (1984), "Das solipsistisch-intuitionistische Konzept der Vernunft und des Verstehens: traditionskritische Bemerkungen," *Zeitschrift für philosophische Forschung* 38: 263–77.

Bonner, K. (1994), "Hermeneutics and Symbolic Interactionism: The Problem of Solipsism," *Human Studies* 17: 225–49.

Borst, C. (1992), "Solipsism," in J. Dancy and E. Sosa (eds.), *A Companion to Epistemology*, Oxford: Blackwell, 487–88.

Bouveresse, J. (1987), *Le mythe de l'intériorité: Expérience, signification et langage privé chez Wittgenstein*, Paris: Minuit.

Bradley, F. H. (1893), *Appearance and Reality: A Metaphysical Essay*, Oxford: Clarendon Press, 1962.

Brockhaus, R. J. (1985), "On Pulling up the Ladder: *Tractatus* 6.54," *Idealistic Studies* 15: 249–70.

Brockhaus, R. J. (1991), *Pulling up the Ladder: The Metaphysical Roots of Wittgenstein's Tractatus Logico-Philosophicus*, La Salle, IL: Open Court.

Brouwer, L. E. J. (1975), *Collected Works 1: Philosophy and Foundations of Mathematics*, ed. A. Heyting, Amsterdam: North Holland Publishing Co.

Burnyeat, M. F. (1976), "Protagoras and Self-Refutation in Plato's Theaetetus," *The Philosophical Review* 85: 172–95.

Camus, A. (1942), *The Outsider*, trans. S. Gilbert, Harmondsworth: Penguin Books, 1961.

Candlish, S. (2007), *The Russell/Bradley Dispute and Its Significance for Twentieth-Century Philosophy*, Basingstoke: Palgrave Macmillan, 2009.

Carnap, R. (1963), "Replies and Systematic Expositions," in P. A. Schilpp (ed.), *The Philosophy of Rudolf Carnap*, La Salle, IL: Open Court, 859–1013.

Carnap, R. (1967), *The Logical Structure of the World & Pseudoproblems in Philosophy* (1928), trans. R. A. George, Berkeley: University of California Press, 1969.

Carr, D. (1977), "Kant, Husserl, and the Nonempirical Ego," *The Journal of Philosophy* 74: 682–90.

Carr, D. (1987), *Interpreting Husserl: Critical and Comparative Studies*, Dordrecht: Nijhoff.

Carr, D. (1999), *The Paradox of Subjectivity: The Self in the Transcendental Tradition*, New York: Oxford University Press.

Cavell, S. (1979), *The Claim of Reason: Wittgenstein, Skepticism, Morality, and Tragedy*, Oxford: Clarendon Press.

Cavell, S. (1981), *The Senses of Walden*, rev. ed., Chicago: The University of Chicago Press, 1992 (1st ed. 1972).

Child, W. (1996), "Solipsism and First Person / Third Person Asymmetries," *European Journal of Philosophy* 4: 137–54.

Choudhury, P. J. (1953), "Vindication of Solipsism," *The Review of Metaphysics* 6: 381–85.
Clark, M. (1964), "A Note on Ethics and Solipsism," *Mind* 73: 127–28.
Cockburn, D. (1990), *Other Human Beings*, Houndmills: Macmillan.
Coffa, J. A. (1991), *The Semantic Tradition from Kant to Carnap: To the Vienna Station*, ed. L. Wessels, Cambridge: Cambridge University Press, 1997.
Collins, A. (1999), *Possible Experience: Understanding Kant's* Critique of Pure Reason, Berkeley: University of California Press.
Conant, J. (1990), "Introduction," in H. Putnam, *Realism with a Human Face*, ed. J. Conant, Cambridge, MA: Harvard University Press, xv–lxxiv.
Cook, J. W. (1994), *Wittgenstein's Metaphysics*, Cambridge: Cambridge University Press.
Cook, J. W. (2000), *Wittgenstein, Empiricism, and Language*, New York: Oxford University Press.
Cortens, A. J. (2000), *Global Anti-Realism: A Metaphilosophical Inquiry*, Boulder, CO: Westview Press.
Coyne, M. U. (1982), "Eye, 'I', and Mine: The Self of Wittgenstein's *Tractatus*," *The Southern Journal of Philosophy* 20: 313–23.
Craig, E. (1998), "Solipsism," in E. Craig (ed.), *Routledge Encyclopedia of Philosophy*, vol. 9, London: Routledge, 25–26.
Crary, A., and Read, R., eds. (2000), *The New Wittgenstein*, London: Routledge.
Critchley, S., and Bernasconi, R., eds. (2002), *The Cambridge Companion to Levinas*, Cambridge: Cambridge University Press.
Critchley, S., and Dews, P., eds. (1996), *Deconstructive Subjectivities*, Albany: State University of New York Press.
Crowell, S. G. (1999), "The Project of Ultimate Grounding and the Appeal to Intersubjectivity in Recent Transcendental Philosophy," *International Journal of Philosophical Studies* 7: 31–54.
Cruz, M. (2001), "On Pain, the Suffering of Wrong, and Other Grievances: Responsibility," in M. P. Lara (ed.), *Rethinking Evil: Contemporary Perspectives*, Berkeley: University of California Press, 198–209.
DeArmey, M. H. (1982) "William James and the Problem of Other Minds," *The Southern Journal of Philosophy* 20: 325–36.
Descartes, R. (1637, 1641), *The Philosophical Writings of Descartes*, 2 vols, ed. and trans. J. Cottingham, J. R. Stoothoff, and D. Murdoch, Cambridge: Cambridge University Press, 1985. (Contains *Discourse on the Method of Rightly Conducting the Reason and Seeking Truth in the Sciences* [1637] and *Meditations on the First Philosophy* [1641]).
Diamond, C. (1992), "Wittgenstein, Ludwig [Josef Johann] (1889–1951)," in L. C. Becker and C. B. Becker (eds.), *Encyclopedia of Ethics*, vol. 2, New York: Garland, 1319–22.

Diamond, C. (2000), "Does Bismarck Have a Beetle in His Box? The Private Language Argument in the *Tractatus*," in A. Crary and R. Read (eds.), *The New Wittgenstein*, London: Routledge, 262–92.
Dilman, I. (1974), "Wittgenstein on the Soul," in G. Vesey (ed.), *Understanding Wittgenstein*, London: Macmillan, 162–92.
Dilman, I. (2004), "Wittgenstein and the Question of Linguistic Idealism," in D. McManus (ed.), *Wittgenstein and Scepticism*, London: Routledge, 162–77.
Dingle, H. (1955), "Solipsism and Related Matters," *Mind* 64: 433–54.
Dore, C. (1989), *God, Suffering and Solipsism*, Houndmills: Macmillan.
Dovel, Y. (2007), *Time and Realism: Metaphysical and Antimetaphysical Perspectives*, Cambridge, MA: The MIT Press.
Duff, R. A., and Marshall, S. E. (1982), "Camus and Rebellion: From Solipsism to Morality," *Philosophical Investigations* 5: 116–34.
Ehman, R. R. (1966), "Subjectivity and Solipsism," *The Review of Metaphysics* 20: 3–24.
Elias, N. (1982), *The Loneliness of the Dying*, Oxford: Blackwell.
Europaeus, L. C. [pseudonym] (1648), *Monarchia solipsorum*, Venetum.
Fichte, J. G. (1794–95), *Science of Knowledge*, ed. and trans. P. Heath and J. Lachs, Cambridge: Cambridge University Press, 1982 (1st ed. 1970).
Fichte, J. G. (1988), *Early Philosophical Writings*, trans. and ed. D. Breazeale, Ithaca, NY: Cornell University Press.
Findlay, J. N. (1984), *Wittgenstein: A Critique*, London: Routledge.
Floyd, J. (1998), "The Uncaptive Eye: Solipsism in Wittgenstein's *Tractatus*," in L. S. Rouner (ed.), *Loneliness*, Notre Dame, IN: University of Notre Dame Press, 79–114.
Fodor, J. A. (1975), *The Language of Thought*, New York: Crowell.
Fodor, J. A. (1980), "Methodological Solipsism Considered as a Research Strategy in Cognitive Psychology," *The Behavioral and Brain Sciences* 3: 63–73.
Franchella, M. (1995), "Like a Bee on a Windowpane: Heyting's Reflections on Solipsism," *Synthese* 105: 207–51.
Fretz, L. (1992), "Individuality in Sartre's Philosophy," in C. Howells (ed.), *The Cambridge Companion to Sartre*, Cambridge: Cambridge University Press, 67–99.
Friedman, M. (1999), *Reconsidering Logical Positivism*, Cambridge: Cambridge University Press.
Gabriel, G. (1995), "Solipsismus," in J. Ritter and K. Gründer (eds.), *Historisches Wörterbuch der Philosophie*, vol. 9, Darmstadt: Wissenschaftliche Buchgesellschaft, 1018–23.
Gaita, G. (2000), *A Common Humanity: Thinking about Love and Truth and Justice*, London: Routledge.

Gaita, R. (2004), *Good and Evil: An Absolute Conception*, rev. ed., London: Routledge (1st ed. 1991).
Gava, G. and Stern, R., eds. (2016), *Pragmatism, Kant, and Transcendental Philosophy*, London: Routledge.
Gellner, E. (1998), *Language and Solitude: Wittgenstein, Malinowski and the Habsburg Dilemma*, Cambridge: Cambridge University Press.
Glendinning, S. (1998), *On Being with Others: Heidegger – Derrida – Wittgenstein*, London: Routledge.
Glock, H.-J. (1999), "Schopenhauer and Wittgenstein: Representation as Language and Will," in C. Janaway (ed.), *The Cambridge Companion to Schopenhauer*, Cambridge: Cambridge University Press, 422–58.
Gmür, F. (2000), *Ästhetik bei Wittgenstein: Über Sagen und Zeigen*, Freiburg: Karl Alber.
Golomb, J. (1995), *In Search of Authenticity: From Kierkegaard to Camus*, London: Routledge.
Grey, D. (1952), "The Solipsism of Bishop Berkeley," *The Philosophical Quarterly* 2: 338–49.
Griffiths, A. P. (1974), "Wittgenstein, Schopenhauer, and Ethics," in G. Vesey (ed.), *Understanding Wittgenstein*, London: Macmillan, 96–116.
Guetti, J. (2004), "Monologic and Dialogic: Wittgenstein, *Heart of Darkness*, and Linguistic Skepticism," in J. Gibson and W. Huemer (eds.), *The Literary Wittgenstein*, London: Routledge, 251–66.
Haack, S. (1976), "The Pragmatist Theory of Truth," *The British Journal for the Philosophy of Science* 27: 231–49.
Haack, S. (1977), "Carnap's 'Aufbau': Some Kantian Reflections," *Ratio* 19: 170–75.
Haack, S. (1987), "'Realism'," *Synthese* 73: 275–99.
Hacker, P. M. S. (1986), *Insight and Illusion: Themes in the Philosophy of Wittgenstein*, rev. ed., Oxford: Clarendon Press (1st ed. 1972).
Hacker, P. M. S. (1996), *Wittgenstein's Place in Twentieth-Century Analytic Philosophy*, Oxford: Blackwell.
Hacker, P. M. S. (2001), *Wittgenstein: Connections and Controversies*, Oxford: Clarendon Press.
Haller, R. (1988), *Questions on Wittgenstein*, London: Routledge.
Hanna, R. (2001), *Kant and the Foundations of Analytic Philosophy*, Oxford: Clarendon Press.
Hare, C. J. (2009), *On Myself, and Other, Less Important Subjects*, Princeton, NJ: Princeton University Press.
von Hartmann, E. (1877), *Neukantianismus, Schopenhauerianismus und Hegelianismus in ihrer Stellung zu den philosophischen Aufgaben der Gegenwart*, Berlin: Carl Duncker.
Hausman, A. (1968), "Solipsism and Berkeley's Alleged Realism," *Revue Internationale de Philosophie* 22: 403–12.

Heidegger, M. (1927), *Sein und Zeit*, 9th ed., Tübingen: Max Niemeyer, 1960.
Heinämaa, S. (2012), "The Body," in S. Luft and S. Overgaard (eds.), *The Routledge Companion to Phenomenology*, London: Routledge, 222–32.
Hertzberg, L. (1994), *The Limits of Experience*, Acta Philosophica Fennica 56, Helsinki: The Philosophical Society of Finland.
Hessell, C. (2018), "Solipsism and the Self in Wittgenstein's *Tractatus*," *Journal of the History of Philosophy* 56: 127–54.
Hintikka, J. (1958), "On Wittgenstein's 'Solipsism'," in I. M. Copi and R. W. Beard (eds.), *Essays on Wittgenstein's Tractatus*, New York: Macmillan, 1966, 157–61.
Hintikka, J. (1996), *Ludwig Wittgenstein: Half-Truths and One-and-a-Half-Truths*, Dordrecht: Kluwer.
Hintikka, M. B., and Hintikka, J. (1986), *Investigating Wittgenstein*, Oxford: Blackwell.
Hölscher, T. (1998), "Logical Solipsism – Reading Wittgenstein's Notebooks," *Acta Analytica* 21: 57–66.
Horster, D. (1982), "Der kantische 'methodische Solipsismus' und die Theorien von Apel und Habermas," *Kant-Studien* 73: 463–71.
Howells, C. (1992), "Conclusion: Sartre and the Deconstruction of the Subject," in C. Howells (ed.), *The Cambridge Companion to Sartre*, Cambridge: Cambridge University Press, 318–52.
Hume, D. (1739–40), *A Treatise of Human Nature*, ed. L. A. Selby-Bigge, 2nd ed., P. H. Nidditch, Oxford: Clarendon Press, 1985.
Hume, D. (1748), *Enquiries Concerning Human Understanding and Concerning the Principles of Morals*, ed. L. A. Selby-Bigge; rev. P. H. Nidditch, 3rd ed., Oxford: Clarendon Press, 1996 (1st ed. 1975).
Humpston, C. S. (2018), "The Paradoxical Self: Awareness, Solipsism and First-Rank Symptoms in Schizophrenia," *Philosophical Psychology* 31: 210–31.
Husserl, E. (1931), *Cartesianische Meditationen: Eine Einleitung in die Phänomenologie*, ed. E. Ströker, Hamburg: Felix Meiner, 1995 (*Cartesian Meditations*, trans. D. Cairns, The Hague: Nijhoff, 1982).
Husserl, E. (1935), *Die Krisis der europäischen Wissenschaften und die transzendentale Phänomenologie: Eine Einleitung in die phänomenologische Philosophie*, ed. E. Ströker, Hamburg: Felix Meiner, 1982.
Hyslop, A. (1995), *Other Minds*, Dordrecht: Kluwer.
Inchofer, M. (1753), *La Monarchie des Solipses*, trans. H. Uytwerf, Amsterdam.
van Iten, R. J. (1962), "Berkeley's Alleged Solipsism," *Revue Internationale de Philosophie* 16: 447–52.

van Iten, R. J. (1968), "Berkeley's Realism and His Alleged Solipsism Re-examined," *Revue Internationale de Philosophie* 22: 413–22.
Jacques, F. (1982), *Difference and Subjectivity: Dialogue and Personal Identity*, trans. A. Rothwell, New Haven, CT: Yale University Press, 1991.
Jacquette, D. (1997), "Wittgenstein on the Transcendence of Ethics," *Australasian Journal of Philosophy* 75: 304–24.
Jacquette, D. (2002), "Wittgenstein on Thoughts as Pictures of Facts and the Transcendence of the Metaphysical Subject," in R. Haller and K. Puhl (eds.), *Wittgenstein and the Future of Philosophy: A Reassessment after 50 Years*, Vienna: öbv&hpt, 160–70.
Jager, R. (1972), *The Development of Bertrand Russell's Philosophy*, London: George Allen & Unwin.
James, W. (1897), *The Will to Believe and Other Essays in Popular Philosophy*, eds. F. H. Burkhardt, F. Bowers, and I. K. Skrupskelis, Cambridge, MA: Harvard University Press, 1979.
James, W. (1907, 1909), *Pragmatism: A New Name for Some Old Ways of Thinking* (1907) & *The Meaning of Truth* (1909), eds. F. H. Burkhardt, F. Bowers, and I. K. Skrupskelis, Cambridge, MA: Harvard University Press (one-volume ed.), 1978.
James, W. (1912), *Essays in Radical Empiricism*, ed. R. B. Perry, Lincoln: University of Nebraska Press, 1996.
Janaway, C. (1989), *Self and World in Schopenhauer's Philosophy*, Oxford: Clarendon Press.
Janik, A. (1985), *Essays on Wittgenstein and Weininger*, Amsterdam: Rodopi.
Janik, A. (2001), *Wittgenstein's Vienna Revisited*, New Brunswick, NJ: Transactions Publishers.
Janik, A., and Toulmin, S. (1973), *Wittgenstein's Vienna*, New York: Simon & Schuster.
Johnston, M. (2010), *Surviving Death*, Princeton, NJ: Princeton University Press.
Johnstone, A. A. (1991), *Rationalized Epistemology: Taking Solipsism Seriously*, Albany: SUNY Press.
Kannisto, H. (1986), *Thoughts and Their Subject: A Study of Wittgenstein's Tractatus*, Acta Philosophica Fennica 40, Helsinki: The Philosophical Society of Finland.
Kant, I. (1781/1787), *Kritik der reinen Vernunft*, ed. R. Schmidt, Leipzig: Felix Meiner, 1990.
Kant, I. (1993), *Opus postumum*, ed. E. Förster, trans. E. Förster and M. Rosen, Cambridge: Cambridge University Press.
Kast, B. (1998), "'Habt nur den Muth, destructiv zu sein': Die Destruktion des Anderen als Voraussetzung für die Entdeckung des Eigenen – Unbekanntes von Max Stirner," *Synthesis Philosophica* 13: 227–37.

Kekes, J. (1971), "A Refutation of Solipsism," *The Personalist* 52: 44–60.
Kivistö, S., and Pihlström, S. (2016), *Kantian Antitheodicy: Philosophical and Literary Varieties*, Basingstoke: Palgrave Macmillan.
Kolakowski, L. (2001), *Metaphysical Horror*, rev. ed., ed. A. Kolakowska, Harmondsworth: Penguin (1st ed. 1988).
Kremer, M. (2004), "To What Extent Is Solipsism a Truth," in B. Stocker (ed.), *Post-Analytic Tractatus*, London: Routledge, 2017.
Kremer, T. (1960), "The Significance of Solipsism," *Proceedings of the Aristotelian Society* 60: 35–60.
Kripke, S. A. (1982), *Wittgenstein on Rules and Private Language: An Elementary Exposition*, Oxford: Blackwell.
Kuhlmann, W. (1990), "Solipsism in Kant's Practical Philosophy and the Discourse Ethics," *Graduate Faculty Philosophy Journal* 13: 159–79.
Kuhlmann, W. (2017), "Transcendental-Pragmatic Foundation of Ethics: Transcendental Arguments and Ethics," in J. P. Brune, R. Stern, and M. H. Werner (eds.), *Transcendental Arguments in Moral Theory*, Berlin: Gruyter, 247–63.
Lachs, J. (1987), *Mind and Philosophers*, Nashville, TN: Vanderbilt University Press.
Lafleur, L. J. (1952), "Solipsism," *The Review of Metaphysics* 5: 523–28.
Lalla, S. (2002), *Solipsismus bei Ludwig Wittgenstein: Eine Studie zum Früh- und Spätwerk*, Frankfurt am Main: Peter Lang.
Langton, R. (1997), "Love and Solipsism," in R. E. Lamb (ed.), *Love Analyzed*, Boulder, CO: Westview Press.
Langton, R. (2009), *Sexual Solipsism: Philosophical Essays on Pornography and Objectification*, Oxford: Oxford University Press.
Lauener, H. (1992), "Transcendental Arguments Pragmatically Relativized: Accepted Norms (Conventions) as an *A Priori* Condition for any Form of Intelligibility," in C. Dilworth (ed.), *Idealization IV: Intelligibility in Science*, Poznan Studies in the Philosophy of the Sciences and the Humanities 26, Amsterdam: Rodopi, 47–69.
Lear, J. (1998), *Open Minded: Working Out the Logic of the Soul*, Cambridge, MA and London: Harvard University Press.
Leibniz, G. W. von (1714), *The Monadology*, trans. R. Latta, Oxford: Oxford University Press, 1898.
Leman-Stefanovic, I. (1987), *The Event of Death: A Phenomenological Inquiry*, Dordrecht: Nijhoff.
LePore, E., and Loewer, B. (1986), "Solipsistic Semantics," in P. A. French et al. (eds.), *Midwest Studies in Philosophy 10*, Minneapolis, MN: University of Minnesota Press, 595–614.
Levinas, E. (1971), *Totalité et infini: Essai sur l'extériorité*, Dordrecht: Kluwer, 1994.
Levinas, E. (1987), *Outside the Subject*, trans. M. B. Smith, London: Athlone Press, 1993.

Levinas, E. (1989), *The Levinas Reader*, ed. S. Hand, Oxford: Blackwell.
Levinas, E. (1998), *Discovering Existence with Husserl*, ed. and trans. R. A. Cohen and M. B. Smith, Evanston, IL: Northwestern University Press.
Levinas, E. (1999), *Alterity and Transcendence*, trans. M. B. Smith, London: The Athlone Press.
Levine, J. (2013), "Logic and Solipsism," in P. Sullivan and M. Potter (eds.), *Wittgenstein's Tractatus: History and Interpretation*, Oxford: Oxford University Press, 170–238.
Linder, M. (1992), *Farewell to the Self-Employed: Deconstructing a Socioeconomic and Legal Solipsism*, New York: Greenwood Press.
Linhe, H. (1996), "Philosophy as Experience, as Elucidation and as Profession: An Attempt to Reconstruct Early Wittgenstein's Philosophy," *Grazer Philosophische Studien* 51: 23–46.
Linhe, H. (2002), "Wittgenstein and Schopenhauer," in R. Haller and K. Puhl (eds.), *Wittgenstein and the Future of Philosophy: A Reassessment after 50 Years*, Vienna: öbv&hpt, 112–20.
Litwack, E. B. (2009), *Wittgenstein and Value: The Quest for Meaning*, London: Continuum.
Locke, J. (1690), *An Essay Concerning Human Understanding*, ed. R. Woolhouse, Harmondsworth: Penguin, 1997.
Luft, S., and Overgaard, S., eds. (2012), *The Routledge Companion to Phenomenology*, London: Routledge.
Luntley, M. (1995), *Reason, Truth and Self: The Postmodern Reconditioned*, London: Routledge.
Lycan, W. G. (1986), "Semantics and Methodological Solipsism," in E. LePore (ed.), *Truth and Interpretation: Perspectives on the Philosophy of Donald Davidson*, Oxford: Blackwell, 245–61.
Malcolm, N. (1982), "Wittgenstein and Idealism," in G. Vesey (ed.), *Idealism: Past and Present*, Cambridge: Cambridge University Press, 249–67.
Maleuvre, D. (2006), *The Religion of Reality: Inquiry into the Self, Art, and Transcendence*, Washington DC: The Catholic University of America Press.
Maloney, J. C. (1985), "Methodological Solipsism Reconsidered as a Research Strategy in Cognitive Psychology," *Philosophy of Science* 52: 451–69.
Maloney, J. C. (1991), "Saving Psychological Solipsism," *Philosophical Studies* 61: 267–83.
Malpas, J., and Solomon, R. C., eds. (1998), *Death and Philosophy*, London: Routledge.
Margolis, J. (1995), *Historied Thought, Constructed World: A Conceptual Primer for the Turn of the Millennium*, Berkeley: University of California Press.

Marras, A. (1985), "The Churchlands on Methodological Solipsism and Computational Psychology," *Philosophy of Science* 52: 295–309.

Matthews, E. (1996), *Twentieth-Century French Philosophy*, Oxford: Oxford University Press.

McCulloch, G. (1995), *The Mind and Its World*, London: Routledge.

McGreal, I. (1948), "The Solipsist's *Apologia*," *The Philosophical Review* 57: 176–80.

McGuinness, B. (2001), "'Solipsism' in the *Tractatus*," in D. Charles and W. Child (eds.), *Wittgensteinian Themes: Essays in Honour of David Pears*, Oxford: Clarendon Press, 1–11.

McManus, D., ed. (2004a), *Wittgenstein and Scepticism*, London: Routledge.

McManus, D. (2004b), "Solipsism and Scepticism in the *Tractatus*," in D. McManus (ed.), *Wittgenstein and Scepticism*, London: Routledge, 137–61.

McRae, R. (1982), "As Though Only God and It Existed in the World," in M. Hooker (ed.), *Leibniz: Critical and Interpretive Essays*, Minneapolis: University of Minnesota Press, 79–89.

Mensch, J. R. (1988), *Intersubjectivity and Transcendental Idealism*, Albany: State University of New York Press.

Merleau-Ponty, M. (1962), *Phenomenology of Perception* (1945), trans. C. Smith, London: Routledge, 2002.

Miller, R. W. (1980), "Solipsism in the *Tractatus*," *Journal of the History of Philosophy* 18: 57–74.

Minar, E. H. (1998), "Wittgenstein on the Metaphysics of the Self: The Dialectic of Solipsism in *Philosophical Investigations*," *Pacific Philosophical Quarterly* 79: 329–54.

Mitroff, I. I. (1971), "Solipsism: An Essay in Psychological Philosophy," *Philosophy of Science* 38: 376–94.

Mohanty, J. N. (1985), *The Possibility of Transcendental Philosophy*, Dordrecht: Nijhoff.

Mohanty, J. N. (1989), *Transcendental Phenomenology: An Analytic Account*, Oxford: Blackwell.

Mondadori, F. (1982), "Solipsistic Perception in a World of Monads," in M. Hooker (ed.), *Leibniz: Critical and Interpretive Essays*, Minneapolis: University of Minnesota Press, 21–44.

Moore, A. W. (1910), *Pragmatism and Its Critics*, Chicago: University of Chicago Press.

Moore, A. W. (1996), "Solipsism and Subjectivity," *European Journal of Philosophy* 4: 220–34.

Moore, A. W. (1997), *Points of View*, Oxford: Clarendon Press.

Moore, G. E. (1959), *Philosophical Papers*, London: George Allen & Unwin.

Morgan, M. (2007), *Discovering Levinas*, Cambridge: Cambridge University Press.
Morris, K. J. (1984), "In Defense of Methodological Solipsism: A Reply to Noonan," *Philosophical Studies* 45: 399–411.
Mounce, H. O. (1981), *Wittgenstein's Tractatus: An Introduction*, Oxford: Basil Blackwell.
Mounce, H. O. (1997), "Philosophy, Solipsism and Thought," *The Philosophical Quarterly* 47: 1–18.
Mulhall, S. (1996), *Heidegger and Being and Time*, London: Routledge.
Mulhall, S. (2008), "'Hopelessly Strange': Bernard Williams' Portrait of Wittgenstein as a Transcendental Idealist," *European Journal of Philosophy* 17: 386–404.
Nagel, T. (1970), *The Possibility of Altruism*, Oxford: Clarendon Press.
Nagel, T. (1979), *Mortal Questions*, Cambridge: Cambridge University Press, 1991.
Nagel, T. (1986), *The View from Nowhere*, New York, 1989: Oxford University Press.
Nagel, T. (1987), *What Does It All Mean? A Very Short Introduction to Philosophy*, New York: Oxford University Press.
Natanson, M. (1981), "The Problem of Others in *Being and Nothingness*," in P. A. Schilpp (ed.), *The Philosophy of Jean-Paul Sartre*, La Salle, IL: Open Court, 1991, 326–44.
Neumer, K., ed. (2000), *Das Verstehen des Anderen*, Frankfurt am Main: Peter Lang.
Niiniluoto, I. (1999), *Critical Scientific Realism*, Oxford: Oxford University Press.
Noonan, H. W. (1981), "Methodological Solipsism," *Philosophical Studies* 40: 269–74.
Noonan, H. W. (1985), "Methodological Solipsism: A Reply to Morris," *Philosophical Studies* 48: 285–90.
Noonan, H. W. (1986), "Russellian Thoughts and Methodological Solipsism," in J. Butterfield (ed.), *Language, Mind and Logic*, Cambridge: Cambridge University Press, 67–90.
Nuttall, A. D. (1974), *A Common Sky: Philosophy and Literary Imagination*, London: Chatto & Windus.
O'Brien, L. F. (1996), "Solipsism and Self-Reference," *European Journal of Philosophy* 4: 175–94.
Oliver, W. D. (1970), "A Sober Look at Solipsism," in N. Rescher (ed.), *Studies in the Theory of Knowledge*, Oxford: Blackwell, 30–39.
O'Neill, O. (1989), *Constructions of Reason: Explorations of Kant's Practical Philosophy*, Cambridge: Cambridge University Press, 1990.
Overgaard, S. (2002), "Epoché and Solipsistic Reduction," *Husserl Studies* 18: 209–22.

Overgaard, S. (2007), *Wittgenstein and Other Minds: Rethinking Subjectivity and Intersubjectivity with Wittgenstein, Levinas, and Husserl*, New York: Routledge.
Park, B.-C. (1998), *Phenomenological Aspects of Wittgenstein's Philosophy*, Dordrecht: Kluwer.
Pears, D. (1987–88), *The False Prison: A Study of the Development of Wittgenstein's Philosophy*, vols 1–2, Oxford: Clarendon Press.
Pears, D. (1993), "The Ego and the Eye: Wittgenstein's Use of an Analogy," in A. Burri and J. Freudiger (eds.), *Relativism and Contextualism: Essays in Honor of Henri Lauener*, Amsterdam: Rodopi, 59–68.
Pears, D. (1996), "The Originality of Wittgenstein's Investigation of Solipsism," *European Journal of Philosophy* 4: 124–36.
Pears, D. (1998), "Saying and Doing: The Pragmatic Aspect of Wittgenstein's Treatment of 'I'," in P. Weingartner, G. Schurz, and G. Dorn (eds.), *The Role of Pragmatics in Contemporary Philosophy*, Vienna: Hölder-Pichler-Tempsky, 382–94.
Pears, D. (2001), "Was the Early Wittgenstein a Solipsist?," in G. Oliveri (ed.), *From the Tractatus to the Tractatus and Other Essays*, Frankfurt am Main: Peter Lang, 13–22.
Pears, D. (2006), *Paradox and Platitude in Wittgenstein's Philosophy*, Oxford: Clarendon Press.
Peperzak, A. T., ed. (1995), *Ethics as First Philosophy: The Significance of Emmanuel Levinas for Philosophy, Literature and Religion*, New York: Routledge.
Petrik, J. (1988), "The Metaphysical Self and Solipsism in the *Tractatus*," in O. Weinberger, P. Koller, and A. Schramm (eds.), *Philosophy of Law, Politics, and Society*, Vienna: Hölder-Pichler-Tempsky, 321–23.
Pettersson, T. (1982), *Consciousness and Time: A Study in the Philosophy and Narrative Technique of Joseph Conrad*, Acta Academiae Aboensis A61:1, Åbo: Åbo Akademi.
Philipse, H. (1995), "Transcendental Idealism," in B. Smith and D. W. Smith (eds.), *The Cambridge Companion to Husserl*, Cambridge: Cambridge University Press, 239–322.
Phillips, D. Z. (1992), *Interventions in Ethics*, Albany: SUNY Press.
Pihlström, S. (1996a), *Structuring the World: The Issue of Realism and the Nature of Ontological Problems in Classical and Contemporary Pragmatism*, Acta Philosophica Fennica 59, Helsinki: The Philosophical Society of Finland.
Pihlström, S. (1996b), "A Solipsist in a Real World," *Dialectica* 50: 275–90.
Pihlström, S. (2000), "Two Kinds of Methodological Solipsism," *Sats* 1(2): 73–90.

Pihlström, S. (2001), "Death – Mine or the Other's?," *Mortality* 6: 265–86.
Pihlström, S. (2003), *Naturalizing the Transcendental: A Pragmatic View*, Amherst, NY: Prometheus/Humanity Books.
Pihlström, S. (2004), *Solipsism: History, Critique, and Relevance*, Tampere: Tampere University Press.
Pihlström, S. (2005), *Pragmatic Moral Realism: A Transcendental Defense*, Amsterdam: Rodopi.
Pihlström, S. (2008), *"The Trail of the Human Serpent Is over Everything": Jamesian Reflections on Mind, World, and Religion*, Lanham, MD: University Press of America.
Pihlström, S. (2009), *Pragmatist Metaphysics: An Essay on the Ethical Grounds of Ontology*, London: Continuum.
Pihlström, S. (2011), *Transcendental Guilt: Reflections on Ethical Finitude*, Lanham, MD: Lexington.
Pihlström, S. (2013), *Pragmatic Pluralism and the Problem of God*, New York: Fordham University Press.
Pihlström, S. (2014), *Taking Evil Seriously*, Basingstoke: Palgrave Macmillan.
Pihlström, S., ed. (2015), *The Bloomsbury Companion to Pragmatism*, New York: Bloomsbury.
Pihlström, S. (2016), *Death and Finitude: Toward a Pragmatic Transcendental Anthropology of Human Limits and Mortality*, Lanham, MD: Lexington.
Pihlström, S. (2020), *Pragmatic Realism, Religious Truth, and Antitheodicy: On Viewing the World by Acknowledging the Other*, Helsinki: Helsinki University Press, forthcoming (open access).
Placek, T. (1999), *Mathematical Intuitionism and Intersubjectivity: A Critical Exposition of Arguments for Intuitionism*, Dordrecht: Kluwer.
Plato (1961), "Theaetetus," in E. Hamilton and H. Cairns (eds.), *The Collected Dialogues of Plato*, Princeton, NJ: Princeton University Press.
Plaut, H. C. (1962), "Empiricism, Solipsism, and Realism," *British Journal for the Philosophy of Science* 13: 216–28.
Popper, K. R. (1983), *Realism and the Aim of Science*, ed. W. W. Bartley, III, Totowa, NJ: Rowman & Littlefield.
Popper, K. R. (1994), *Knowledge and the Body–Mind Problem: In Defence of Interaction*, ed. M. A. Notturno, London: Routledge.
Puhl, K. (1999), *Subjekt und Körper: Untersuchungen zur Subjektkritik bei Wittgenstein und zur Theorie der Subjektivität*, Paderborn: Mentis.
Putnam, H. (1975), *Mind, Language, and Reality*, Cambridge: Cambridge University Press.
Putnam, H. (1981), *Reason, Truth and History*, Cambridge: Cambridge University Press.

Putnam, H. (1983), *Realism and Reason*, Cambridge: Cambridge University Press.
Putnam, H. (1987), *The Many Faces of Realism*, La Salle, IL: Open Court.
Putnam, H. (1990), *Realism with a Human Face*, ed. J. Conant, Cambridge, MA: Harvard University Press.
Putnam, H. (1992), *Renewing Philosophy*, Cambridge, MA: Harvard University Press
Putnam, H. (1994), *Words and Life*, ed. J. Conant, Cambridge, MA: Harvard University Press.
Putnam, H. (1995), *Pragmatism: An Open Question*, Oxford: Blackwell.
Putnam, H. (1999), *The Threefold Cord: Mind, Body, and World*, New York: Columbia University Press.
Putnam, H. (2012), *Philosophy in an Age of Science: Physics, Mathematics, and Skepticism*, eds. M. De Caro and D. Macarthur, Cambridge, MA: Harvard University Press.
Putnam, H., and Putnam, R. A. (2017), *Pragmatism as a Way of Life: The Lasting Legacy of William James and John Dewey*, ed. D. Macarthur, Cambridge, MA: The Belknap Press of Harvard University Press.
Quine, W. V. (1995), *From Stimulus to Science*, Cambridge, MA: Harvard University Press.
Razzaque, A. (1995), "Linguistic Solipsism: A Defense," *Indian Philosophical Quarterly* 22: 207–14.
Read, R. (2010), "Wittgenstein's *Philosophical Investigations* as a War Book," *New Literary History* 41: 593–612.
Reichenbach, H. (1951), *The Rise of Scientific Philosophy*, Berkeley: University of California Press, 1956.
Rhees, R. (1999), *Moral Questions*, ed. D. Z. Phillips, Houndmills: Macmillan.
Richardson, A. (1998), *Carnap's Construction of the World: The Aufbau and the Emergence of Logical Empiricism*, Cambridge: Cambridge University Press.
Ridge, M. (2001), "Taking Solipsism Seriously: Nonhuman Animals and Meta-Cognitive Theories of Consciousness," *Philosophical Studies* 103: 315–40.
Robinson, H. J. (1978), "The Opposite of Solipsism," *Idealistic Studies* 8: 162–68.
Rogers, T. J. (1970), *Techniques of Solipsism: A Study of Theodor Storm's Narrative Fiction*, Cambridge: The Modern Humanities Research Association.
Rollins, C. D. (1967), "Solipsism," in P. Edwards (ed.), *The Encyclopedia of Philosophy*, vol. 7, London: Macmillan, 487–91.
Römpp, G. (1992), *Husserls Phänomenologie der Intersubjektivität und ihre Bedeutung für eine Theorie intersubjektiver Objektivität und*

die Konzeption einer phänomenologischen Philosophie, Dordrecht: Kluwer.

Roth, P. A. (1987), *Meaning and Method in the Social Sciences: A Case for Methodological Pluralism*, Ithaca, NY: Cornell University Press.

Rowlands, M. (1991), "Towards a Reasonable Version of Methodological Solipsism," *Mind and Language* 6: 39–57.

Rowlands, M. (1995), "Against Methodological Solipsism: The Ecological Approach," *Philosophical Psychology* 8: 5–24.

Rudrun, D. (2005), "Living Alone: Solipsism in *Heart of Darkness*," *Philosophy and Literature* 29: 409–27.

Russell, B. (1912), *The Problems of Philosophy*, London: Oxford University Press, 1964.

Russell, B. (1948), *Human Knowledge: Its Scope and Limits*, London: George Allen & Unwin.

Russell, B. (1983), *Theory of Knowledge: The 1913 Manuscript*, in *The Collected Papers of Bertrand Russell*, vol. 7, eds. E. R. Eames and K. Blackwell, London: George Allen & Unwin.

Russell, J. E. (1906), "Solipsism: The Logical Issue of Radical Empiricism," *Philosophical Review* 15: 606–13.

Sagal, P., and Borg, G. (1993), "The Range Principle and the Problem of Other Minds," *British Journal for the Philosophy of Science* 44: 477–91.

Sandis, C. (2012), "Understanding the Lion for Real," in A. Marques and N. Venturinha (eds.), *Knowledge, Language and Mind: Wittgenstein's Thought in Progress*, Berlin: de Gruyter, 138–61.

Sandis, C. (2015), "'If Some People Looked like Elephants and Others like Cats': Wittgenstein on Understanding Others and Forms of Life," *Nordic Wittgenstein Review* 4: 131–53; https://www.nordicwittgen steinreview.com/article/view/3372/pdf.

Santayana, G. (1923), *Scepticism and Animal Faith: Introduction to a System of Philosophy*, New York: Dover, 1955.

Sartre, J.-P. (1943), *Being and Nothingness: A Phenomenological Essay on Ontology*, trans. H. E. Barnes, New York: Philosophical Library, 1956/1966.

von Savigny, E. (1996), *Der Mensch als Mitmensch: Wittgensteins "Philosophische Untersuchungen"*, München: Deutscher Taschenbuch Verlag.

von Savigny, E., and Scholz, O. R., eds. (1995), *Wittgenstein über die Seele*, Frankfurt am Main: Suhrkamp.

Schachter, J.-P. (1997), "The Angel in the Machine," *Journal of Philosophical Research* 22: 445–60.

Schantz, R. (2000), "Selbstbewusstsein und Objektbewusstsein bei Kant: Eine Studie zu den Paralogismen der reinen Vernunft," *Grazer Philosophische Studien* 60: 151–69.

Schantz, R. (2008), "Review Essay on Sami Pihlström's *Solipsism: History, Critique, and Relevance*," *Philosophy and Phenomenological Research* 77: 268–71.

Scheffler, S. (2013), *Death and the Afterlife*, Oxford: Oxford University Press.

Schiller, F. C. S. (1907), *Studies in Humanism*, London: Macmillan.

Schiller, F. C. S. (1912), *Humanism: Philosophical Essays*, 2nd ed., London: Macmillan (1st ed. 1903).

Schiller, F. C. S., Joad, C. E. M., and Richardson, C. A. (1923), "Is Neo-Idealism Reducible to Solipsism?," *The Aristotelian Society, Supplement* 3: 129–47.

Schlick, M. (1936), "Meaning and Verification," in H. Mulder and B. F. B. van de Valde-Schlick (eds.), *Schlick, Philosophical Papers*, vol. 2, Dordrecht: D. Reidel, 1979, 456–81.

Schopenhauer, A. (1844), *The World as Will and Representation*, vols I–II, trans. E. F. J. Payne, New York: Dover, 1969.

Schroeder, S. (2006), *Wittgenstein: The Way Out of the Fly-Bottle*, Cambridge: Polity.

Schurman, S. (1987), *The Solipsistic Novels of Samuel Beckett*, Köln: Pahl-Rugenstein.

Searle, J. R. (1995), *The Construction of Social Reality*, London: Penguin.

Seigfried, C. H. (1990), *William James's Radical Reconstruction of Philosophy*, Albany: SUNY Press.

Shelley, Mary (1826), *The Last Man*, London: Wordsworth, 2004.

Shook, J. R. (1998), *Pragmatism: An Annotated Bibliography 1898–1940*, Amsterdam: Rodopi.

Sluga, H. (1996), "'Whose House Is That?' Wittgenstein on the Self," in H. Sluga and D. G. Stern (eds.), *The Cambridge Companion to Wittgenstein*, Cambridge: Cambridge University Press, 320–53.

Smith, B., and Smith, D. W., eds. (1995), *The Cambridge Companion to Husserl*, Cambridge: Cambridge University Press.

Sober, E. (1995), "Why Not Solipsism?," *Philosophy and Phenomenological Research* 55: 547–66.

Solomon, R. C. (1998), "Death Fetishism, Morbid Solipsism," in J. Malpas and R. C. Solomon (eds.), *Death and Philosophy*, London: Routledge, 152–76.

Sorell, T. (2001), "Cartesian Method and the Self," *Philosophical Investigations* 24: 55–74.

Sorell, T. (2005), *Descartes Reinvented*, Cambridge: Cambridge University Press.

Sorensen, R. A. (1998), "Self-Strengthening Empathy," *Philosophy and Phenomenological Research* 58: 75–98.

Sorensen, R. A. (2018), "Diary of a Telepathic Solipsist," *Ratio* 31: 1–19.

Spinoza, B. de (1677), *The Ethics*, trans. R. H. M. Elwes, New York: Dover, 1955 (1st ed. 1883).
Sprigge, T. L. S. (1993), *James and Bradley: American Truth and British Reality*, Chicago: Open Court.
Srzednicki, J. (1972), "The Transcendental Impossibility of Solipsism," *Ratio* 14: 131–43.
Steeves, H. P. (1998), *Founding Community: A Phenomenological-Ethical Inquiry*, Dordrecht: Kluwer.
Stein, E. (1989), *On the Problem of Empathy* (1917), trans. W. Stein, 3rd ed., Washington DC: ICS Publications.
Stenius, E. (1960), *Wittgenstein's Tractatus: A Critical Exposition of Its Main Lines of Thought*, Oxford: Blackwell, 1964.
Stern, A. (1947–48), "Toward a Solution of the Problem of Solipsism," *Philosophy and Phenomenological Research* 8: 679–87.
Stern, D. G. (1995), *Wittgenstein on Mind and Language*, New York: Oxford University Press.
Stern, D. G. (1996), "The Availability of Wittgenstein's Philosophy," in H. Sluga and D. G. Stern (eds.), *The Cambridge Companion to Wittgenstein*, Cambridge: Cambridge University Press, 442–76.
Stern, R., ed. (1999), *Transcendental Arguments: Problems and Prospects*, Oxford: Clarendon Press.
Stirner, M. (1845), *Der Einzige und sein Eigenthum*, Leipzig: Otto Wigand.
Stokhof, M. (2002), *The World and Life as One: Ethics and Ontology in Wittgenstein's Early Thought*, Stanford, CA: Stanford University Press.
Strawson, P. F. (1959), *Individuals: An Essay in Descriptive Metaphysics*, London: Routledge, 1993.
Strawson, P. F. (1966), *The Bounds of Sense*, London: Methuen.
Stroll, A. (2000), *Twentieth-Century Analytic Philosophy*, New York: Columbia University Press.
Sturgeon, N. L. (1974), "Altruism, Solipsism, and the Objectivity of Reasons," *Philosophical Review* 83: 374–402.
Sullivan, P. M. (1996), "The 'Truth' in Solipsism, and Wittgenstein's Rejection of the A Priori," *European Journal of Philosophy* 4: 195–219.
Tang, H. (2011), "Transcendental Idealism in Wittgenstein's *Tractatus*," *The Philosophical Quarterly* 61: 598–607.
Taylor, C. (1995), *Philosophical Arguments*, Cambridge, MA: Harvard University Press.
Tejedor, C. (2015), *The Early Wittgenstein on Metaphysics, Natural Science, Language and Value*, London: Routledge.
Thomas, E. V. (1999), "From Detachment to Immersion: Wittgenstein and 'the Problem of Life'," *Ratio* 12: 195–209.
Thomas, E. V. (2001), *Wittgensteinian Values: Philosophy, Religious Belief and Descriptivist Methodology*, Aldershot: Ashgate.

Thornton, S. P. (2004), "Solipsism and the Problem of Other Minds," *Internet Encyclopedia of Philosophy*, online: http://www.iep.utm.edu/solipsis/print (accessed October 2013).
Tipton, I. (1992), "Descartes' Demon and Berkeley's World," *Philosophical Investigations* 15: 111–30.
Tlumak, J. (1976), "On a Defective Transcendental Refutation of Solipsism," *Ratio* 18: 50–55.
Todd, W. (1968), *Analytical Solipsism*, The Hague: Nijhoff.
Tollefsen, O. (1987), "The Equivocation Defense of Cognitive Relativism," in S. J. Bartlett and P. Suber (eds.), *Self-Reference: Reflections on Reflexivity*, Dordrecht: Nijhoff, 209–17.
Tuomela, R. (1989), "Methodological Solipsism and Explanation in Psychology," *Philosophy of Science* 56: 23–47.
Ushenko, A. P. (1948), "The Solipsist Phenomenon," *The Philosophical Review* 57: 505–8.
Vaaja, T. (2015), *The Problem of Other Minds: Themes from Wittgenstein*, Diss., Jyväskylä, University of Jyväskylä, online: https://jyx.jyu.fi/handle/123456789/46742 (accessed September 2015).
Valberg, J. J. (2007), *Dream, Death, and the Self*, Princeton, NJ: Princeton University Press.
Vesey, G. (1974a), "Other Minds," in G. Vesey (ed.), *Understanding Wittgenstein*, London: Macmillan, 149–61.
Vesey, G., ed. (1974b), *Understanding Wittgenstein*, London: Macmillan.
Vinci, T. (1995), "Solipsism," in R. Audi (ed.), *The Cambridge Dictionary of Philosophy*, Cambridge: Cambridge University Press, 751.
Vossenkuhl, W. (1995), *Ludwig Wittgenstein*, München: C.H. Beck.
Vossenkuhl, W. (1999), "Wittgensteins Solipsismus," in W. Lütterfelds and A. Roser (eds.), *Der Konflikt der Lebensformen in Wittgensteins Philosophie der Sprache*, Frankfurt am Main: Suhrkamp, 213–43.
Vossenkuhl, W. (2009), *Solipsismus und Sprachkritik: Beiträge zu Wittgenstein*, Berlin: Parerga.
Wallgren, T. (2006), *Transformative Philosophy: Socrates, Wittgenstein, and the Democratic Spirit of Philosophy*, Lanham, MD: Lexington.
Watzka, H. (2000), *Sagen und Zeigen: Die Verschränkung von Metaphysik und Sprachkritik beim frühen und beim späten Wittgenstein*, Stuttgart: Kohlhammer.
Weininger, O. (1905), *Geschlecht und Charakter: Eine prinzipielle Untersuchung*, Berlin: Gustav Kliepenheuer, 1932.
Weissman, D. (1993), *Truth's Debt to Value*, New Haven, CT: Yale University Press.
Wider, K. (1990), "Overtones of Solipsism in Thomas Nagel's 'What is it Like to Be a Bat?' and *The View from Nowhere*," *Philosophy and Phenomenological Research* 50: 481–99.

Wider, K. (1991), "A Nothing about which Something Can Be Said: Sartre and Wittgenstein on the Self," in R. Aronson and A. van den Hoven (eds.), *Sartre Alive*, Detroit: Wayne State University Press, 324–39.
Wider, K. (1995), "*Truth and Existence*: The Idealism in Sartre's Theory of Truth," *International Journal of Philosophical Studies* 3: 91–109.
Williams, B. (1974), "Wittgenstein and Idealism," in G. Vesey (ed.), *Understanding Wittgenstein*, London: Macmillan, 76–95.
Williams, B. (1993), *Shame and Necessity*, Berkeley: University of California Press.
Winch, P. (1972), *Ethics and Action*, London: Routledge and Kegan Paul.
Winch, P. (1987), *Trying to Make Sense*, Oxford: Blackwell.
Wisdom, J. (1965), *Other Minds*, 2nd ed., Oxford: Blackwell.
Wittgenstein, L. (1921), *Tractatus Logico-Philosophicus*, Frankfurt am Main: Suhrkamp, 1960 (English trans. D. F. Pears and B. F. McGuinness, London: Routledge & Kegan Paul, 1974).
Wittgenstein, L. (1953), *Philosophical Investigations*, eds. G. E. M. Anscombe and G. H. von Wright, trans. G. E. M. Anscombe, Oxford: Blackwell, 1958.
Wittgenstein, L. (1956), *Remarks on the Foundations of Mathematics*, eds. G. H. von Wright, R. Rhees, and G. E. M. Anscombe, trans. G. E. M. Anscombe, Oxford: Blackwell.
Wittgenstein, L. (1958), *The Blue and Brown Books*, ed. R. Rhees, New York: Harper & Row, 1965.
Wittgenstein, L. (1961), *Notebooks 1914–1916*, eds. G. H. von Wright and G. E. M. Anscombe, trans. G. E. M. Anscombe, 2nd ed., Oxford: Blackwell, 1973.
Wittgenstein, L. (1965), "Lecture on Ethics," *The Philosophical Review* 74, 3–16 (reprinted in Wittgenstein 1993).
Wittgenstein, L. (1967a), *Zettel*, eds. G. E. M. Anscombe and G. H. von Wright, trans. G. E. M. Anscombe, Oxford: Blackwell.
Wittgenstein, L. (1967b), *Wittgenstein und der Wiener Kreis: Gespräche, aufgezeichnet von Friedrich Waismann*, ed. B. F. McGuinness, Frankfurt am Main: Suhrkamp, 1996.
Wittgenstein, L. (1969), *On Certainty*, eds. G. E. M. Anscombe and G. H. von Wright, trans. D. Paul and G. E. M. Anscombe, Oxford: Blackwell.
Wittgenstein, L. (1975), *Philosophical Remarks*, ed. R. Rhees, trans. R. Hargreaves and R. White, Oxford: Blackwell.
Wittgenstein, L. (1992), *Geheime Tagebücher*, ed. W. Baum, Vienna: Turia & Kant.
Wittgenstein, L. (1993), *Philosophical Occasions 1912–1951*, eds. J. Klagge and A. Nordmann, Indianapolis: Hackett.

Wittgenstein, L. (1998), *Culture and Value: A Selection from the Posthumous Remains*, 2nd ed., eds. G. H. von Wright and H. Nyman, trans. P. Winch, Oxford: Blackwell.

Wittgenstein, L. (2016), *Wittgenstein: Lectures, Cambridge 1930–1933: From the Notes of G.E. Moore*, eds. D. G. Stern, B. Rogers, and G. Citron, Cambridge: Cambridge University Press, 2018.

Woodfield, A., ed. (1982), *Thought and Object: Essays on Intentionality*, Oxford: Clarendon Press.

Worthington, B. A. (1988), *Selfconsciousness and Selfreference: An Interpretation of Wittgenstein's Tractatus*, Aldershott: Avebury.

Yagisawa, T. (1993), "The Cost of Meaning Solipsism," in J. A. Fodor (ed.), *Holism: A Consumer Update*, Amsterdam: Rodopi, 213–30.

Young, J. (2005), *Schopenhauer*, London: Routledge.

Zahavi, D. (1996), "Husserl's Intersubjective Transformation of Transcendental Philosophy," *The Journal of the British Society for Phenomenology* 27: 228–45.

Zahavi, D. (2001), *Husserl and Transcendental Intersubjectivity: A Response to the Linguistic-Pragmatic Critique*, Athens: Ohio University Press.

Zahavi, D. (2003), *Husserl's Phenomenology*, Stanford, CA: Stanford University Press.

Zahavi, D. (2005), *Subjectivity and Selfhood: Investigating the First-Person Perspective*, Cambridge, MA: The MIT Press, 2008.

Zahavi, D., ed. (2012), *The Oxford Handbook of Contemporary Phenomenology*, Oxford: Oxford University Press.

INDEX

Absolute, the 32
acknowledgment 160–1
Allison, H. E. 102
Anscombe, E. 97
antirealism 80–1, 101
Apel, K.-O. 4, 10, 155
Arendt, H. 159
argument(s) from analogy 84
asymmetry 84–5
attitude towards a soul 120–1
Atwell, J. E. 54
Ayer, A. J. 40

Bach, J. S. 73
Barrett, A. 21
Bauman, Z. 135
Beckett, S. 3
behaviorism 60
Bell, D. 19, 72, 79–80, 97, 99
Berkeley, G. 24, 29, 169
Borst, D. 6, 8, 30, 45
Bradley, F. H. 30–2
Brockhaus, R. 114, 131
Brouwer, L. E. J. 170

Camus, A. 3, 136, 197
Carnap, R. 9, 40–4, 172–3
Carr, D. 180
Cavell, S. 94–5, 97, 122–3, 159, 191–2, 201
Child, W. 80
classical solipsism 19, 24–5, 35, 45, 64, 75
Cockburn, D. 118, 122
cogito 28, 154

compassion 13
Conrad, J. 3, 120
consciousness 108
Cook, J. W. 185
Coyne, M. U. 113
Craig, E. 8
credo realism 104

Dasein 60–1, 132–3, 135
death 129–48
Descartes, R. 4, 15, 21–30, 39, 49–51, 55, 83–4, 134, 152, 154, 167
determinism 1
Dore, C. 84

egoism 10, 21, 53–4
Eliot, T. S. 3
emotivism 10
empathy 150
empiricism 29, 33
epistemological solipsism 8
ethical monism 131
ethical solipsism 10, 71, 118, 120, 134, 146–7
ethics 79, 113–15, 119, 128–9, 197–8
evil 145–6
existentialism 59, 130

fallibilism 8, 106
Fichte, J. G. 22, 52–4, 176–7
Findlay, J. 85, 193
Fodor, J. 9
foundationalism 8

INDEX

Gaita, R. 123
Gellner, E. 25
Gmür, F. 117
God 27–8, 32, 53, 83–4
God's-Eye View 45, 149
Golomb, J. 149
grammatical solipsism 98
guilt 147

Haack, S. 23
Hacker, P. M. S. 76
Hegel, G. W. F. 52, 176
Heidegger, M. 60–1, 63, 132–4, 149
Heyting, A. 170
Hintikka, J. 9, 66–7, 97, 184–5
Hintikka, M. B. 9, 66
Hölscher, T. 78
horizon, the 138–40
Hume, D. 29, 169
Husserl, E. 4, 13, 54–63, 124, 134, 136, 154, 178–81
Hyslop, A. 5, 85, 163

idealism 23, 50, 66, 92, 102, 109, 152, 193, 206
inexhaustibility 127
intersubjectivity 55–7, 109, 125, 179–80

Jacques, F. 124–5
Jacquette, D. 115–16
James, W. 35, 46, 95, 107–8, 112, 153, 157–9, 171–2, 195–6
Jesus 10
Johnston, M. 138, 140–1
Johnstone, A. A. 36–9, 172

Kannisto, H. 72–4, 87, 99
Kant, I. 4, 15–16, 20, 24, 47–54, 66, 69, 77, 87, 102, 105, 134, 152, 154, 159, 175–7

Kierkegaard, S. 149
Kolakowski, L. 169–70
Kripke, S. A. 97

Lafleur, L. J. 130
Lalla, S. 99–100, 194–5
Lauener, H. 104, 106
Leibniz, G. W. 28, 169
Levinas, E. 111, 123–5, 127–8, 131–7, 139, 146, 153–6, 200–5
lifeworld 56
limit(s) 68, 71, 87, 127, 142
linguistic solipsism 9
Locke, J. 22, 29
logical positivism 40
look, the 60
love 196

McGuinness, B. 72
Maimon, S. 52
Margolis, J. 4, 10
materialism 84
Mensch, J. 58
Merleau-Ponty, M. 61–3, 107, 154, 196
metaphilosophy 160
metaphysical realism 101, 144
metaphysical solipsism,
    see ontological solipsism
methodological doubt 27
methodological solipsism 9–10, 39–46, 66
Minar, E. H. 207
Moore, A. W. 168
Moore, G. E. 22, 31
moral law 53
mortality 130, 148
Mounce, H. O. 69, 72
Mulhall, S. 185
Müller, F. E. 21
mystical, the 126
mysticism 128

Nagel, T. 25–6, 36, 114, 168, 199
narcissism 14
natality 159–60
naturalism 131, 144
Nietzsche, F. 149
Niiniluoto, I. 6
normativity 90, 112, 122
nothing(ness) 75, 139, 143–4

O'Brien, L. F. 77
Occam's Razor 81, 87
Oliver, W. D. 89, 157
ontological solipsism 6–7, 19, 40
other minds (problem) 5, 30, 32, 43, 50, 84–5, 163
other(ness) (the other) 13, 57, 112, 123, 145, 148, 160, 203
Overgaard, S. 58, 135–6, 204

panpsychism 164
Park, B.-C. 59
Pears, D. 64, 67–73, 90, 124, 183–4
Peirce, C. S. 46
phenomenological reduction 58
phenomenology 55–63, 124, 142
philosophical temperaments 151
Popper, K. R. 23, 26, 36, 73
practical solipsism 165
practices 91–3, 100
pragmatic maxim 46, 174
pragmatic realism 102, 131
pragmatism 30, 35, 91–4, 100, 107
prescriptivism 10
private language (argument) 43, 64, 90, 97
problem of life, the 78, 156
Protagoras 22, 167
psychological solipsism 164–5
Putnam, H. 15–16, 41–6, 81, 94–5, 104–6, 154, 158–9, 173–4

qualia 98
Quine, W. V. 173

rationalism 28–9
Razzaque, A. 9
Read, R. 207
realism 6, 16, 65–6, 70, 72, 79–81, 86–9, 92–3, 97, 101, 105, 109, 118–19, 131
Reichenbach, H. 40
Reinhold, K. 52
relativism 13, 22, 154
Robinson, H. J. 36, 158
Rollins, C. D. 4, 9–10, 21, 24
Russell, B. 11, 13, 15, 22, 30–9, 70

Santayana, G. 33–5
Sartre, J.-P. 3, 12–13, 59–61, 63, 75, 107–8, 136, 181
Schachter, J.-P. 28
Schopenhauer, A. 16, 52, 54, 76–7, 150, 177, 187–8
scientism 114
Scotti, G. C. 21
Searle, J. 4
Seigfried, C. H. 107
self, the, *see* subject
selflessness 121–2
semantic solipsism 8–9
Shakespeare, W. 73
sharing 206
skeptical solipsism 19, 27, 30
skepticism 1, 3, 8, 26, 30, 36–7, 48, 159
Sluga, H. 78
Sober, E. 44
solipsism of the present moment (temporal solipsism) 7, 26, 30, 34, 71, 74–5, 133
Spinoza, B. 28
Stein, E. 177
Stenius, E. 66

Sterne, L. 3
Stirner, M. 178
Storm, T. 3
Strawson, P. F. 49, 85
subject (self) 12, 38, 51–2, 73–80, 108, 114, 116, 121, 133, 138, 141, 143, 187
subjective idealism 6
subjectivism 10, 22
subjectivity 26, 63, 77–9, 109, 144, 190
suffering 117–18, 129, 145, 147–8, 150
suicide 126, 136–7

things in themselves 98
Thomas, E. V. 121–2, 199
Thornton, S. 6
Todd, W. 43
Tollefsen, O. 89
transcendence 116–17, 127
transcendental anthropology 92
transcendental argument(s) 85, 90–1, 94, 103, 149, 189
transcendental deduction 49
transcendental idealism 49–53, 66, 72, 76, 99, 102
transcendental illusion 64
transcendental intersubjectivity 57
transcendental philosophy 54, 56, 142, 159, 179
transcendental realism 45, 49
transcendental solipsism 47–82, 111, 118, 130, 136–44, 152, 154, 160, 182
transcendental subject (self, ego) 15, 39, 41, 48–52, 55–6, 61, 63, 90, 93, 139–43
transcendental vs. transcendent 116–17

Valberg, J. J. 137–44, 204–5
von Hartmann, E. 21
Vossenkuhl, W. 72, 96–100

Watzka, H. 96
Weininger, O. 137
Wider, K. 75
Wilcox, J. T.
Williams, B. 97, 166–7
will to believe, the 95–6, 105, 107, 112–13, 149, 153
Winch, P. 121, 123
Wittgenstein, L. 2, 4, 9–13, 16, 20–2, 30–1, 42, 47, 54, 56, 64–81, 84–106, 113–43, 152–4, 156, 158, 162, 181–202, 207
Wordsworth, W. 3

Zahavi, D. 56–7, 179
zombies 95